Elizabeth Sewell

A first history of Greece

Elizabeth Sewell

A first history of Greece

ISBN/EAN: 9783742816092

Manufactured in Europe, USA, Canada, Australia, Japa

Cover: Foto ©ninafisch / pixelio.de

Manufactured and distributed by brebook publishing software (www.brebook.com)

Elizabeth Sewell

A first history of Greece

A FIRST HISTORY OF GREECE.

A

FIRST HISTORY OF GREECE.

BY THE

AUTHOR OF "AMY HERBERT,"
"THE CHILD'S FIRST HISTORY OF ROME,"

ETC. ETC.

NEW EDITION.

LONDON:
LONGMANS, GREEN, AND CO.
1868.

PREFACE.

The history of Greece is, in general, very perplexing to children, from its involving events connected with a number of small states, the names of which are for the most part new to them. Even to read it with a map does not materially lessen the difficulty; for children, especially girls, rarely know much of ancient geography; and whilst they are laboriously searching for the unknown places, the thread of the history is interrupted, and their attention perhaps irrecoverably distracted.

With the view of lessening this evil, a short chapter has been prefixed to the following history, containing the names of the Grecian states, and the chief places mentioned as connected with them. And it may perhaps be found that, by giving children a lesson in the ancient geography of Greece, before they begin to study its history; and making them as well acquainted with the divisions of the country as they are with those of England, they may be better able to comprehend what otherwise might appear only a confused account of petty wars; — uninteresting, and unimportant.

The facts contained in the history have been mainly derived from the work of Bishop Thirlwall.

GEOGRAPHY OF GREECE, &c.

GRECIAN STATES.

Countries.	Chief Towns, &c.
Attica	Athens, with its ports,—Piræus, Phalerum, and Munychia. Eleusis, Decelea, Marathon. The river Ilissus, Mount Pentelicus, Mount Parnes.
Megaris	Megara.
Bœotia	Thebes, Platæa, Leuctra, Cheronæa, Thespiæ, Tanagra, Mount Cithæron, Mount Helicon.
Phocis	Delphi, Mount Parnassus.
Locri Epicnemidii	Alpeni.
Locri Opuntii	
Locri Ozolæ	Amphissa, Naupactus.
Doris	
Ætolia	
Acarnania	
Thessalia	Thermopylæ, Demetrias, the Vale of Tempe, the district of Magnesia, Mount Olympus, Mount Œta, Mount Ossa, the Hills of Cynoscephalæ

THE PELOPONNESUS.

Achaia	
Argolis	Argos, Mycenæ, Træzen, Halia.
Elis	Olympia.
Messenia	Ithome, Messene.
Laconia	Sparta, Helos, Sellasia, the river Eurotas
Corinthia	Corinth.
Sicyonia	Sicyon.
Arcadia	Mantinea, Megalopolis.

COUNTRIES AND ISLANDS ADJOINING GREECE.

Macedonia	Pydna, Amphipolis, the Peninsula of Chalcidice, containing the towns of Olynthus and Potidæa.
Thrace	The peninsula called Chersonesus, containing the towns of Ægos Potami and Sestos. The river Strymon.
Epirus	The district of Molossia, Dodona.
Illyria	
Italy	Crotona, Rhegium.
Sicily (Island)	Syracuse, Segesta, Selinus, Catana.
Eubœa (Island)	Eretria, Chalcis, Artemisium.
Lesbos (Island)	Mitylene.

The Islands of Salamis, Ægina, Thera, Melos, Delos, Paros, Andros, Paros, Scyros, Crete, Corcyra, Ithaca, Samos, Zacynthus, Cephalenia. The three small islands of Arginusæ off the coast of Æolis in Asia Minor. Sphacteria (off the coast of Messenia.)

ASIA MINOR.

Countries	Chief Towns, &c
Pamphilia	The river Eurymedon.
Mysia	Lampsacus, Abydos.
Bithynia.	
Lydia	Sardis, Magnesia. The river Pactolus
Ionia	Miletus, Ephesus.
Caria	Myus.
Cilicia	Issus.
Æolis.	

PERSIA, INDIA, &c.

Media	Ecbatana.
Susiana	Susa.
Parthia.	
Sogdiana	The river Oxus.
Bactriana.	
Gedrosia.	
Armenia.	
Assyria	Babylon, Arbela or Gaugamela.
Phœnicia	Tyre.
Palestine	Jerusalem.

The Rivers Hydaspes, Zaradrus, and Indus.

EGYPT.

The desert of Libya, and the city of Alexandria.

The Pontus Euxinus; now called the Black Sea.
The Propontis; now the Sea of Marmora.
The Ægean Sea; now the Archipelago.
The Hellespont (straits connecting the Propontis with the Ægean Sea);
 now the Straits of the Dardanelles.

CONTENTS.

CHAPTER I.
The Siege of Troy - - - - - 1

CHAPTER II.
The Return of the Heracleids - - - - 5

CHAPTER III.
The Laws of Lycurgus - - - - 12

CHAPTER IV.
The First Messenian War - - - - 21

CHAPTER V.
The Second Messenian War - - - 26

CHAPTER VI.
The Conspiracy of Cylon at Athens - - - 30

CHAPTER VII.
Solon gives Laws to Athens - - - - 34

CHAPTER VIII.
Pisistratus, Tyrant of Athens - - - 39

CHAPTER IX.
Hippias expelled from Athens - - - 46

CHAPTER X.
The Burning of Sardis - - - - 51

CHAPTER XI.
The Battle of Marathon — 61

CHAPTER XII.
The Battle of Thermopylæ — 68

CHAPTER XIII.
The Battle of Salamis — 82

CHAPTER XIV.
The Battle of Platæa — 98

CHAPTER XV.
The Rebuilding and Fortification of Athens — 113

CHAPTER XVI.
Cimon banished from Athens — 128

CHAPTER XVII.
The Building of the Parthenon, the Propylæa — 140

CHAPTER XVIII.
The Beginning of the Peloponnesian War — 146

CHAPTER XIX.
The Plague at Athens — 158

CHAPTER XX.
The Siege of Platæa — 163

CHAPTER XXI.
Pylos taken and fortified — 172

CHAPTER XXII.
The Peace of Nicias — 179

CHAPTER XXIII.
Commencement of the Sicilian War - - 187

CHAPTER XXIV.
Continuation of the Sicilian War - - - 194

CHAPTER XXV.
Conclusion of the Sicilian War - - 201

CHAPTER XXVI.
The Return of Alcibiades - - - 213

CHAPTER XXVII.
The Battle of Arginusæ, and the unjust Sentence against the Athenian Generals - - - - 219

CHAPTER XXVIII.
The Battle of Ægos Potami - - - 225

CHAPTER XXIX.
The Government of the Thirty Tyrants - 228

CHAPTER XXX.
The Death of Socrates - - - - 234

CHAPTER XXXI.
The Retreat of the Ten Thousand Greeks - 238

CHAPTER XXXII.
The Peace of Antalcidas - - 249

CHAPTER XXXIII.
The Battle of Leuctra - - - - 255

CHAPTER XXXIV.
The Battle of Mantinea - - 261

CONTENTS.

	Page
CHAPTER XXXV.	
Commencement of the Sacred War	260
CHAPTER XXXVI.	
The Battle of Chæronea	274
CHAPTER XXXVII.	
The Invasion of Persia by Alexander the Great	280
CHAPTER XXXVIII.	
The Battle of Issus	285
CHAPTER XXXIX.	
The Battle of Arbela, or Gaugamela	291
CHAPTER XL.	
Alexander defeats Porus	295
CHAPTER XLI.	
Death of Alexander the Great at Babylon	303
CHAPTER XLII.	
Athens taken by Antipater	309
CHAPTER XLIII.	
Athens submits to Cassander	315
CHAPTER XLIV.	
Agis IV. endeavours to reform Sparta	321
CHAPTER XLV.	
The Death of Philopœmen	326
CHAPTER XLVI.	
Corinth destroyed, and Greece made a Roman Province	332
CHAPTER XLVII	
Conclusion	335

HISTORY OF GREECE.

CHAPTER I.

THE SIEGE OF TROY.

B.C. 1184.

THE History of Greece is more confused at first than that of many other countries. It goes back into years so long past away, that we cannot learn anything certain about them; and, instead of being the account of what happened to one great nation, it tells us of the events which befel several small states.

Greece is in the south-east of Europe. If we were to describe it now, we should say that it is bounded on the north by Turkey; on the east by the Archipelago and Asia-Minor; and on the south and west by the Mediterranean. In former times the Archipelago was called the Ægeum Mare, or Ægean Sea; and Turkey was divided into Macedonia, Illyria, Thrace, Epirus, and other kingdoms.

Greece is a beautiful and fertile country, producing olives, vines, figs, corn, and all the necessaries of life; and, being so far to the south, the climate is very warm and pleasant. But it must have been much more beautiful in ancient days, when it contained a number of cities and towns, adorned with splendid buildings; besides temples ornamented with rows of pillars, and statues, and carvings. These things are now in ruins, but even the portions that are left are far superior to the works of the present day: for the Greeks were especially famous for their skill and taste; and, indeed, no nation has ever equalled them in these respects.

The southern part of Greece was in ancient days called the Peloponnesus. It is joined to the northern part by the Isthmus of Corinth.

The whole country, but particularly the Peloponnesus, is full of mountains, which seem to have been the natural cause of the number of small states; since they shut in the people who lived in the valleys, something in the same way as walls shut in the inhabitants of a town. There are a great many rivers in Greece, but they are narrow, and generally dry in the summer. The sea flows round Greece on three sides, and, as it is encircled by a great number of lovely islands, we may well imagine that the inhabitants soon learnt the use of ships and boats, and made voyages from their own land to visit those who dwelt so near them. The animals of Greece were very much the same as ours, except that there were wild boars, and wolves, and bears, amongst the forests and hills, which persons who were bold and hardy used to take pleasure in hunting.

The people who first dwelt in Greece were descended from Japhet the son of Noah. It was from him that all the original inhabitants of Europe came; as the greater part of Asia was peopled by the children of Shem, and Africa by the children of Ham.

Thus we are told in the Bible that "the sons of Noah that went forth out of the ark, were Shem, and Ham, and Japhet;—and of them was the whole earth overspread."[*]

We do not know how many years passed after

---

[*] Genesis ix. 18, 19.

the deluge before Greece was peopled, but we learn from ancient writers that the earliest inhabitants were the Pelasgi. They do not appear to have been at all like the savage tribes we read of as being found in parts of America, or Australia, or New Zealand; for they are said to have understood how to cultivate their land, and keep sheep, and carry on a trade with the neighbouring countries; and their buildings, though they were very rough, were so strong that the ruins are to be seen in these days. The Greeks used themselves to believe that the old castles of the Pelasgi were the work of a race of giants called Cyclops, for they could not imagine it possible that such huge stones could have been put together by common men.

The next race of people whom we hear of as inhabiting Greece were the Hellenes; from them the whole country used to be called Hellas. The name of Greece was given to it by the Romans. It is supposed that the Hellenes came from the west, and gained possession of the country by degrees; not conquering all at once, but living amongst the Pelasgi, and being mixed up with them, until at length, from being only a small tribe, they became masters of the whole land. They were not governed by one king any more than the Pelasgi. There were still different states having their own rulers, though they all spoke nearly the same language. It is also said, that by this time colonies of strangers had settled in Greece from Egypt and Asia, but we know very little about them. The only fact we are quite sure of is, that the Greeks learnt how to form the letters of their alphabet from the Phœnicians, who dwelt on the coasts of Asia-Minor. This gives us an idea that they must have been accustomed to trade with the Phœnicians and be a good deal with them.

All these ancient people were idolaters. Their

gods were supposed to have their abodes upon the top of a high mountain called Olympus, between Thessaly and Macedonia. The chief of all was Zeus, but there were a great number of inferior deities; indeed, the Greeks seem to have taken delight in fancying that every town, and river, and hill, had a god or goddess of its own. These special gods are called tutelary deities. The Greeks also supposed that at some peculiar places the will of the gods was declared to persons who went to ask it. They built temples on these spots, and paid great respect to the priests and priestesses who had the charge of them. The most famous of the Oracles, as they were termed, were those of Dodona in Epirus, and Delphi in Phocis. The god Zeus was worshipped at Dodona, and Apollo at Delphi.

There are a great many wonderful stories told of the events which took place in these early times, but there is only one which it is necessary to mention here — the account of the siege of Troy.

Troy was a city of Asia-Minor, and the capital of a small state called Troas. It stood near the sea coast, and was surrounded by strong high walls. About the time when the Israelites were governed by judges, Troy was governed by a king named Priam. Paris, the son of Priam, travelled to Greece, and there was very kindly received by Menelaus king of Sparta, one of the chief cities in Peloponnesus. But instead of being grateful for the attentions which were shown to him, Paris was wicked enough, when he went back to Troy, to carry away with him the beautiful wife of Menelaus — a lady called Helen. Menelaus, as may well be supposed, was exceedingly angry, and so were all his friends, and they agreed to join their armies and go to besiege Troy. For ten years they tried in vain to break down the walls of the city; and, at last, when they found that all their endeavours were of no use, they formed a plan for getting into it secretly. They made a great hollow wooden horse, which they filled with armed men, and having done this the whole Grecian army moved away, as if they were intending to give up their attempt. The people of Troy were quite deceived, and very foolishly were persuaded by a man, who was in reality a Greek, but who pretended to be a friend of the Trojans, to make a breach in the wall and take the horse in. They thought then that all their troubles were at an end. But when it became dark night, the soldiers who were hidden inside the wooden horse stole out very quietly, and went as quickly as they could to the gates, and opened them. The Greek armies had returned by this time and were waiting outside the walls. As soon as the gates were opened they rushed in, killed the inhabitants, plundered their houses, and, at last, burned the city to the ground. And thus ended this long war: — B.C. 1184. Almost all that we know about it is from the writings of Homer, the oldest of the Greek poets, who composed two beautiful poems, called the Iliad and the Odyssey. The Iliad describes the war and the siege of Troy; and the Odyssey tells of the adventures which befel Ulysses, king of the Isle of Ithaca, as he was returning from Troy to his own country.

CHAP. II.

THE RETURN OF THE HERACLEIDS.

ABOUT B.C. 1124.

THE next great change which took place in Greece was the invasion of the southern part of the country, or Peloponnesus,—so named from Pelops an ancient Greek prince, — by a tribe known as the Heracleids, or descendants of Hercules. The Heracleids are called Dorians, from their having dwelt in Doris in the north of Greece; but it was always said that they originally came from Peloponnesus, and had a right to return there.

The following is the account which the ancient Greek writers give of these people. We shall see at once, that like almost all old histories of this kind it cannot be quite true.

Hercules, the ancestor of the Heracleids, was said to have been the son of the god Zeus; for the Greeks were very fond of fancying that their great heroes were descended from the gods. They declared he was stronger than any person who ever lived; and they kept an account of some of his wonderful deeds which were called the twelve labours of Hercules. The mother of Hercules was supposed to have been the grand-daughter of a king of Argos in Peloponnesus, and Hercules therefore had a right to be king of that state. One of his cousins, however, who was his great enemy, took possession of the throne, and treated Hercules very shamefully during his life, and after his death drove all his children away from Argos. They went for safety to Attica, another Grecian state to the north of Peloponnesus; and Eurystheus, their cruel cousin, followed them with a great army. The people of Attica were friends to the Heracleids, and helped them in their distress; and when a battle was fought, the Heracleids conquered, and Eurystheus fled away in his chariot. He was overtaken in a narrow pass amongst great rocks, by Hyllus, the eldest son of Hercules, and there slain. Then the Heracleids returned in triumph to Argos; but they were not allowed to stay there very long. A dreadful plague broke out which destroyed an immense number of people, and as the chief persons in Argos believed it was a sign that the gods were angry with them, they sent to the Oracle at Delphi, to ask the cause. The answer given them was, that the plague was sent because the Heracleids had returned to Argos too soon. Of course after such a warning they did not dare remain, and once more they left their country and went to Attica.

Several years went by after this, and then Hyllus, the eldest of the race of Hercules, sent again to the Oracle of Delphi, to know if the time had arrived when they might go back to Argos. "Wait," replied the Oracle, "for the third crop, and then return by the Straits." The Heracleids thought they understood this. They waited for three years, till three crops or harvests had been gathered in; and then they set out for their ancient home across the Isthmus of Corinth. But they were met by the inhabitants of Peloponnesus and defeated. Again and again they tried, and still they never could succeed. More than a hundred years passed during these misfortunes. Hyllus died, and his son; and it might have been thought that the Heracleids, having suffered so many disappointments, would have given up all idea of being restored to their country. But in the third generation, that is, in the time of the grandson of Hyllus, the Oracle of Delphi was once more consulted, and the answer given before was made clear. "The third crop," meant the third generation, and by "the Straits," it was intended that they were to pass over to Peloponnesus by sea, and not by land. Then, at last, the Heracleids gained their wishes, and, having crossed the Straits, defeated their enemies, and took possession, not only of Argos, but of the whole of Peloponnesus.

This was the story told by the Grecian poets, but

all that we can really believe about it is, that the Dorians did really cross over to Peloponnesus and settle themselves there by degrees.

After this, no great change took place for a great many years. The different states of Greece were like persons belonging to one family, living apart and often quarrelling with each other, but still not liking strangers to interfere with them. They worshipped the same gods, and consulted the same oracles; and in order to decide questions which concerned all, or many of the states, they chose particular persons to meet together at stated times and settle what was to be done. These persons formed what was called Amphictyonies, or Amphictyonic councils. There were several of these councils, but the most celebrated is that which used to meet twice a year to arrange all affairs concerning the temple at Delphi.

The Greeks, however, did not keep entirely to their own land and the islands near it. Some of the ancient people, who were driven out of Peloponnesus when the Heracleids or Dorians took possession of the country, went over to Asia-Minor, and settled themselves near the coast; and in time others followed their example. The Greeks were always inclined to be restless, and to like moving to new places; and by degrees there were Greek states and cities not only in Asia-Minor, but also in Sicily, and the south of Italy, and the island of Cyprus, and even in Egypt, and Libya, in Africa. The different states were also in the habit of founding colonies in the countries adjoining Greece. There were several of these colonies on the coast of Macedonia. A strong feeling of union existed between the colonies and the state from which they came. The colonies were careful to help what was called the mother-country, whenever it was in any distress.

The same gods, it was believed, watched over them both. And in order to remind themselves that they were still one people, the colonists, when they left their native place, were accustomed to carry with them a portion of a fire which the Greeks kept burning in the council hall of the city, where the magistrates met; and which was therefore considered sacred. This fire they managed to keep lighted, whilst they were on their voyage or journey, and then it was used for the same purpose as before in their new home. It was also a rule amongst them, that if the colonies, in their turn, wished to found new cities in distant countries, the leader of the expedition was always to be brought from the mother country. These colonies greatly increased the power of the Greeks, but they also frequently brought them into difficulties. As they were settled in foreign countries, the monarchs of those countries often interfered with them, and this brought on a war with the parent state. It would not be easy for us to have cities scattered about as the Greeks had; but in those days, many of the lands near Greece were only inhabited by barbarous tribes, and it was not difficult to land on their coasts and build a town. The difficulty was to keep these towns afterwards, when the tribes were more civilised and united under one king.

But that which more than anything else made the states look upon themselves as one nation, was their custom of all meeting together, at stated times, to amuse themselves with public games.

There were four different kinds of these public games: the Olympic, the Pythian, the Isthmian, and the Nemean. The Olympic were the most celebrated; indeed the fame of them spread all over the world.

The place where these games were held was a

lovely valley, shut in by mountains, and by two rivers, in the state of Elis, in Peloponnesus. For ages and ages this spot was considered sacred. The Greeks thought that it was peculiarly blessed by Zeus, the chief of their gods; and the people of Elis were allowed to live quietly in times of war, and to enjoy themselves in their homes without being disturbed, because no one liked to interfere with a state in which there was a place so sacred as Olympia.

There is little now to be seen in the plain of Olympia but a few ruins of brick. The mountains stand as they did in the old times, and trees flourish upon them year after year, and the rivers flow in the same tracks; but all the great buildings and statues have crumbled to dust, and the valley is silent and deserted.

It was very different in the ancient days when the Greeks were a great people. Every fourth year, when the summer days were long, and the moon was bright and full, crowds from all the various Grecian states, and from the colonies in Europe, Africa, and Asia, hastened to Olympia to amuse themselves with the public games, and do honour to the great Olympian Zeus. The temple of the god stood in the middle of the sacred ground. It was a beautiful building, ornamented on the outside with carved figures or sculpture, for which the Greeks were always famous. A golden statue of Victory was placed in front, and a golden vase at each end of the roof. Beneath the statue hung a shield likewise of gold. Within the temple was the figure of the god, the work of one of the most famous sculptors that ever lived. It was of an enormous size, and made of ivory and gold; the ivory was coloured so as to look like flesh. Precious stones, and painting, and gold adorned not only the figure of the god but the throne on which he sat; and the whole looked so dazzling and wonderful, that the Greeks forgot that the image was made by the hands of a human being, and they worshipped it. There were several buildings at Olympia besides the temple: in one the victors in the games dined; in another the regulations relating to the games were made; and others contained treasures — offerings from the various states.

But the public games brought people to Olympia, as well as the respect paid to Zeus. The Greeks indeed thought that they showed their devotion to the god by going to these festivals which were dedicated to him; and the greatest honour which any one could have was to gain the prize on such occasions. There were chariot races, and horse races, and foot races, and boxing and wrestling matches, all of which seem to us of very little importance, but which the Greeks thought of great consequence. And yet the prize which was given was only a garland made of the leaves of the wild olive. For the Greeks cared more for honour than riches,—and no one who had gained the olive wreath at the Olympic games would have parted with it for thousands of pounds.

It was the same at the Pythian, and Isthmian, and Nemean games. Persons were very anxious to gain the prizes, but only because it was an honour to do so.

The Pythian games were held near Delphi, in honour of a victory supposed to have been gained by the god Apollo over a great serpent. The prize given was a wreath of laurel.

The Isthmian games were so named because they were celebrated on the Isthmus of Corinth. They were held in honour of Poseidon (called Neptune by the Romans), the god of the sea, and the prize was a wreath of pine leaves.

St. Paul makes mention of these games in his first epistle to the Corinthians; where he tells the early Christians who lived in the City of Corinth, that they were to strive as hard to obtain heaven, as other persons did to obtain the fading crown or wreath at the public games.

The prize at the Nemean games was a wreath of parsley. These games were celebrated on the plains of Nemea, in the state of Argolis, in Peloponnesus. They were in honour of Hercules, who was said to have killed a savage lion in a forest near.

After some time the Greeks used to date their history from the years when the Olympic games were celebrated. They began to do this about the year B.C. 776, and every four years they called an Olympiad. In speaking, therefore, of any particular event, instead of saying as we might, — it happened so many years after the world was created, or so many years before the birth of our Lord; they would say — it happened in the first, second, or third year of such an Olympiad.

CHAP. III.

THE LAWS OF LYCURGUS.

B.C. 884.

It would be very confusing to give an account of each of the Grecian states separately, neither is it necessary, since there were two, which were always considered the chief; and in learning their history we at the same time learn the principal events which took place in the others.

It may, however, be desirable to give a list of the chief divisions of Greece, as it will make the history which follows more clear. In Peloponnesus, or Southern Greece, were Laconia, Messenia, Elis, Arcadia, Argolis, Corinth, Sicyon, and Achaia. In Greece Proper, or Northern Greece, were Attica, Megaris, Bœotia, Phocis, Ætolia, Locris, Doris, Acarnania, and Thessaly. We shall perhaps gain a better idea of the country by remembering that these divisions were not larger than many of our English counties. The small size of Greece is indeed very remarkable. The whole country was not more than 250 miles in length, and 180 in breadth.

A division sometimes consisted of several small states, so independent of each other that they would often make peace or war by themselves; and yet united together, in other respects, and governed by the same magistrates. There were, for instance, fourteen little states in Bœotia, which were all governed by a number of magistrates, called Bœotarchs, chosen from all the states every year. Thebes was the principal of these states, and the others were considered its subjects. But this arrangement naturally caused a great deal of disturbance. The little states still thought themselves free, and whenever they chose they made an alliance with the people of some distant city or district, and then the inhabitants of the chief state became very angry, and often war was the consequence. It is necessary also to remember that the chief state is often spoken of by itself, when, in fact, the little states were joined with it. In the same way as we often now talk of England's making war or peace, when we mean not England alone, but Scotland, Ireland, and Wales also. This is particularly the case in regard to Thebes.

The principal events of Grecian history are

C

however, connected with the two great cities of Athens and Sparta. Sparta was the capital of the state of Laconia in Peloponnesus. The Heracleids or Dorians settled themselves there, when first they invaded Peloponnesus; and though they allowed the people, who had lived in the country before they came, to remain, yet they made them pay tribute, and would not let them help in the government. In fact the Dorians treated the people they had conquered very much in the same way as the Normans, under William the Conqueror, treated the Anglo-Saxons, after the battle of Hastings.

The Dorians who lived in the city were called Spartans, and the conquered people, Lacedæmonians. But in speaking of them — especially in describing the battles which they fought — they are often called by one name, — Spartans. The true Spartans always, however, considered themselves superior to the Lacedæmonians. They were in fact the nobles of the country. There was one town in Laconia which would not yield to the Spartans. This was Helos, a place near the sea coast. The inhabitants, it is said, tried very much to keep their freedom, but their endeavours were of no use; and they were not only conquered like the rest of the inhabitants of Laconia, but were made slaves for ever.

The Spartans were hard masters, and though probably they were not as cruel to the Helots as some writers have declared, yet we know that many of the laws respecting these slaves were very severe. A Helot was forced to live always in the same place, and to wear a peculiar dress, and was kept so distinct from the Spartans that he did not dare even to sing a Spartan song.

The Helots, in consequence of these hardships, were often inclined to rebel, and the Spartans were always suspecting them. It has been asserted that every year a number of young Spartans were ordered to go about the country secretly, with daggers, and kill every Helot who was remarkable for cleverness or strength, or was likely to make a disturbance in the country. On one occasion, when the Spartans were afraid that the Helots intended to rebel, they sent for the bravest and best, who had distinguished themselves in war, pretending that they were going to reward them by making them free; and when two thousand had assembled, full of joy and gratitude, the cruel Spartans caused them all to be killed.

The Spartans indeed were always a severe, determined people, having customs and manners which made them in many ways unlike other nations; and as their country was shut in by mountains, they lived a good deal to themselves, and became too proud of their own laws and government to have any wish to improve them.

The person who is supposed to have quite fixed the peculiar habits of the Spartans was Lycurgus, the younger son of a Spartan king, named Eunomus. Lycurgus is said to have lived about 900 years before the birth of our Blessed Saviour, about the same time that king Jehoshaphat was reigning in Judea. Polydectes, the elder son of Eunomus, came to the throne after his father, and died before a child which he was expecting was actually born to him; so that it seemed as if Lycurgus had a claim to succeed. But Lycurgus was too honourable to take possession of any dignity that might not strictly be his. He therefore told the queen, his brother's widow, that if, when her child was born, it should be a boy, he would not attempt to take the crown for himself, but would only be guardian to the little infant, until he should be old enough to rule for himself. One evening as he was sitting at supper with the magistrates of the city, some messengers came to him, bringing with them a little prince, just born. Lycurgus did not show the least annoyance, but taking the baby in his arms, he laid him in the seat set apart for the king, and turning to the persons present, exclaimed: "Spartans! a king is born to us." Then, to show how truly glad he was himself, and how much the people ought to rejoice, he gave to the infant the name of "Charilaus," or "People's joy."

But Lycurgus was not rewarded for his right conduct as he deserved. The queen could not bear him, and in order to make the people dislike him, pretended that he wished to murder the little king. Lycurgus did not try to defend himself, but thought it best to go away, in order to put a stop to the evil reports which were set on foot. He therefore left Sparta, intending to visit foreign countries, and enquire into their laws and customs, so that he might be able in after years to improve those of his own nation. He is said to have gone to the Island of Crete first. The Cretans were, like the Spartans, a Dorian race, and were famous for their wise government; and Lycurgus is supposed to have learnt a great deal from them. From Crete he went to Asia-Minor and Egypt; and when at last he had gained the knowledge he wished, he prepared to go back to his own country, where his friends were very anxious to see him, as everything had gone wrong during his absence, because king Charilaus did not know how to govern properly. Having a great reverence for the gods, Lycurgus resolved, before he returned to Sparta, to go to Delphi, and ask of the Oracle whether his wish of making better laws for Sparta was wise, and whether he was the proper person to undertake such a task. The priestess at Delphi praised him excessively, and told him that he was more like a god than a man, and Lycurgus went away quite satisfied that his intentions would be blest.

On his arrival at Sparta he began at once to carry out his plan. He went to some of the principal persons in the city, and informed them that he was wishing to make some alteration in the laws, and asked them to help him. Many promised that they would; and when the day was fixed on which he was to propose the changes to the people, Lycurgus begged thirty of his friends to arm themselves and station themselves in the market place, so that if any disturbance were made they might be near to aid him.

King Charilaus found out what was going on, and being much alarmed fled to a temple for safety; but he was soon persuaded to come back, and give his own consent to the plan which his uncle Lycurgus had formed.

It took some time to arrange every thing properly, and many persons hated Lycurgus, and did all they could to annoy him, and stop what he was doing; but he went on steadily, inquiring into wrong customs, and putting an end to them; and making new and wise laws; and at length he had the great satisfaction of seeing the country improving and the people happier. Then he had gained his chief wish, and as he was determined, if possible, to prevent the Spartans from ever returning again to their bad laws, he one day assembled the king and all the chief magistrates, and told them that he was obliged to go away from the city for a little time, and therefore begged they would take an oath to observe the new laws till he came back.

No one liked to refuse, and Lycurgus once more left Sparta. Again he journeyed to Delphi, and this time the question which he asked was, whether the laws that he had framed would make the people happy. He was told that there was nothing wanting to them, and that Sparta would flourish as long as they were observed. Lycurgus sent back this answer to his fellow countrymen; but he never returned to them himself; and wandered in other lands till his death. The Spartans therefore were still bound by their oath. They kept the laws, and soon learnt to like them; and as years went by, and they knew that Lycurgus must be dead, they honoured him as a god.

It is usual to call the Spartan laws the laws of Lycurgus, but it must not be thought that they were all framed by him. No doubt he made a great many of them; but some must have been only brought into use again, after having been forgotten, for we find that they were common in other places besides Sparta, where the Dorians settled.

One of the most remarkable things in the way the Spartans were governed was, that they had always two kings, who were descended from two of the descendants of Hercules. Their kings, however, had not much more power than all chief magistrates generally have. They could not make laws by themselves, but were obliged to consult a council or senate, chosen by the people, and composed of twenty-eight persons who had reached the age of sixty.

When a law was to be made, the kings and the senate met together, to decide whether it would be wise to propose it to the people. If they agreed that it was, they brought forward the subject at a public meeting, which was held every month, in the open air, in a place outside the city. All Spartans who were thirty years old, might attend this meeting. They were not allowed to discuss the law which was to be made, but were only asked if they would consent to it. If they did, the law was considered as settled.

But the persons who really had the chief power in Sparta were five magistrates, called Ephors. They were chosen by the people and were so much looked up to, that even the kings were obliged to appear before them if any complaint was made against them.

The habits of living of the Spartans were very different from any we are accustomed to. They did not care for luxury or grandeur, and even the kings did not dress better or have better dinners than the rest of the people.

All the men dined together in public; the two kings as well as their subjects. Fifteen persons sat down at one table, and each person was obliged to bring a certain quantity of provisions every month. The little boys used to sit on stools, at their fathers' feet; but the elder boys had tables for themselves.

They were not at all particular about their food and never had rich dishes, but were contented generally with what they called black broth, which is said to have had a very disagreeable taste, together with cheese and figs.

It was the great wish of the Spartans to be brave and hardy themselves, and to bring up their children to be the same. And it is said that when a sickly child was born, the chief persons of the family to which it belonged would take it from its mother, and send it away to some caverns in a mountain, where the poor little infant was left to die. The healthy children remained with their parents. When the little boys were seven years old they were sent to school, not to learn reading and writing as children do now, but to be taught how to fight and wrestle, and understand every thing which might be of use when they went to war. In order to make them hardy they wore the same kind of clothes both in winter and summer; their beds were made of reeds; and now and then they were obliged to go without any dinner, and were beaten, not because they had done wrong, but in order to teach them how to bear pain. It was indeed thought such a noble thing to endure suffering silently, that the bravest boys used to take a pride in standing upon the altar in one of the temples and allowing themselves to be lashed so dreadfully, that at times some of them died; yet even in these cases they often expired without uttering a groan.

There was another custom which appears strange to us, but which the Spartans approved, because they thought that it trained their children to be quick and clever. They used now and then to order the boys to go and steal whatever they could find in the fields or houses of their neighbours; and if the child managed well, and took away what he wanted, he was praised for it; but if he failed he was punished.

This was considered very different from common stealing, but it certainly must have taught the children to be cunning.

After being accustomed to this severe life from childhood, the Spartans, it may easily be supposed, cared very little for the hardships of war. In fact, they liked war better than peace; and when a young Spartan knew that a battle was to take place, he dressed himself as gaily, and looked as cheerful and happy as if he was going to a great entertainment. Even the women wished nothing more for their husbands or children than that they should be good soldiers: and a Spartan mother is said to have given her son his shield, as he was setting forth for battle, telling him that he was either to bring it home himself, or to be borne upon it dead. The idea of running away never seems to have entered their minds.

One of the worst things we know about the Spartans is that they were very fond of money, and were often tempted to behave dishonorably, if they were offered a reward. This is particularly extraordinary, because they were not allowed to coin gold or silver, but were obliged to use iron bars for money; so that they could never have a great deal at a time, as it would have been very inconvenient. Their lands were divided into shares, which were given to different families. The best shares belonged to the Spartans, and the others were left for the Lacedæmonians.

CHAP. IV.

THE FIRST MESSENIAN WAR.

B.C. 743.

As the Spartans were so well trained for war, they were not likely to remain for any length of time without finding some cause for quarrelling with their neighbours. The first dispute we know of, which was of much consequence, was with the Messenians.

Messenia was a state close to Laconia, and it had been peopled in the same way by the Dorians. But the laws and customs were not entirely like those of Sparta, and the inhabitants were more peaceably inclined. The country was very fertile and pleasant. It had many streams and woody valleys, and plains where the flocks and herds might feed, and the hills were not as high as those in Laconia, so that the sun shone brightly upon the land, and ripened the fruits, and caused the trees and shrubs to flourish. All these advantages made the Spartans wish to have it for their own. Two or three different reasons have been given for the first beginning of this war; and it is certain that the Spartans and Messenians disliked each other some time before they actually took up arms; but the circumstances which at last caused the war to commence were the following :—

A rich Messenian, whose name was Polychares, possessed some herds of cattle, which he sent to graze on lands that belonged to a Spartan; making an agreement with the Spartan to let him have a share in the profits of the cows. The Spartan sold the cows, and then told Polychares that they had been carried off by pirates. Polychares, however, found out the truth, and the Spartan being very much frightened, entreated to be forgiven, and promised to pay as much money as the cows were worth; only, he said, the son of Polychares must go with him to fetch it. Polychares did not think that any harm was intended, and allowed his son to go; but they had no sooner left Messenia, and entered Laconia, than the wicked Spartan turned upon the poor young man and killed him. Polychares was exceedingly angry, and very unhappy when the news reached him. He went to Sparta and begged that the murderer might be punished; but the kings and the ephors would not listen to him; and Polychares then resolving to revenge himself, waylaid the persons who crossed the borders of the two countries, and killed every Spartan who came in his way. This was very dreadful, and the Spartans could not allow it to go on. They declared that Polychares must be given up to them; but the Messenians would not consent, and after long disputes war broke out.

The real object of the Spartans in beginning this war was soon made clear. They bound themselves by a solemn oath never to end it, until the lands of the Messenians became their own; and then, without giving any warning of their plans, marched across the border when it was dark night, entered one of the Messenian towns, and killed the inhabitants when they were lying quietly asleep in their beds.

This cruel act roused the spirit of the Messenians to the utmost. They saw that the Spartans were determined to conquer them, and did all they could to defend themselves. But they had never been taught to fight as well as the Spartans, and though they carried on the war year after year, their case became gradually hopeless. The farmers and labourers did not care to till the ground, when the Spartans might come and carry away every thing they possessed; and in consequence every one suffered from hunger and dreadful illness, besides the dangers of the battles.

At last, when they were nearly in despair, they determined to shut themselves up in Ithomé, a town which was built on the top of a very steep hill, from whence they thought they might watch all that the Spartans did, and prevent them from advancing further into the country. They even talked of building a new town there, because the old one was not large enough to hold all the persons who wished to settle in it. But before beginning this work they sent to the Oracle at Delphi, to know what they were to do in order to succeed in defending themselves from the Spartans. The answer declared that a sacrifice must be offered to the gods, of a young maiden belonging to the royal family, who was to be chosen by lot. If the lot should fall upon a wrong person, one, for instance, who was not of the royal family, another maiden was to be offered willingly by her relations. The lot did fall wrongly, or at least the soothsayer declared it did, and then Aristodemus, a prince of the royal house, came forward of his own accord, and said that his daughter should die. She was a young girl just engaged to be married, and her intended husband was overcome with horror at the thought of losing her. In order to save her he pretended that the gods would not be satisfied, even if she were sacrificed, because they required a good person as an offering, and he knew her to have been wicked.

This accusation enraged Aristodemus beyond imagination; and seizing his weapon, he killed his daughter with his own hands.

The soothsayer still asserted that the gods would not be contented. The young maiden they said had been murdered, and not offered as a sacrifice. The Messenian king, however, interfered, and persuaded the people that all had been done which was necessary, and they prepared to carry on the war with fresh hope. The Spartans were frightened when they heard of the sacrifice which the Messenians had made, and feared that the gods would no longer be on their side, but as the war went on the Messenians still lost ground. Their king was killed in battle, and Aristodemus was chosen in his stead. The soothsayers warned the people, that because he had murdered his daughter, he would not be approved by the gods, but he was so good and brave that every one liked him, and for some time after he came to the throne, there seemed a prospect that the Messenians might be able to drive away their enemies. Aristodemus, however, felt a doubt of this himself, for he heard of wonderful things being seen and heard, which he thought showed that the gods were against him. At last he had a horrible dream. He imagined that his daughter appeared to him, dressed in black, and showed him the wound by which he had killed her; and then taking away the armour which he wore, clothed him with a white robe, and put a golden crown upon his head. This was the dress in which the kings of Messenia were prepared for burial. Aristodemus believed that the dream was sent from heaven, and that it foretold his own death and the ruin of his country; and in bitter sorrow, thinking that his life could be of no use, he went to the place where his child was buried, and killed himself upon her grave.

The war lasted but a short time after Aristodemus was dead. The Messenians, indeed, chose another chief, but they were quite unable to defend themselves any longer, and after the war had continued for twenty years, they fled from the town of Ithomé, and gave up their beautiful country to their enemies.

The Spartans treated them very hardly; indeed they were oppressed as much as the Helots, and when a Spartan king died, both the Messenians and the Helots were obliged to appear with their wives as mourners at his funeral.

CHAP. V.

THE SECOND MESSENIAN WAR.

B.C. 685.

THIRTY-EIGHT years passed after the first Messenian war, before the people of Messenia tried to free themselves from the Spartans; for it was very difficult to begin a rebellion, because the Spartans were so powerful. There were, however, two neighbouring states, Argos and Arcadia, which were willing to help them. The Spartans had long been enemies of the Argives, and had conquered part of their country; and, in consequence, the Argives were very willing to assist the Messenians and Arcadians in a war against the Spartans. The people of Elis, too, were inclined to join with them, so that the Spartans had a great many enemies to fight against.

At this time, B.C. 685, there lived in Messenia a brave prince of the ancient royal family, named Aristomenes. He had long grieved for the hardness which his fellow-countrymen suffered from the Spartans, and when he found that they could have help from the neighbouring states, he resolved at once to rouse the people and begin the war. A battle was fought in which Aristomenes distinguished himself extremely, and the Messenians offered to make him their king; but he refused, for he had no wishes for his own glory; his only thought was how to save others. He consented, however, to be the chief general.

The great object of Aristomenes now was to raise the hopes of the Messenians; and, in order to give them, what they would consider a happy omen, he crossed by night a mountain which divided Laconia from Messenia, and entering the city of Sparta, he went secretly to the temple of the goddess Athene (or Minerva), and fixed against the wall a shield, on which was engraved: "Aristomenes, to the goddess, from the Spartans." This was meant as a triumph over the Spartans. He had taken the shield from a Spartan in battle, and now he sent it back as a present to the goddess.

The Spartans soon found out that their enemies were very powerful; and they sent to the Oracle at Delphi for counsel. The reply of the Oracle was, that they were to seek advice from the Athenians.

The Athenians were the inhabitants of Athens, the capital of Attica, to the north of Peloponnesus. Athens was quite as famous a city as Sparta, and the two states were always rivals. Instead of helping the Spartans by giving them good counsel, or men, or money, the Athenians, it is said, sent them a poet named Tyrtæus. This did not appear as if it would be much use at first, but in the end it helped the Spartans extremely; for the songs that Tyrtæus made, gave them such courage, that they were able to fight much more bravely than perhaps they would otherwise have done.

There are many strange and wonderful tales related by the Grecian writers of the adventures of Aristomenes; and it is certain that he led the Messenians and their allies bravely to battle, and often gained victories over the Spartans. But, at length, after the war had lasted about three years, he fell, we are told, into the hands of his enemies, together with fifty of his friends. They were all carried to Sparta, and thrown into a deep pit. Aristomenes reached the bottom of the pit safely, but his unfortunate companions were dashed to pieces. The cavern was quite dark, and its sides

were so steep and rocky that it seemed next to
impossible for any one to clamber up; and when
Aristomenes looked up he could see the sky appearing far above his head, showing him how deep the
pit was into which he had been cast. For three
days he remained alone in the cavern. On the
third day he heard a noise, as if something alive
was moving about near him. It was a fox which
had made its way into the pit through a passage
that led up to the open air, and which the Spartans
do not seem to have known anything about. Aristomenes seized the creature by the tail, and followed
it, creeping as well as he could, through the narrow
way by which it tried to escape. After some time
the fox came to a hole. Aristomenes then let him
go, and set himself to work to make the hole larger,
and succeeded so well that at last, by his own hands,
he dug a way through the ground and escaped.

The Messenians had at this time shut themelves
up in a strong place amongst the mountains, called
Eira, in the same way as they had before done at
Ithomé. Aristomenes joined them as soon as he
possibly could, and no doubt his friends were over-
joyed to receive him in safety after all his dangers.
His wisdom and bravery were now again of the
greatest use to them. For eleven long years the
Spartans besieged Eira, and still Aristomenes and
his countrymen defended themselves; but the day
of destruction came at last.

It happened that Aristomenes had received a
wound, which prevented him from going about
amongst his men to see that they were all keeping
proper guard over the citadel; and the Messenian
soldiers took advantage of this to go away from their
posts, when they chose. One dark, stormy night,
when it seemed as if the Spartans could not possibly
think of making an attack, a Messenian soldier left

his watch and went back to his home. His wife did not at all expect him, and during his absence she had allowed a Spartan herdsman to come and see her. The Spartan was naturally enough very frightened when he found that the Messenian was returned, and in a great hurry hid himself, but in such a way that he could hear all which the husband and wife said to each other. The Messenian began to tell his wife about Aristomenes and his wound, and that the watch was not kept as strictly as usual; and the Spartan listened and thought that he would make good use of the news. When the Messenian had finished talking, and left the room, the Spartan hastened from the house and went back to the camp to tell his general that he had better at once order an attack to be made, for that the sentinels were off their guard. The Spartans accordingly set forth, caring nothing for the dark night. They clambered up the walls, and entered the citadel. The Messenians were sleeping peacefully, when they were awakened by a dreadful howling of the dogs in the city; and soon learnt that their enemies were within the gates. The night was so dark that neither the Spartans nor the Messenians could do much either in attack or defence till the morning. But when daylight came Aristomenes urged his people to fight desperately to the last. Even the women fought, for they were all in despair, and the torrents of rain, and the fearful flashes of lightning, and the rolling thunder, seemed to make their situation more terrible. They went on in this way for three days and nights; but whilst the Spartans were bringing fresh soldiers continually into the citadel, the poor Messenians were dying one after the other from their wounds and their hunger. Aristomenes at last saw that he must give up He collected his men together, and made them stand in the form of a square, with a hollow in the middle, in which he placed the women and children. They then went forward together to meet their enemies, and Aristomenes made signs to show that they wished to be allowed to leave the city. The Spartans not liking to refuse, opened a way amongst the ranks of their soldiers; Aristomenes and the Messenians passed safely through, and leaving Eira and their native country to be taken possession of by the Spartans, set forth themselves for Arcadia.

It must have been a sad and weary journey, but there was comfort for them at the end, for the Arcadians received them most kindly. Aristomenes attacked the Spartans many times after this, but all his efforts failed, and Messenia was now quite subject to Sparta, though an Oracle declared that it should not always remain so. After his warlike life, Aristomenes died peacefully in the house of his son-in-law, in the Island of Rhodes.

Thus ended the second Messenian war, b.c. 668. The Spartans treated the people they had conquered with the same severity as before, and many went away to other countries. Some of the descendants of Aristomenes, in after years passed over to Sicily, and took a town which they named Messene, in remembrance of their own country; and to this day it is called Messina.

CHAP. VI.

THE CONSPIRACY OF CYLON AT ATHENS.

b.c. 612.

WE must now turn to the history of Athens, a state which has been mentioned before as the rival of Sparta. The Spartans were a Dorian people; the Athenians came from a race called Ionians; and there was as great a distinction between them as between the French and the English, at least in many respects. They spoke the same language, indeed, but it was with another accent; a like difference could be discovered amongst several of the other Grecian states. Some were Dorian and some Ionian. The Dorian states usually sided with the Spartans, and the Ionian with the Athenians. Attica, of which Athens was the capital, was but a small state, yet in the earliest times it is said to have been divided into several districts, each governed by a chief, who took the title of king. Athens was one of these districts, and Cecrops, a king of Athens, persuaded his people and those of the other districts to form a union or confederacy, to protect themselves from pirates and invaders. In after years the districts were united into one state, by Theseus, one of the early Grecian heroes, about whom almost as many wonderful stories are told as about Hercules. Theseus was the king of Athens, and he made his city the capital of the country, and it soon became of so much importance that the name of Athenians is used commonly for the inhabitants of the whole state.

The last king of Athens was Codrus; he was king about the time that the Dorians were preparing to invade Peloponnesus, and the following story is related of him:—

On one occasion, the Dorians, it is said, came near Athens, and were going to attack it, but they were not sure of success, because it had been declared by an Oracle that they should only gain the victory in case of their not doing any harm to the Athenian king. Codrus heard what the Oracle had said, and, as he loved his country better than his own life, he disguised himself as a peasant, entered the camp of the Dorians, and managed to quarrel with one of the soldiers, who, becoming very angry, killed him When the Athenians learnt that Codrus was dead, they sent to ask for his body. The Dorians knew directly that they could not hope to conquer, for the command given by the oracle had been broken. They withdrew therefore from Attica, and the Athenians, in order to show their gratitude by doing honour to Codrus, made a law that no one should ever be allowed to bear the same title of king again. From that time, the chief ruler in Athens was called Archon, instead of king.

Only one archon at first ruled in Athens, and he was always chosen from among the relations of Codrus; but after some time a change was made, and nine archons were appointed, who were taken from amongst the chief persons in the state, and held their office only for a year.

The Athenians could not have been very happy under the government of the archons, for the poor people were treated very harshly by the rich nobles, who were called Eupatrida. If any poor person borrowed money which he was not able to repay, he and his children might be made slaves. Besides, there were no written laws, so that the people did not know by what rules they were to be governed. At length, however, they saw the evil of this state of things, and Draco, one of the archons, determined to try and improve it. He framed a set of laws which he thought would be useful, but his notions were so very hard and strict, that it was found to be quite impossible to act up to them. Almost every offence, according to Draco's laws, was to be punished by death; because, he said, the least offence deserved death, and yet he could not find any thing worse for the greatest crime.

The Athenians, finding that Draco's laws did not help them, went on for several years in the same way as before; but the disorder and confusion in the state daily increased.

At length one of the nobles, named Cylon, formed a plot for taking the government into his own hands, and making himself the king, or, — as the chief ruler of a state was in those days often called, — the tyrant of Athens. For the word tyrant did not then mean a cruel hard-hearted person, but only a chief who governed according to his own will.

Cylon's plot was discovered, and he himself was obliged to flee away. Some of his friends, finding themselves in danger of being taken, sought refuge in the temple of Athene. Athene was the tutelary goddess of the Athenians, and there were several temples to her honour in the Acropolis, or the citadel of Athens. It was to one of these temples that Cylon's friends fled for safety; for whilst they were there, it would have been considered a profane act to do them any injury. The archons finding what they had done, sent them a message to say that if they would give themselves up they should not be killed.

This message induced Cylon's friends to leave the temple, but they were probably a little in doubt whether the archons would keep their word; for in order that they might be considered still under the protection of the goddess, they fastened a string to her statue, and held it in their hands as they came into the midst of their enemies. The string broke as they were passing a temple dedicated to the Eumenides, or furies; and Megacles, one of the archons, of the family of the Alcmæonids, declared it was a sign that the goddess Athene had given them up. The rest of the archons agreed with him, and instantly the unfortunate men were seized and killed.

This act of the archons was much condemned by many of the Athenians. It was considered an insult to the goddess, and it was declared that she would take vengeance upon the city, unless the archons were punished. There were great disputes upon the subject, and at length thirty of the Alcmæonids were sentenced to exile, and the bones of those who had died before the sentence was passed, were dug up and cast out of the land. Then it was hoped the goddess might be appeased; but in the after history of Greece, we shall hear continually of the stain which remained on the family of the Alcmæonids, and the evils which followed their cruel action.

CHAP. VII.

SOLON GIVES LAWS TO ATHENS.

B.C. 594.

WHILST the Athenians were thus in confusion and discord, the neighbouring states took advantage of their condition, and attacked and plundered their possessions. The island of Salamis, which once belonged to them, had been taken from them by the people of Megara; and the power of the Athenians was so broken down by their divisions that they had never been able to succeed in retaking it. They were so weary at last of making the attempt, and so provoked at constantly losing men and money without gaining any advantages, that a law was passed forbidding any person, on pain of death, even to propose that another endeavour should be made to recover Salamis. The people in general

agreed to this law readily, but there was one person
who was very much ashamed of it, and thought it a
disgrace to his country. This was Solon, an Athenian noble, and one of the descendants of Codrus.
Salamis was his native place, and he could not bear
to think that it should belong to the Megarians;
yet, as the law was made, he did not dare openly to
advise any thing against it. As, however, he was
very clever, he set himself to work to write a poem
upon the loss of Salamis, and when it was finished
he ran into the market place, pretending he was
mad, and began to repeat it. The Athenians, who
were always easily excited by anything strange,
gathered about him to listen. Solon went on recit-
ing his poem, declaring, in a strange wild way, that
it was a shame to let such a lovely island remain in
the hands of their enemies, and by degrees the people came round to his notions, and loudly protested
that the law should be done away with, and they
would go to war.

Solon was made their general, and by his skill
Salamis was retaken. But, as the Megarians after
a time conquered it again, it was agreed that
the Lacedæmonians should decide which it should
belong to. Five judges were sent from Sparta to
settle the question. Solon was the person who spoke
for his countrymen, and all he said was so convinc-
ing that the judges, after proper consideration,
determined that Salamis was to belong to the
Athenians.

Solon was now looked up to as the chief person
in the state, and as he had travelled a great deal,
and was well acquainted with the laws and customs
of other countries, he was considered able to put
an end to the disturbances of the country, by fram-
ing good laws for the government of the people.
Solon did not like, however, to begin such a task

by himself. He wished to improve the habits of the people, and to give them better notions of religion than they had before, and he therefore sent for Epimenides, the Cretan, to assist him in instructing and reforming them.

Epimenides was a very wise man, and was supposed for that reason to be taught by the gods. It was said of him, that when he was a little boy, his father one day sent him into the country to bring home some sheep, and that Epimenides being very hot and tired, and seeing a cool cave by the way side, went into it and lay down to rest. After a little while he fell asleep, and when he woke up again, he of course supposed that it was time for him to continue his journey. When he began to look about him, however, he observed that every thing he saw was very much altered; the country looked different, and the people he met were not at all what he expected; and at last he found out that he had been asleep for fifty years, instead of a few hours. This of course is a very untrue story, but it shows that people imagined Epimenides to be unlike common persons. He knew a great deal about herbs and plants, and how to cure diseases, and he was very particular in attending to the worship of the gods. He wrote poetry also, and was supposed to be able to foretell what was going to happen; and it is he whom St. Paul mentions in the epistle to Titus, bishop of Crete, when he declares that "one of themselves, even a prophet of their own, said: 'the Cretans are always liars, evil beasts, slow bellies.'"*

From all this we can understand how anxious Solon must have been to have the assistance of Epimenides, when he proposed to reform the religion and the laws of Athens. And yet,—to show how

* Titus i. 12.

little even the wisest heathens understood of true religion—we are told that Epimenides, when he arrived at Athens, allowed a human sacrifice to be offered, in order to make atonement for the crime committed by Megacles, the Alcmæonid.

After soothing the fears of the Athenians, by telling them what they were to do to appease the gods, Epimenides gave them further instruction as to some of their religious ceremonies, and then returned to Crete; refusing to receive any honours or gifts, except a branch from the sacred olive tree, which was believed to have been planted on the Acropolis by the goddess Athene.

Solon's work was now to begin, and the changes he made were so wisely ordered, that they continued a blessing to the people for years afterwards. The rich were no longer allowed to oppress the poor, or sell them as slaves, when they could not pay their debts. The laws of Draco were done away with, except those which concerned murder and blood-shedding; persons who had been sent into exile were recalled,—the Alcmæonids amongst them; and the citizens were divided into four classes, according to their rank and wealth, and those who were the richest were obliged to pay the most towards the government.

The power of the archons was also at this time very much lessened; and there was a council formed, consisting of four hundred persons, all of whom were to be more than thirty years of age. The principal business of the council was to prepare the laws which required to be made, and then to bring them before the Assembly of the people for their approval.

This Assembly of the people at Athens was not quite the same as at Sparta. At Sparta the people were only allowed to say whether or not they approved of the laws proposed to them; they could not talk about them, or alter them; but at Athens they might do both. The Assemblies were held every month, in a large open space called the Pnyx. Every man who had reached the age of twenty was allowed to be present and vote by holding up his hand; and when any one wished to address the Assembly, he stood upon a pedestal called the Bema, and spoke from thence, so that all might hear him.

Solon also appointed councils or courts to judge criminals, and to settle disputes. The most celebrated was the court of Areopagus, which is mentioned in the Bible, in the seventeenth chapter of the Acts of the Apostles, where it is said, that when St. Paul was at Athens, some of the most learned persons in the city "took him and brought him to Areopagus," and that "he stood in the midst of Mars' hill," which was where the court was held, and taught the people how they were to worship the true God. This court of Areopagus had existed before Solon's time, but he gave greater power to the persons who belonged to it. It was composed of the wisest and best persons in the state, and no one was allowed to be a member of it who had not been an archon. When there was any difficulty to be decided in a religious question, the case used to be brought before the Areopagus; which was the reason of the Athenians' taking St. Paul before it. Or if a murder had been committed, or any person had taken a false oath, the court of the Areopagus judged the cause. In fact it was the business of these judges to watch over the conduct of the people; and they were so much respected, that even other states and nations used sometimes to send to them to beg them to settle disputed points.

There was a great difference between the **laws** of

Lycurgus and Solon respecting children, for Solon did not think of taking boys from their parents till they were sixteen years old; when they were obliged to go to public schools for two years. Afterwards they were taught to be soldiers for two years more; and they were then considered as citizens, and might have a share in the government if they were fitted for it.

CHAP. VIII.

PISISTRATUS, TYRANT OF ATHENS.

B.C. 560.

WHEN Solon had settled all that seemed necessary for the prosperity of Athens, we are told that he travelled in different countries, visiting Cyprus, Egypt, and Asia Minor, and the court of Crœsus, the rich king of Lydia; but the account that is given of this part of his life cannot quite be depended upon.

After a long time he went back to Athens, where he found that many troubles had arisen during his absence. The people had begun to quarrel, and had divided into three sets or parties, each of which wished to be chief over the other. The leader of one of these parties was a clever and brave, but very ambitious man, named Pisistratus, who was one of Solon's relations.

In order to win favour, Pisistratus pretended to be a great friend to the poor. He was very generous to them, and kind in his manner, and, in consequence, became a great favourite with them. But Solon soon discovered that all which Pisistratus really cared for, was to gain power for himself. He talked to him, and tried to persuade him to give up his scheme for making himself chief. But Pisistratus only listened for a little time, and then went away to follow his own will.

One day, Pisistratus appeared in the marketplace, in a chariot drawn by mules which had evidently been very much hurt. He himself also was disfigured with wounds; and when the people came to inquire what had happened, he told them that, as he was travelling into the country, a band of his enemies had fallen upon him, and tried to kill him, because he was the friend of the poor.

This story was quite untrue, for Pisistratus had wounded himself and his mules on purpose. But as almost every one believed him, the people were very earnest that he should have a guard to protect him; and they proposed that fifty persons, armed with clubs, should attend him wherever he went. Solon was the only person who ventured to oppose this suggestion. He saw at once, that when Pisistratus had a guard of his own, he could act in any way he pleased without fear of being punished, and he therefore tried to persuade the Athenians to give up the idea; but they would not listen to him, and the guard was appointed.

The consequences were just what Solon had expected: Pisistratus made himself more and more powerful, and at last induced so many people to join him, that he was able to take possession of the Acropolis, and keep it for his own, as if it had been his castle. This was in the year B.C. 560.

Pisistratus was now quite the master of Athens, for some of his enemies left the city, and those who remained submitted to him.

He still paid great respect to Solon, and consulted him in cases of difficulty; and as he seemed inclined to rule wisely and mercifully, Solon was willing to be his friend. The following year, however, we are told that Solon died, and then Pisistratus was left without any check.

He was not long allowed to rule in peace. There were many persons in Athens who hated him, and in a short time they joined together against him, and forced him to leave the city. But there was less peace then than there had been before. The men who had driven Pisistratus away began to quarrel amongst themselves; and for five years they went on fighting and disputing. At last Megacles, an Alcmæonid, and the grandson of Megacles, the archon, who was exiled, sent to Pisistratus to invite him back, and to know whether, if help were given him to regain his power, he would take the daughter of Megacles for his wife. Pisistratus agreed to the proposal, and Megacles then tried to persuade the Athenians that it was the will of the gods that Pisistratus should return to Athens. For this purpose, he dressed up a tall and beautiful woman in a suit of armour, to represent the goddess Athene, and made her drive into the city in a chariot, whilst Pisistratus rode by her side. Two heralds went before them, proclaiming that Athene was bringing back the governor. Whether the people really believed that this woman was a goddess, we cannot of course tell, but they certainly allowed Pisistratus to return quietly; and soon afterwards he kept his promise, and married the daughter of Megacles. Still there was no rest for Athens. Pisistratus did not behave well to his wife, and Megacles was very angry in consequence. He soon turned against Pisistratus, drove him from the city, and obliged him to fly to the island of Eubœa. There Pisistratus remained ten years, still hoping that he should get back to Athens. He collected money and soldiers, and sent to his friends to come and join him; and, at length, when he thought that his army would be sufficiently powerful, he made them cross the sea, and advance close to Athens. His enemies came out against him, but he overcame them, and they fled; and once more Pisistratus was made governor of Athens.

That was the last great change which took place in his life. The Alcmæonids and some other powerful families left the city, and Pisistratus was allowed to remain in peace. For ten more years he ruled gently and wisely, and then he died, and left his government to his three sons, Hippias, Hipparchus, and Thessalus.

Pisistratus did many useful things for Athens. He would not allow any one to be idle, and employed a great many of the poor in building splendid temples and other public edifices. There was one temple, especially, dedicated to the same god as that at Olympia, the plan of which was so vast, that it was not quite finished for 700 years. This temple is usually known by the name of the temple of Jupiter Olympius. Jupiter and Zeus meant the same god. Jupiter was the Roman name, and Zeus the Greek. Pisistratus also planted a shady garden called the Lyceum, at a short distance from Athens, and caused buildings to be erected in it, where young men might study, and practise all sorts of exercises to make them strong and active. He was besides very fond of books, and is said to have been the first Greek who formed a regular library. It is supposed that he collected together the poems of Homer, the celebrated poet, which had before been scattered about in different places.

The sons of Pisistratus appear to have been very like their father. They were merciful and gentle in their government, they took care to have the people properly instructed, and they gave great encouragement to all who were distinguished for talents or accomplishments.

Under their rule Athens prospered for some time; but, at length, an event happened, which proved the ruin of the tyrants, as they were called, and brought, in the end, years of misery upon Greece.

At that time there were two young men in Athens, named Harmodius and Aristogeiton, both of whom Hipparchus, the tyrant, had grievously offended.

Being great friends, these two young men consulted with each other as to the surest mode of revenging themselves, and agreed that they would never rest until the power of the tyrants should be overthrown.

A plot was soon formed; for several other persons in Athens were discontented, and wished for a change of government. It was proposed that Hippias should first be attacked, on the occasion of a great festival, held yearly in honour of Athene, and called the Panathenæa.

The citizens were then allowed to march in a procession with spears and shields; and it was thought that when Hippias was dead, the rest of the conspirators, being armed, would be able to take advantage of the tumult which was sure to follow, to rid themselves of their other enemies. The scheme, however, did not turn out quite as was intended. The day fixed upon arrived, and Hippias, wishing to assist in arranging the procession properly, went to a suburb of the city called the Ceramicus, from which it was to set out. There he staid for some time giving orders. Presently a man, who was one of the conspirators, came up and began talking to him. Harmodius and Aristogeiton, perceiving this, were frightened; they did not know what the man could be saying, and fancied he must be betraying them. Without waiting to consult with their friends, they rushed forward into the city, determined to revenge themselves upon the tyrants, whatever might be the consequence. Hipparchus met them in the way. They fell upon him and slew him. A few minutes afterwards the guards came up, seized Harmodius, and killed him upon the spot. Aristogeiton escaped through the crowd, but was soon retaken.

He was put to the torture, in order to make him confess who were his accomplices; and a woman named Leæna, who was supposed to know all his secrets, was treated in the same cruel manner, in the hope of forcing her to tell what she knew. It is said that in order to prevent herself from betraying her friend in the agony of pain, she bit off her own tongue, and spat it in the face of Hippias, who was watching her torments.

Numbers of the people were seized; for all who carried daggers on the day of the festival were known to be the friends of Harmodius and Aristogeiton; as it was contrary to the laws for the citizens to have any arms on that occasion, except spears and shields.

The discovery of this plot seems to have worked a great change in the disposition of Hippias; or perhaps it only brought out the evil qualities hidden in his heart, to which before he was not tempted to give way. He became cruel and suspicious, and treated the Athenians hardly, making them pay large sums of money for taxes. We know very little of his youngest brother Thessalus; he seems never to have come forward in public matters.

Hippias no doubt felt himself unsafe amongst his own people, for he tried to make friends with foreigners; and for this purpose gave his daughter as a wife to the son of the tyrant of Lampsacus, a city of Mysia, in Asia Minor. This tyrant was in great favour with the king of Persia, and Hippias thought probably that through his means he might obtain help from the Persian monarch if he should need it. But the worst enemies of Hippias were the Alcmæonids, who, having been again banished by Pisistratus, were anxiously watching for an opportunity of overthrowing the power of Hippias, and returning to the city themselves.

The Alcmæonids had at that time great influence with the Oracle of Delphi. Some years before, the front of the temple of Delphi had been destroyed by fire, and the Alcmæonids had engaged to rebuild it for a certain sum. As they wished to be considered liberal and generous, they spent a great deal more money upon it than they were obliged to do; using beautiful Parian marble instead of common stone. The Greeks, who were very fond of the temple at Delphi, and considered it as belonging to them all, praised the Alcmæonids extremely for this conduct, and the priestess at Delphi was very willing to favour them in any way possible.

Cleisthenes was now the head of the family of the Alcmæonids. He was a clever cunning man, and knew well in what way it would be best to act in order to obtain the restoration of his family. He managed to inform the priestess of Delphi of his wishes, and, in order to please him, whenever any persons came from Sparta to ask questions of the Oracle, the answer given always was, that it was their duty to make Athens free; which of course meant that they were to assist in expelling Hippias from the city. The Spartans hearing this command so often, felt that they ought to attend to it. They had always been friends with the family of Pisistratus before, but in spite of this friendly feeling, they determined now to raise an army, and send it by sea to invade Attica.

CHAP. IX.

HIPPIAS EXPELLED FROM ATHENS.
B.C. 510.

THE interference of the Spartans in the affairs of Athens was but the beginning of a succession of changes in the government; for Hippias was defeated, and obliged to leave the country; and Cleisthenes and the Alcmæonids returned to their native city, and took the government upon themselves. This happened the very same year that the last king of Rome was dethroned. But as the Alcmæonids had no rightful claim to be rulers over their fellow citizens, so the people were not content to obey them. Constant quarrels arose between those who wished the rich and the noble alone to have power, and those who desired that the lower classes should share it with them. Cleisthenes being elected an archon, took the side of the poor, and made several changes in the laws in their favour. Amongst other things, he introduced a custom, by which any man who was considered to have too much influence in the state might be exiled for ten years. This was called ostracism, because the citizens were in the habit of writing the name of the person they dreaded upon an oyster shell or a tile. Six thousand citizens were obliged to vote in order to pass the sentence of ostracism. They were not compelled to say who it was they had fixed upon, but they wrote the name secretly, and the person whose name was found to be written the oftenest was exiled.

These new laws naturally caused a great many disputes, especially amongst the nobles, who very much disliked them. They sent to the Spartans to assist them in overthrowing Cleisthenes; and the

Spartans, though they had been the means of restoring the Alcmæonids, now turned against them; for in reality they always hated them, and considered them an accursed race.

War soon broke out over the whole country; for several of the other Grecian states joined with Sparta in attacking Athens; and the Athenians, alarmed at the number of their enemies, despatched ambassadors to Sardis to beg for the aid of the Persians. None, however, was given them, and they were obliged to carry on the war by themselves.

All this time Hippias had been living in Asia Minor, watching what was going on in Greece, and no doubt hoping that whilst so many changes were taking place, something might occur to give him an opportunity of returning to Athens. That time seemed now arrived. The Spartans, bent upon the destruction of the Alcmæonids, sent a message to Hippias, begging him to go to Sparta, and join in a consultation with them and their allies; and Hippias immediately set out on his journey.

On his arrival, the Spartans called a great meeting of deputies from the different Peloponnesian states which were friendly to them. In the presence of the whole assembly they declared that Hippias and the Pisistratids — as the family of Pisistratus were named — had been wronged, and that the time was come when the injury which had been committed ought to be repaired; and they summoned their allies to assist in restoring Hippias to the power he had lost.

No answer was made. The allies saw that the proposal was unjust; since they had no right to force the Athenians to accept a ruler whom they disliked. Yet no one at first dared openly to object. At length the deputy from Corinth rose up. He had reason to fear the power of tyrants, for Corinth had, like Athens, been long subject to the rule of one family, and the most celebrated of the race, who was named Periander, had brought grievous misery upon his people, by his cruelty and oppression.

The Corinthian deputy reminded the assembly of this fact. He told them that it would be a disgrace to make the Athenians submit to a form of government which the Spartans themselves detested; and he described most earnestly how wretched the Corinthians had been when Periander ruled over them.

His speech made a great impression upon the other deputies. With one voice they declared that the proposal of the Spartans should be rejected, and the assembly dispersed. The Spartans were compelled to give up their plan, and Hippias returned to Asia, feeling very angry and disappointed; and soon afterwards proceeded to the court of Darius, king of Persia, hoping to obtain there the help which he saw it would be vain to expect from the states of Greece.

We are now coming to a time when the affairs of the Greeks were very much mixed up with those of the Persians. But before we begin a new subject, it will perhaps be well to consider what the knowledge and civilisation of the Greeks was, at the period of their history which we have already reached.

Even in these early days the Greeks showed such skill in drawing, painting, sculpture, and architecture, as to excite our admiration and astonishment. Their public buildings were generally erected according to certain rules, called "Orders of Architecture." The two principal orders were the Doric and the Ionic; but there was another, the Corinthian, which was introduced afterwards.

The pillars of a Doric building were almost

without ornament. In an Ionic building the tops, or capitals of the pillars, were twisted like rams' horns; and in a Corinthian building they were beautifully cut into the form of leaves. The Grecian statues were carved in marble, or moulded in some metal, generally brass. They were mostly placed as ornaments to the temples; sometimes on the outside, and sometimes in the inside. Now and then they were made of wood overlaid with ivory or gold.

With regard to their writers, the Greeks were as distinguished as they were in arts. Homer, Hesiod, Pindar, Simonides, Anacreon, Corinna, Sappho, and Alcæus were all celebrated poets, who lived before and about the time when the Persian wars began. Corinna was a Bœotian lady. She is said to have instructed Pindar, who was a Theban by birth; and she was pronounced superior to him five times, and gained the prize for poetry at a public festival.

Sappho was a native of Mitylene, in the island of Lesbos. She was the most celebrated woman of her age, and exceedingly courted and flattered. One of her poems, it is said, affected Solon so much, that he expressed an earnest desire to learn it before he died. It is unfortunate that her writings were not as good as they were beautiful. She was a friend of the poet Alcæus, who lived in the same island. There is a story also told that Anacreon was very much in love with her, but it is not supposed to be true.

Besides poets, there were many learned men, or philosophers, in those days; persons who accustomed themselves to think a great deal upon such subjects as the creation of the world — why human beings were made to live upon the earth — what become of them after death; with many other questions of the kind, which must have been extremely perplexing to them, as they had never learnt the truth in all these matters from the Bible.

Seven of these philosophers are known by the name of the seven wise men of Greece. Solon was one of them. Thales, of Miletus; Pittacus, of Mitylene; and Bias, a native of Ionia, in Asia Minor, were also of the number. Who the others were is not quite certain. Periander, of Corinth, is sometimes named amongst them. It may seem strange to hear of him as one of the seven wise men; but although he was harsh and severe in his government, he was a very clever man, and a great encourager of learning.

But the most famous of all the philosophers of those days was Pythagoras. He taught his followers to believe that their souls were immortal; but he also thought that every person's soul had been living in some other form before it was joined to his body; and he fancied that when the body died, that soul would again be sent to dwell in another body. This notion was called the doctrine of the transmigration of souls. Pythagoras was a native of the island of Samos, and travelled a great deal in Egypt and the East, where it is supposed he learnt many of his notions. He afterwards went to live at Crotona, in Italy, amongst the Greeks who had settled in that country. There he formed a society consisting of three hundred young men, who lived together, and whom he instructed in all things which he knew himself, such as medicine, astronomy, &c. He made them lead very strict lives, and was especially careful that they should be religious according to his notions of religion. Pythagoras was very much respected, and many persons were anxious to be taught by him; but he and his followers meddled with the government of the country, and, in consequence, great disturbances arose, and they were obliged to leave Italy. Pythagoras died soon afterwards, but his followers were still known by his name, and were called Pythagorean philosophers.

CHAP. X.
THE BURNING OF SARDIS.
B.C. 499.

WE must now turn to the wars of the Greeks and Persians. The kings of Persia are connected with many events of sacred history. We read in the Bible that the prophet Daniel "prospered in the reign of Darius, and in the reign of Cyrus the Persian." So again we are told, in the book of Ezra, that the Lord "stirred up the spirit of Cyrus, king of Persia, that he made a proclamation" to allow the Israelites, who were captives in Babylon, to return to their own land. This Cyrus was a mighty and virtuous prince; one especially appointed by God to be the means of good to the Jews; and who had been mentioned by name by the prophet Isaiah, nearly 200 years before he began to reign. The people over whom he at first ruled dwelt amongst the mountains near the shores of the Persian Gulf. They were divided into different tribes, and for the most part were shepherds, who wandered from place to place, taking care of their flocks. The members of one family called the Achæmenids were esteemed more noble than the rest, and to this family Cyrus belonged. The Persians had no king of their own before Cyrus, but were subject to the Medians, a people who originally inhabited the mountains by the south coast of the

Caspian Sea, and who, shortly before the time of Cyrus, had conquered a great portion of the ancient kingdom of Assyria. Near to Media was Lydia, the country of Crœsus, the rich king, to whose court it is sometimes supposed that Solon travelled after he had given laws to Athens. The extent of the kingdom of Lydia varied at different times. In the time of Crœsus it was in its greatest prosperity, for he was one of the most powerful monarchs of his age. He was brother-in-law to the king of Media. The two countries, therefore, were likely to help each other in case of a war with any other nation; and when their forces were united, it would not seem possible for a poor people like the Persians to rebel and overcome them.

Still we may be quite sure that, whatever has been foretold by Almighty God, will certainly come to pass. Cyrus had been especially named as the king who was to be the means of setting the Jews free from their captivity in Babylon; and, in due course of time, the event which was prophesied so long beforehand came to pass. The Persian mountaineers being a bold independent spirited people, could not bear to be subject to the Medes, and rose up in arms against them, and Cyrus became their leader. The Medes were soon conquered, for they had become indolent and luxurious, and were not able to withstand such a hardy race as the Persians; and Cyrus then was king of Media and Persia. He next conquered Crœsus, king of Lydia, who was very much afraid of having such a mighty neighbour as Cyrus, and began the war, hoping to subdue him, instead of being subdued himself. The history of this conquest is one of the most interesting in all history, for Crœsus had proved himself in many respects to be a great and noble prince; and no one can help feeling sorry for him, who reads the account of the terrible misfortunes which befell him in his latter years, when his dominions and his treasures were taken from him, and he was made prisoner by Cyrus. It is said that he then remembered bitterly a remark made by the wise Solon, when visiting him at his splendid court at Sardis.

Crœsus was showing Solon his ornaments, and displaying his riches, hoping to excite the philosopher's envy. Whilst exhibiting them, he asked Solon whether he did not consider him as the happiest of mankind. "No," replied Solon, "I know one man more happy,— a poor peasant of Greece, who has but few wants, and can supply them with his labour." Crœsus was vexed at the reply, and inquired again, whether Solon did not at least think him happy,—even if he was not the most happy of all. "Alas!" exclaimed Solon, "what man can be pronounced happy before he dies!"

In the days of his misfortune, Crœsus remembered this speech. It had been meant as a warning to him of the great changes which might take place in his lot in life ; but, at the time, he had not understood it, for it was difficult to believe that any one could rise up who should be able to dethrone so mighty a prince. The account of this visit of Solon to Crœsus is given by a celebrated Greek historian; but it seems, upon calculation, that it cannot be strictly true. We must not, however, dwell longer upon the history of Crœsus and of Cyrus. After conquering Media and Lydia, Cyrus laid siege to Babylon, and took it, and it was then that he fulfilled the prophecy of Isaiah, and gave permission to the Jews to return to their own land.

Cambyses, the son of Cyrus, succeeded him as king of the Persian empire, which was now a very large one. Then followed Smerdis, the Magian.

who was an impostor, and not really one of the
Persian princes, and was only allowed to reign for
a few months; and then came Darius Hystaspes,
one of the royal family of the Achæmenids, though
not directly descended from Cyrus. He, it was,
who was reigning at the time that Hippias left
Sparta in anger and disappointment, and determined to seek for help in another country.

All this time, whilst Crœsus and Cyrus, and the
other great eastern princes, had been conquering
each other, and forming new kingdoms, the Greeks,
who were settled in Asia Minor, had been far from
living in peace.

Whoever might be the conqueror, was sure to
invade their province; for they were a rich people,
dwelling in the midst of plenty and comfort, and
every monarch in his turn was anxious to have
them as his subjects. At one time they were very
much under the power of Crœsus; then, when he
was conquered by Cyrus, they became subject to
the Persians, and so they remained when Darius
Hystaspes ascended the throne.

The Greeks, however, were not a people likely
to continue quietly subject to any one; their wish
always was to be allowed to be free, and govern
themselves in their own way, and, in consequence,
there were frequent revolts and disturbances. For,
whenever any governor of the Greek provinces was
out of favour with his master, the king of Persia, it
was easy for him to persuade his people that it
would be a good thing to rebel.

This was the case during the reign of Darius
Hystaspes. The rebellion was caused by the following circumstances. Histiæus, governor of Miletus, the capital of Ionia, had, on one occasion,
conferred a great favour on Darius, by preventing
his being betrayed into the hands of his enemies,

when he was making war upon the Scythians, a wild people who inhabited the country now called Southern Russia. Darius rewarded Histiæus by bestowing upon him a district in Thrace, where there were rich mines of gold, and fine trees which could be used for ship-building. But when this was done, the Persian king began to fear that his friend would become too powerful. He sent for him to Susa, the capital of Persia, and told him that he must not go away again, as his advice was very much wanted, and he could be of great use in the government. Histiæus knew that this was merely a pretence, and that, in fact, he should be a prisoner; but it would have been useless to refuse, and he therefore remained at Susa, whilst his brother-in-law, Aristagoras, was left to govern Miletus.

Some time after this, Aristagoras undertook a warlike expedition with some Persians, which was not successful, and he was afraid of getting into disgrace at court in consequence. This put it into his mind to excite a revolt, and he began to form plans, and consider how the rebellion could most safely be managed. Whilst he was pondering upon the subject, a messenger arrived from Susa from Histiæus. The messenger was a slave; Aristagoras ordered him to be admitted into his presence, but when the man appeared, the only message that he gave was, that Histiæus desired Aristagoras to shave off the hair of his head and look at the skin. Aristagoras obeyed, and when the slave's hair was shaved off, there was found traced on the skin, by a hot iron, what Histiæus wished to say, but had been afraid to write or tell by word of mouth.

The message, which was sent in such a strange way, was to this purpose: that Histiæus was tired of remaining at Susa, but was afraid to try and escape, and could think of no other way of freeing himself but that of raising a rebellion amongst the people of Miletus, which very probably he should be sent himself to quell. He therefore begged Aristagoras to aid him by exciting a revolt. This request, which exactly agreed with the plans that Aristagoras had been forming, of course gave him great encouragement, and he now determined to lose no time in putting his scheme into action.

The first thing Aristagoras did was to take counsel with the chief persons in the Ionian cities, who, he believed, would be likely to help him; and then, when it was thought necessary that he should seek assistance from some powerful state, he set out himself for Lacedæmon, taking with him a good deal of money, and a brass plate, on which a map of the world was traced, according to the notions of the wisest men in his province.

On his arrival at Sparta, he went immediately to Cleomenes, one of the kings, hoping to persuade him that it would be a good thing for the Spartans to help the Ionians in their rebellion. He brought forth the brass map, and pointed out the vast empire of Persia; he described the riches of the country, how fertile the land was, and how much wealth was laid up at Susa. All this, he told Cleomenes, might one day belong to the Spartans, if they would only make up their minds to assist the Ionians; for when once they had crossed over to Asia Minor, they might soon march to Susa, and make themselves masters of the city and its treasures. Aristagoras having finished all he had to say, Cleomenes asked him to wait for three days, and he should then have an answer to his proposal. At the end of this time, Aristagoras and Cleomenes met again. The Spartan king was anxious to make inquiries before he engaged himself in such an important undertaking. "How many days' journey," he asked,

"lie between the sea and the palace at Susa?"
"The distance is a three months' march," replied
Aristagoras, hastily, not considering how much
Cleomenes might be startled by the idea of such a
long journey. The next moment he saw what a
mistake he had committed. Cleomenes broke off
the conversation, gave up all thought of joining in
the enterprise, and ordered Aristagoras to quit
Sparta before the sun should that night set. Instead of attending to the command, Aristagoras
followed Cleomenes to his own house, taking in his
hand an olive-branch, which was a symbol of peace,
and a token that he had a favour to ask. Cleomenes could not refuse to see a person who came to
him so humbly, and he allowed Aristagoras to be
admitted to the room in which he was sitting with
his little daughter, Gorgo, a child of about eight or
nine years of age. Aristagoras had a different
temptation now to bring before the Spartan king.
He offered him money: if he would consent to
assist the Ionians in their revolt, he should at once
receive a great reward. Cleomenes refused, and
Aristagoras offered more and more. Gorgo stood
by, unnoticed herself, but carefully watching all
that was going on. At length, feeling quite sure
that her father was being tempted to do something
which his conscience told him was wrong, the little
girl exclaimed, " Go away, father, the stranger will
do you harm!"

The warning came at the right moment: Cleomenes turned away from the bribe, and Aristagoras,
without further delay, left Sparta.

He next proceeded to Athens: there the people
were very differently disposed from the Spartans;
they knew more of Persia, and were inclined,
almost without being asked, to enter into the war.
We may remember that, a few years before, when

the Spartans attacked Athens, and wished to expel the Alcmæonids, the Athenians sent to ask for help from the Persians. The person they applied to was Artaphernes, governor of Lydia, the brother of king Darius. Artaphernes promised to aid them, if they would consent to give earth and water to the king of Persia. This was the eastern way of expressing that Athens was to become subject to Persia. The Athenian envoys consented, not perhaps quite knowing all that was meant by the demand for earth and water; but when they went back to their own country, they were very much blamed for what they had done, and their fellow citizens openly declared that they would never agree to any thing of the kind. Artaphernes, therefore, gave no help, and from that time, probably, had a feeling of indignation against Athens. Some time afterwards, Hippias went to him, and begged him to assist in restoring him to his former power; and Artaphernes willingly consented, being glad of any opportunity of doing what the Athenians disliked.

It was well known at Athens what Hippias was aiming at; and the Athenians, forgetting how they had offended Artaphernes before, despatched ambassadors, to request him not to interfere in their affairs, by supporting their old tyrant. The only answer they received was, that they should be safe, if they would recall Hippias.

This message had arrived just at the moment when Aristagoras of Miletus reached Athens. The Athenian people were furious against the Persians, and needed but little persuasion to induce them to join in a war against them. They agreed to send twenty ships to assist the Ionians in their rebellion, and Aristagoras returned to Miletus, well satisfied with his success.

The twenty Athenian vessels set sail, accompa

nied by five other vessels belonging to the Eretrians, the inhabitants of the chief city and district in the island of Eubœa, who had been persuaded to join in the expedition. On reaching the coast of Asia Minor, the troops landed, and being joined by a good many Ionians, they hired guides, and proceeded, all together, through a valley, called the vale of the Cayster, and ascended a high mountain, on the other side of which was Sardis, the capital of Lydia.

The citadel of Sardis was very strong, but the houses of the town were principally made of wickerwork, and those which were built of brick were thatched with reeds. This was done because earthquakes were very common in that part of the country, and it was therefore safer to have the houses covered with light materials, which would not hurt any one if they were thrown down. The Greek soldiers stood on the top of Mount Tmolus, and looked down upon this rich eastern city, and then, like a mountain torrent, they rushed down the side of the hill and attacked it. Artaphernes was in Sardis himself, but knowing that it was useless to think of defending the town, he shut himself up with his soldiers in the citadel. The Greeks were in a very short time masters of the city, and wandered from house to house, plundering everything of value that came in their way. At last, one of the soldiers, in his eagerness and anger, set fire to a house. The flames spread in every direction. The inhabitants of Sardis, driven from their homes, rushed together to the market-place, which was built close to the river Pactolus, and determined to defend themselves there bravely whilst defence was possible. The Athenians remained in the midst of the burning city. It was a situation of great danger for them, conquerors though they were; for help might be sent to Artaphernes, at any moment, from the neighbouring cities, and then they could not expect to escape. Retreat seemed their only hope, and, as quickly as possible, they marched out of the city, ascended Mount Tmolus, passed down the vale of the Cayster, and proceeded on their way to the sea-coast. But, before reaching it, they were overtaken by a great army, which had been raised as soon as the people of Lydia knew of their invasion. A battle followed, and the Greeks were defeated. Those amongst them who belonged to the provinces in Asia fled to their own cities; and the Athenians and Eretrians got on board their ships, and sailed back to Greece with all speed.

The anger of Darius, when he heard of the burning of Sardis, surpassed all bounds. That which seemed mostly to irritate him was, that the action had been committed by a small body of unknown strangers from a distant land. One of the first questions he asked was, who were the people that had ventured upon so bold a deed; and from his heart he prayed that he might live to punish them.

The feeling was not allowed to die away. Each day, before Darius began his meal, an attendant was ordered to appear before him, and recall to him the name of the Athenians, and preparations were soon begun to enable him to take his revenge.

It was necessary, however, first, to subdue the Greek provinces in Asia Minor. Histiæus, the former governor of Miletus, who had been the prime mover of the Ionian revolt, was now suspected by Darius, but he managed to clear himself, and was sent, as he had wished, to Ionia, to endeavour to quiet his rebellious people. He found, however, when he arrived there, that he was still an object of suspicion to Artaphernes, the king's brother, who said to him one day, when speaking of the way in which Aristagoras had behaved, "Aristagoras drew the sandal on, but it was of your stitching." This speech frightened Histiæus, and seeing that it would be useless any longer to pretend to be loyal to Darius, he went away secretly by night, and from that time openly joined in the rebellion. The remainder of his history had perhaps better be told at once, for he met with a dreadful fate in return for his selfishness and treachery. He was taken prisoner by the Persians, and carried before Artaphernes, who immediately ordered him to be crucified, and then cut off his head, and sent it to Darius at Susa.

It is said that Darius was very sorry when he heard of the death of Histiæus, and was angry with Artaphernes in consequence; probably he did not really believe how deceitfully Histiæus had behaved. Aristagoras likewise was killed in the course of the war.

CHAP. XL.

THE BATTLE OF MARATHON.

B.C. 490.

SIX years passed after the first revolt of the Ionian Greeks, under Aristagoras, before they were finally subdued by the Persians. During that time, very many lives were lost, and very great sufferings were endured; and when at last Darius had made himself master of the rebel cities, the evil was not at an end. Still the Athenians, who had assisted them, were left unpunished, and the revenge of the great Persian monarch was ungratified. As the provinces in Asia Minor were conquered, he was left more free to turn his thoughts to the distant people who had offended him in Europe, and a great fleet was prepared and sent forth; but a violent storm overtook and destroyed it: and the land army, which reached Europe, and marched through Macedonia, was surprised by night by the people of the country, and so many were killed, that the rest were obliged to retreat.

Darius was not to be stopped by any disasters; his anger against the Greeks had never been satisfied, and even if he had been inclined for peace himself, he would have been constantly urged to war by the entreaties of Hippias, the tyrant of Athens, who had never given up his hope of being one day restored to his country and his power. Greater preparations the next year were made by the Persians; and Darius, being willing to try the spirit of his enemies before he invaded their dominions, sent heralds to Athens and Eretria, and many other of the Grecian cities, requiring, as before, earth and water, in token of submission to his dominion. The two great states of Greece, Athens and Sparta, scorned the demand, and, in their rage, ordered the ambassadors to be put to death. The inhabitants of many of the islands yielded to it, amongst them the people of Ægina; and this submission was the cause of a civil war in Greece, which was st ll going on when, in the year B.C. 490, the Persian king at length fulfilled his long-intended purpose, and actually invaded Greece.

The Persian forces were placed under the command of his generals, Datis and Artaphernes. The latter was the king's nephew, the son of that Artaphernes, governor of Lydia, of whom we have before heard. The fleet which bore the army across the sea, consisted of 600 triremes, or ships of war, and a number of other vessels, for the conveyance of the horses. The Greek island of Naxos was attacked first, and the Persians, on their landing, burned the town, and carried away the people to be slaves. They then proceeded to Delos, but that was a sacred island, supposed to be the birth-place of the gods, Apollo and Artemis, who represented the sun and moon; and as the Persians paid great honour to the sun and moon themselves, they passed on without injuring the place, and even, it is said, sent incense to burn upon the altars of the gods.

Eretria, in the island of Euboea, was next attacked. The inhabitants had joined with the Athenians in the burning of Sardis, and the vengeance of the Persian king was especially directed against them. The Eretrians defended themselves for six days, but some amongst them were treacherous, and, on the seventh day, opened the gates to their enemies. They could not, however, save themselves from destruction, for their city was plundered, burnt, and at last razed to the ground, and the prisoners were kept to be carried in triumph to Persia. All this was done in the hope of terrifying the Athenians. They were the chief offenders, and on them the chief punishment was to fall; and now, as the Persian army drew nearer and nearer to Attica, the plans for invading it began to be more carefully considered.

There was one person whose opinion was well known to be more worthy of attention than that of any other man. This was Hippias, who had accompanied the army from Persia. By this time he was an old man, but his anger against the Athenians, and his selfish, ambitious feelings were as strong as ever, and now, without any hesitation, he gave the advice which might, he well knew, bring his country to ruin.

On the eastern coast of Attica, and opposite to

the island of Eubœa, stretched a plain of about five or six miles in length, and two in breadth. It was in the form of a crescent, the horns or points of which consisted of two promontories, running out into the sea. A stream flowed through the middle of the plain, and near each of the promontories were marshes, overgrown with reeds and rushes. At the back of the plain rose steep slopes, covered with pines, olives, cedars, cypresses, and myrtles; whilst beyond were the sharp, rugged mountains of Pentelicus and Parnes.

This plain was the plain of Marathon, one of the most celebrated spots in the history of the world; and here it was that Hippias advised the Persians to land, under the belief that it would give them room for exercising the skill of their horsemen; whilst the Athenians would, he knew, be only able to oppose them with foot-soldiers.

But before we attempt to describe the events of the battle which followed, we must turn, for a few moments, to the scenes which were passing at Athens, and see in what spirit the inhabitants were preparing to encounter their terrible invaders. The first thought of the Athenians, when the news arrived that the Persians had landed at Marathon, only about six-and-twenty miles from Athens, was to march forth without delay, and boldly to face their enemies. Every man who could bear arms was enlisted, and even the slaves were called upon to fight, with the promise of obtaining their freedom. The danger was so near, that there was but little time to summon the aid of the other states of Greece. The people of Platæa, indeed, who were originally dependent upon Thebes, but had lately placed themselves under the protection of Athens, despatched a thousand men to join the army; but this was the only support offered by any

of the neighbouring states, and Sparta was so far
off, that it seemed scarcely possible to send word of
the landing of the Persians soon enough to obtain
help from thence. The Athenians, however, would not be contented
without making an effort to let the Spartans know
of their great peril, and they accordingly despatched
a messenger to Sparta, named Phidippides, famed
for the extraordinary quickness with which he
could travel. Phidippides journeyed without pause
or rest, and the next day reached Sparta. He delivered his message, entreating for aid; and the
Spartans did not refuse it. But one of their great
festivals was then approaching, and it was a fixed
law of their religion never to begin an expedition
at that season till the moon was at the full. It
wanted some days of that. They were obliged
therefore to wait, and before assistance was sent,
the battle of Marathon had been fought. The
Athenians, having crossed the mountains, which
lay between them and their enemies, descended
into the plain, where the Persians were encamped.
There are said to have been about ten thousand
men in their army, who, by the laws of Athens, were
to be commanded by ten generals, each one having
the command for a day. One amongst them was
Miltiades; he had once been ruler of the Thracian
Chersonesus, a country close to the Hellespont, but
had fled from it to avoid the anger of the Persian
king, whom he had offended. Miltiades was an
exceedingly clever man, and a very excellent general, and though his countrymen were inclined to be
suspicious of him, because he had once been a tyrant, they still looked up to him so much, that
several of the generals were willing to give up their
own authority, and to trust the chief command of the
army to him on this important occasion. Miltiades,

however, would not risk a battle till his own turn came to command, for he did not wish to excite any jealous feeling.

The Persian host consisted of about 120,000 men, gathered from forty-six different nations; and the first sight of them must have been very alarming to the Greeks, who had never been accustomed even to their strange dresses, and had heard enough of their conquests to fear them greatly. The two armies were stationed about a mile distant from each other. The Athenians were on rather higher ground than the Persians, and when the signal was given they rushed down eagerly upon their enemies; whilst the Persians stood looking upon them with contempt, and thinking it madness that such a small body of men should venture to oppose so vast a host.

The Persian army was strongest in the middle, and weakest at the sides; but it was just the reverse with the Athenian. When, therefore, the attack began, the Greeks in the centre were driven back, but those at the sides made up for this loss.

They drove the Persians, who were fighting against them, back to the shore, and into the marshes near the promontories, where they could not find firm ground to stand; and when these were quite defeated, Miltiades made the two side bodies of Greeks join together and attack the Persians, who had been victorious in the centre. In this way he routed them all. The Persians fled to the shore, hoping to get on board their ships, but many perished in the marshes, and numbers also were slain.

Some persons say that Hippias was amongst the killed, but others declare that he escaped, and died afterwards in the island of Lemnos. Seven of the Persian ships were taken. One of them, when pushing off from the shore, was seized by the brother of the famous Greek poet, Æschylus, and held by him until the Persians cut of his hand with a hatchet.

It was evening before the last remains of the mighty Persian host, which had looked so proudly upon the little army of the Greeks, escaped to the ships that were lying in the bay ready to shelter them. Shadows had gathered over the plain, where the dead lay motionless and at rest, but the sharp peak of the mountain of Pentelicus was steeped in the rich rose-coloured mist, which is the peculiar beauty of the sunsets among the hills of Greece. Suddenly, from the summit of the mountain, there flashed a quick brilliant light. It was seen by the Persians and the Greeks at the same moment, and both understood its meaning. It was the reflection of the sun-light on an uplifted shield.

There were traitors at Athens, who were friends to Hippias, and wished the Persians to conquer; and this shield was hoisted on the summit of Pentelicus, to invite the Persians to sail round to the south coast of Attica, and land there before any one could be prepared to stop them.

The Persians followed the signal, and set sail; but the Athenian generals were too quick-sighted for them. As soon as they saw the direction in which the ships steered, they guessed their object. Without a moment's delay, the army set forth on its return to Athens, leaving only a small portion of men at Marathon to bury the dead. When the Persians arrived at the southern coast, they found an Athenian army still ready to oppose them, and their plans being thus totally defeated, they soon after sailed back to Asia.

This ended the first great battle between the Persians and the Greeks.

It was remembered by the Greeks with triumph, and celebrated in every possible way. Pictures

were painted, and poems were written about it,
and the Athenians declared that even the gods
had interfered to save them from their enemies.
The soldiers who died in the battle were considered
as greater than human beings; and when a celebrated Athenian orator, in after years, wished to
assure his hearers of the truth of his words, he
swore, as a sacred oath, by the bones of those
who lay buried at Marathon.

The plain of Marathon is, at this day, in many respects what it was when the battle took place, more
than two thousand years ago. It is bare, without
hedges or houses; but between the two marshes
there stands a lofty mound, beneath which lie the
bones of the 192 Athenians who fell on that celebrated day. At a little distance may also be seen
some large blocks of white marble, the remains of
a monument, which, after the death of Miltiades,
was raised there to his honour. The shepherds
who feed their sheep on the plain of Marathon,
still speak of the battle that was fought there; and
when the howling of the wind, or the roaring of the
sea, are heard in the dark night, they flee with their
flocks to the mountains, for they believe that they
have heard the shouts of spectre warriors, and the
neighing of their phantom horses.

CHAP. XII.

THE BATTLE OF THERMOPYLÆ.

B.C. 480.

WHEN Miltiades returned to Athens, after gaining
the victory at Marathon, he no doubt looked forward
to a life of great honour and glory. Every one admired and respected him; and his influence was so

great, that when he asked for some ships and men in order to carry out an expedition which he had planned, his request was granted at once, though no one knew exactly what he intended to do. He probably meant in the end to take vengeance on the islands that had submitted to the Persians; but his first wish was to revenge some private injuries which he had received from an enemy in the island of Paros. He sailed to Paros, therefore, and laid siege to the chief town, but he could not take it; and whilst he was trying to do so, he accidentally injured his knee, and the wound became so serious, that he was obliged to return to Athens. This was a heavy disappointment to the men who went with him; for he had promised them great riches from the expedition. His enemies took advantage of the complaints made against him, and accused him publicly of having deceived the people. When the case was tried, Miltiades was brought on a couch into the court; but his brother was obliged to defend his cause, because he was too ill to do it himself. The judges pronounced him to be guilty, and his punishment would have been very severe, if it had not been for his late victories. As it was, they ordered him to pay a large fine; and because he could not raise the money directly, he was thrown into prison, where he soon afterwards died of the wound in his leg.

It was a sad end for a great man, though Miltiades certainly deserved some punishment for his selfish conduct. The Athenians paid him great honour after his death, by raising the monument to his memory, the remains of which, as was before said, are to be seen on the plain of Marathon at this day.

The persons in Athens who were of the greatest importance when Miltiades was dead, were Themistocles and Aristides. Themistocles was a man of high birth on his father's side. His mother was a foreigner, and therefore not so much thought of. He was rich, clever, and ambitious. It is said that he used to lie awake at night, thinking upon the greatness of Miltiades, and longing to resemble him; and his one object seems to have been to make Athens a powerful state, and to have the principal honour and influence in it himself.

Aristides was a very different person. He wished, like Themistocles, to make Athens powerful, but he did not care for greatness for himself. His only desire was to do what was just and right; and though he belonged to a rich and noble family, and had a great many opportunities of gaining wealth from the public offices which he held, he cared so little for money, that he lived and died poor.

Such a man was certain of being very much respected; but he also excited a great deal of envy and ill will. Persons, who were not good themselves, disliked to have such an excellent example set them; and Themistocles himself, though he was in many respects noble and honourable, was not willing to follow the plans of Aristides when they interfered with his own ambition. In consequence of these feelings, Aristides was banished from Athens by the sentence of ostracism. No fault was brought against him, but his name was written down by the greater number of persons who had to vote, merely because they hated him for being so much better than themselves. There is a story told that Aristides was asked by a man, who was going to vote, but who could not write, to inscribe his own name upon the shell; and that when he inquired of the man why he wished Aristides to be sent into exile, the reply was: "Because I am tired of hearing him called the Just."

When Aristides was gone, Themistocles had no one to be his rival with the people: and he certainly used his influence well, for he did his utmost to prepare them for an evil which he foresaw to be near at hand—the renewal of the Persian invasion. Every one who thought at all, must have known that Darius would never rest until he had revenged himself for the loss of the battle of Marathon; and, in fact, all Asia was kept in a tumult and excitement for three years afterwards, from the vast preparations which the king of Persia was making to invade Greece again. But it was the will of Providence that Darius himself should never have this favourite wish fulfilled. In the fourth year he was disturbed by great family troubles, which occupied all his attention; and at the same time, an insurrection broke out in Egypt, which was then subject to Persia; and just as he had settled his family disputes, and was thinking of punishing the Egyptians, he died.

His son Xerxes succeeded him. He was a different person from Darius; not so clever, and not so ambitious; and, from having been bred up in a court, more fond of luxury and finery. His mother, Atossa, was the daughter of Cyrus, and Xerxes was proud of such a grandfather, and had from childhood been taught to look upon himself as superior to every one. Probably he would never have troubled himself with such a great undertaking as an expedition against Greece, if he had not been urged to it by the persons about him. There were several members of the family of Hippias at his court, who were always wishing for a war, and used every effort to persuade the young king to engage in it; and at last they succeeded. Xerxes not only resolved upon the war, but determined to carry it on himself; and though his uncle, Artabanus warned him against running such a risk, he was not to be persuaded to give it up.

It took four years to collect the army, and provide for the support of the troops on their long march. Magazines of all things necessary were formed at different places by which they were to pass, and stores were also ordered to be carried by the fleet. Without this care it would have been impossible for such an enormous number of persons to have found food enough to eat, for the accounts given of them almost surpass belief. There were Persians, Medes, Bactrians, Parthians, and soldiers from the provinces next to Persia, wearing light caps on their heads, and coats or tunics, the sleeves of which were covered with scales; Assyrians, with brazen helmets, who carried steel-headed clubs; Indians, dressed in cotton, with cane bows and arrows; Arabs, who wore coats reaching to the feet, and who likewise used bows and arrows, though of greater length; half-naked Ethiopians, also, who covered themselves with the skins of beasts, and painted their bodies in red and white when they went to battle; and a race called Eastern Ethiopians, who are said to have worn the skin of a horse's head instead of a helmet, with the ears standing up, and the mane hanging down behind them; not to mention the inhabitants of Asia Minor, and of the country bordering on the Black Sea; with others, whose names are less commonly known: in all, 1,700,000 foot soldiers, and 80,000 horsemen, besides the men on board more than 1,200 ships of war. The multitude increased as the army travelled on, so that at last it became almost impossible to reckon them.

They set out from Sardis; and when they reached Abydos, on the borders of the Hellespont, a marble throne was erected on a hill above the town, and

Xerxes, seated upon it, looked down upon his mighty
host. It must have been a splendid sight, more
splendid perhaps than any other which we read of
in the history of the world. White tents, and brilliant
banners, horses with gay trappings, and men
with glittering arms, filled the plain; and over the
Hellespont stretched two bridges, framed of boats,
for the passage of the army; a work which no human
being had ever before attempted. Xerxes
might well have imagined himself equal to the
gods: all men seemed subject to him, and even the
mighty sea could not stop his progress. His first
thoughts as he gazed upon his army, were doubtless
full of pride and glory, but a few minutes afterwards
tears rushed to his eyes. Artabanus, his uncle,
drew near and asked the cause. "I weep," replied
Xerxes, "to think that a hundred years hence not
one of these will be alive."

The day after the grand review of the army,
orders were given that they should begin to cross
the Hellespont. The troops were to pass over on
one bridge, the baggage on the other. The bridges
were strewn with myrtle, and incense was burnt
upon them to make them, as the Persians believed,
sacred; and then, 10,000 men, called the Immortals,
the bravest of the Persian soldiers, marched over,
crowned with chaplets. The rest of the army followed,
one body after another. On they went for
seven days and seven nights, those who moved too
slowly being driven forward by whips. Xerxes,
himself, the tallest and grandest-looking man of the
whole army, was the last.

They were now in Europe, but there were many
miles to journey before they could reach Greece.
Xerxes, however, had but little trouble in providing
for his host. All the towns and villages through
which they passed were obliged to furnish them

with provisions; and messengers were sent before
the king, to every place at which he intended to
stop, to order a banquet to be prepared for himself.
These banquets cost so much money, that a citizen
of Abdera, a town in Thrace, advised his fellow-
citizens to offer a solemn thanksgiving to the gods,
through whose kindness it happened that Xerxes was
accustomed to make only one meal a day. The want
of water was the only thing which the army really
suffered from. We are told that they several times
drank rivers dry. This will not appear so difficult
to believe, when we remember that their numbers
went on increasing continually.

Such an immense host could not approach Greece
without causing great alarm, but none of the leading states thought of submission. They remembered
that the Greeks had been conquerors at Marathon,
and they trusted to be so again. Their chief difficulty lay in the quarrels which the different states
had with one another, and which prevented them
from acting together. The Spartans, about this
time, had a dispute with the people of Argos, and
the Argives were more willing to yield to Xerxes,
than to help their enemies in resisting him. The
Achæans, also, kept aloof from a feeling of jealousy
towards Sparta; and the Athenians and the people
of Ægina were enemies. The Athenians, however,
exerted themselves far more than any of the other
states. Themistocles did everything he possibly
could to put an end to all quarrels; and, at length,
it was agreed that a congress, or assembly of deputies
sent by all who were willing to oppose the Persians,
should meet upon the Isthmus of Corinth, to consider what was to be done upon this occasion. It
was determined to ask for assistance from the inhabitants of Crete, Syracuse, and others who might be
able to help them; and as the meeting took place

before Xerxes had left Asia, and they were anxious
to know what the number of his armies might be,
they sent spies to Sardis, to bring back a true re
port. The spies were discovered, and the Persian
generals were about to put them to death; but
Xerxes, in the pride of his heart, ordered that they
should be led through his vast host, and then sent
back to Greece, to tell their countrymen the power
of the mighty monarch of Asia.

The ambassadors who went to beg for aid, in this
time of difficulty, were not very successful. Every
one was afraid. The inhabitants of the island of
Corcyra promised their help, but took care to delay
till it was too late. Gelo, the tyrant of Syracuse,
offered to send a large force to Greece, if he were
allowed to be the chief commander of all the forces,
both by land and sea. But when he was told that
only a Spartan could be allowed to command at sea,
he held back, saying, that they seemed better provided with generals than with troops, and that the
Greeks had lost the spring out of their year: by
which he meant the troops which he intended
to have sent, if they had granted his request. It
was fortunate, however, that they did not do so, for
there was great reason to suppose that Gelo was not
really friendly to the Greeks, and that he would
have gone over to the Persians if it had suited his
purpose.

The next thing to be considered was, at what
point it would be best for the Greeks to station
themselves, in order to oppose the invaders. It was
thought at first that the pass of Tempe, in Thessaly,
would be a desirable place; but this was afterwards
given up, and Thermopylæ was then fixed upon.

Thermopylæ was a pass between Thessaly and
Phocis. The jutting promontory of Mount Œta
towered above it on one side, and on the other it was

washed by the waves of the sea. It was about four or five miles in length, and its breadth at either end was so narrow, that it is said not to have allowed space for the passage of more than a single carriage at a time; but in the middle it was wider. At the foot of the rocks hot streams gushed out, and trickled across the road, and from these came the name, Thermopylæ, which means "the hot gates." The pass of Thermopylæ is now very unlike what it must have been in the time of Xerxes; for the sea has retired, and a river that flows from amongst the hills has brought down a quantity of mud, which has hardened by degrees, so that Thermopylæ is now becoming a broad plain. But when it was chosen by the Greeks as the best place for opposing the Persians, it was easy for a few hundred men to defend it against thousands; and thus, doubtless, thought Leonidas, king of Sparta, when he set forth with 300 Spartans, a body of Helots, and a small number of troops from the other states, to defend his country against the invasion of the Persian monarch. At the time when Leonidas set forth for Thermopylæ, preparations were going on for celebrating the Olympic games; but no one thought it necessary to stop them, or even to delay them; for the festival at which they were held was very sacred in the eyes of the Greeks, and it was supposed that Leonidas would be quite able to prevent the Persians from advancing further into the country before it was over. Every care, however, was taken to oppose Xerxes, both by sea and land, and a fleet was sent to guard the entrance of the channel between the Island of Eubœa and the coast of Greece.

The terror of the Greeks by sea seems to have been greater than on land. When the first fire signals gave notice that a few Persian ships, sent to observe what the Greeks were doing, were in sight, the alarm was so great, that the Spartan commander thought it better to retire, after setting watches on the heights of Euboea to give the earliest intelligence of the enemy's movements. Not many days after, the whole of the Persian fleet was seen approaching. They anchored near the south coast of Magnesia, on a beautiful, still, summer's night, so calm and bright, that no one could have thought of danger. As the morning dawned, a faint ripple, and the gradual swell of the sea, gave notice of an approaching storm. It came from the north-east, and its fury was terrible. For three days and three nights it raged, and when at length it subsided, the Persian fleet was scattered, its mariners were lost, and the sea shore was strewn for miles with the bodies of the unfortunate men who had perished.

The Greeks believed that their gods had raised the storm on purpose to destroy their enemies, and they were full of thankfulness and delight. But the Persians were not so easily defeated. They had indeed lost a great many ships, and a large number of men, but there was an immense force still left, and the Greeks soon found, to their surprise, that their enemies had another fleet ready to oppose them. Themistocles, who was one of the commanders, still however kept up their courage; twice they attacked the Persians, and were successful; but the third time, when the Persians drew near to Artemisium, on the north coast of Euboea, and began the battle themselves, the Greeks were forced to retreat, though it could not really be said that they were conquered, as their enemies suffered almost as much as themselves. Probably one cause of their retiring was the news which at this time reached them of all that had happened at Thermopylæ.

To this place we must now go back. It has been

said that the Greeks were not aware of any pressing danger when they sent Leonidas and his small body of troops to defend the narrow pass of Thermopylæ. There seemed, indeed, but slight cause for alarm. A few men, brave as the Spartans, might well have defended that narrow way, till the Olympic games were over, and the Grecian armies assembled; and if Thermopylæ had been, what they supposed, the only passage for the Persian troops, so it would probably have happened.

But there was another way, difficult indeed, and scarcely known except by persons very well acquainted with the mountains, yet still sufficient to allow at least a portion of the Persian army to pass over the mountain, instead of at its base. It was a track along a mountain torrent, which came out at the town of Alpeni at the southern end of the pass, and when Leonidas reached Thermopylæ, he was, for the first time, told of its existence. A body of Phocians was instantly sent to defend it; and, at the same time, orders were given to repair a ruined wall at the northern end of the pass, which had in former days been built by the Phocians to guard themselves from the incursions of the Thessalians.

As the Persian armies drew near, many of the troops brought from Peloponnesus became alarmed and would willingly have gone back, but the other allies persuaded Leonidas to retain them. The Spartans apparently had no thought of fear. When Xerxes sent forward a horseman to reconnoitre, the man brought back word that the Spartan soldiers were stationed on the outside of the wall, and were engaged in combing their long hair, and practising gymnastic exercises, or feats of strength and activity. Xerxes inquired what the meaning of such conduct could be, and was told by a person who was acquainted with the customs of the Greeks that the action of combing their hair signified their intention to fight even to death. This intention could not however have seemed of much consequence to the lord of such innumerable armies; and Xerxes, supposing that his presence alone would be sufficient to terrify them, waited for four days in the vain expectation that the Greeks would retreat.

On the fifth day, orders were given to a chosen body of Persian troops to attack the insolent enemy, and bring them prisoners to the presence of the Persian monarch, who, seated upon a lofty throne, prepared proudly to witness what he imagined would be his certain victory. But the event was far different from his expectation. Again and again, not only on that day, but on the morrow, the flower of the Persian army, even the 10,000 Immortals, the chosen body guard of the king, were driven back by the intrepid Greeks and thrice the Persian monarch started from his throne in rage and disappointment, as he saw his soldiers yield to the valour of their foes.

Sadness and perplexity filled the heart of the haughty king. If such was the opposition which he met at the commencement of his project, what difficulties must he not expect before it could be completed? Whilst these thoughts were weighing upon his spirits, a secret was made known to him which restored all his former hopes. A traitor from the Greeks, named Ephialtes, betrayed the fact that there was a track over the mountains. This was all that Xerxes needed. A detachment of his army was ordered to follow the guidance of Ephialtes, and when night drew on, they began to ascend the rugged path. For several hours they went on unperceived and unthought of; and by the time that the morning light broke over the sea, they had reached the summit of the mountain. The Phocians who had been left to guard the path were resting, unconscious of danger; but as the Persians came nearer, trampling over the fallen leaves of the trees which covered the hills, the sound was heard in the deep silence of the early summer's morning; and in a moment the Phocians were aroused to the consciousness of their great peril. They seized their arms, and turned bravely upon their enemies. The Persians gave way, but only for a moment. A shower of arrows, aimed at the Greeks, drove them from their position, and retreating to the highest peak of the mountains, they resolved to fight to the last. But the Persians took no trouble to follow them; on they passed, to descend the southern side of the mountains. The tidings of their approach were soon brought to Leonidas, and spread rapidly through the camp. The danger was not to be escaped except by flight. Leonidas and his Spartans could not flee. They had been placed in that post by their country, and to leave it would stamp them with shame for ever. But the allies were at liberty. Leonidas could not ask them to remain, when death must inevitably be their fate. Troop after troop, they retired: all, save a body of men from Thespia, a Bœotian town, who chose to share the glory and the fate of the Spartans; and 400 Thebans, whom Leonidas knew were in reality traitors to the cause of Greece, and whom he retained in order to punish them. Three persons, however, the Spartan king was willing, if possible, to save. Two were his own kinsmen; the third was Megistias, a descendant of a celebrated ancient seer. Megistias was himself a soothsayer, and is said to have foretold the events which had taken place. But though he sent away his only son,—saying he was anxious that the family of his great ancestor should not end with him—he refused to go himself, preferring rather to die, than to see the ruin of his country.

The kinsmen of Leonidas made the same choice. When they were told that they might carry back letters and messages to Sparta; one replied, that he had come to bear arms, not to carry letters; and the other, that his deeds would tell all that Sparta wished to know.

By the middle of the day the Greek allies were in safety; the 10,000 Persians, who had crossed the mountain, were at the southern entrance of the pass, and Leonidas and his friends were ready to oppose them to death. The barbarians, as the Greeks were accustomed to call the Persians, came on, driven forward by the lash of their commanders. The Spartans needed nothing but their own steadfast bravery to urge them to the battle. They sallied forth, attacked the Persians, and four times forced them to retire. But their small numbers were soon thinned. One of the first amongst the slain was Leonidas; and crowding around his body to defend it from the Persians, the Spartans fought in desperation. Their spears were broken, and their swords blunted; and at length, when the Persians had actually entered the pass, they retreated beyond the wall at the northern end, and collecting together on a knoll, there made their last stand.

The Thebans, cowardly and traitorous as they had always been, threw down their arms, begged for mercy, and were saved; whilst the few remaining Spartans, armed only with a few swords, stood as marks for the arrows and the spears of their enemies, and fell at last, happy in the thought—the best thought which could give strength to the mind of a heathen—that they had died for their country, and by their country would be honoured. They were buried on the spot where they perished, and the inscription, engraved upon their tomb in after years, bade the passenger "tell at Sparta, that they had died in obedience to her laws."

The body of Leonidas was carried off by the Persians, but a marble lion was placed on the knoll in memory of him.

Two Spartans, it is said, were absent from the camp when the attack began. They had been sent to Alpeni on account of a distressing complaint in their eyes. When the news was brought of the advance of the Persians, one made his Helot lead him to the place of combat, where he fell with the rest of his countrymen. The heart of the other failed him, and he fled. But when he returned to Sparta he was shunned as if afflicted by a pestilence. No one would speak to him or share the fire of his hearth with him; coward was the name constantly applied to him; and he never regained the favour of his countrymen until his conduct, on an after occasion, showed that he wished to make amends for his former weakness.

CHAP. XIII.

THE BATTLE OF SALAMIS.

B.C. 480.

Whilst Xerxes was thus slowly and with difficulty advancing into Greece, the Athenians were fully occupied in providing for their own safety: It was quite clear that if Xerxes succeeded in reaching Athens, it would be impossible to prevent his taking possession of it; and when news was brought that the Grecian fleet had been obliged to retire from Artemisium, and that Leonidas had been defeated at Thermopylæ, the hope of being able to resist the power of the Persians was nearly at an end. The inhabitants of Peloponnesus, instead of offering assistance, were determined, they said, not to send any force beyond the Isthmus of Corinth, which they intended to fortify with a wall: and as the Athenians were thus left to themselves, their only prospect of safety was to cross to the Island of Salamis, with their wives and children, and, leaving them there, to make a final effort for their country by sea.

Themistocles was the person who urged them to do this. Some time before, when first the alarm about the Persian invasion began, the Greeks had sent to the Oracle at Delphi, to know what it would be right to do in order to save themselves. The answer which the priestess gave only increased their fears. "Fly," she said, "to the uttermost ends of the earth: for, from the crown to the sole, no part of Athens can escape the fire and sword of the barbarian. Begone, and expect your doom." The messengers turned away in despair; but they were cheered by the advice of one of the chief men at Delphi, who entreated them not to be so soon discouraged, but to approach the temple once more, and beg of the god in his pity to give them a more favourable reply. Again therefore they appeared before the priestess; but the second answer was nearly as gloomy as the first, and much more difficult to be understood. "The goddess Athene," they were told, "had earnestly struggled, but could not propitiate her sire to spare her beloved city. It, and the whole land, were irrevocably doomed to ruin. Yet had Zeus granted to her prayer that, when all beside was lost, a wooden wall should still shelter her citizens. Let them not wait to be trampled down by the horse and foot of the invaders, but turn their backs; they might again look him in the face. In seed time or in harvest, thou, divine Salamis, shalt make women childless."

Many were the different opinions in Athens as to the meaning of this strange prophecy. The general idea was that the wooden walls meant ships; but whether the ships were to take them away to some distant land, or whether the Athenians were to defend themselves by their means, seemed very uncertain. Some great event, they saw, was predicted as about to happen near Salamis; and probably the childless women meant their own people; so at least it was supposed; till Themistocles, who is suspected of having secretly persuaded the priestess at Delphi to give this answer, suggested that a Grecian oracle would never have called Salamis "divine," if their barbarous enemies were to gain the victory there. "Rather," he said, "the prophecy meant that Salamis was the place where the Persians were to be destroyed; and, for the present, the best thing the Athenians could do, would be at once to retire there. They might carry away their treasures, and place their wives and children in safety, and the city must be commended to the care of Athene, and then left to its fate."

This was a very sad proposition, especially for the old people, who had long lived in peace and comfort in their native city. Some of the poorest determined to remain; partly because they could not afford the expense of removing; and partly because they still had a hope, that in some wonderful way Athens would be delivered. The rest made up their minds to go; and when all things were ready — the treasures collected, and the women, children, and slaves assembled, — Cimon, the son of Miltiades, set the example of departure. Carrying his horse's bridle in his hand he ascended to the Acropolis, and after hanging up the bridle in the temple of Athene, as being no longer useful to him, he took down one of the shields which were placed against the wall, made his prayers to the goddess, then went down to the water side, and embarked. His fellow citizens followed his example. The ships carried some to Salamis, some to the island of Ægina, and some to Trœzen, a district to the south-east of Argolis, in Peloponnesus. Trœzen was the birthplace of Theseus, who has been mentioned as one of the great heroes of Greece, and the first king of Attica. From this cause, probably, the Trœzenians were particularly touched by the misfortunes of the Athenians, and now, in their distress, they showed the greatest kindness to the poor exiles. Two oboles, or about fourpence-halfpenny a day, were allowed to every person for his support; a schoolmaster was hired to teach the children; and even the vineyards and orchards were thrown open, and the children allowed to eat as much fruit as they pleased.

When the women and their little ones were thus provided for, nothing remained to be done, but to collect all the ships and men possible, and assemble them in readiness for the next attack of the Persians.

It may be as well now to return to Xerxes, whom we left conqueror at the pass of Thermopylæ. This pass was the entrance, or the key, as it has been called, of northern Greece. When Xerxes had once gained possession of it, his way seemed clear before him. Phocis, the first state which lay in his way, was ravaged, whilst the people fled to the high plains, under the loftiest peaks of Mount Parnassus, and left their houses and their gardens, their temples and fields, to be destroyed by their enemies. Doris was spared,

I

because it was considered friendly to the Persians; and the great army moved on to the borders of Bœotia, intending to pass through it to Attica; whilst a small force was ordered to march to Delphi, strip the temple of its treasures, and bring them as a tribute to Xerxes. It was more easy, however, to give this order than to execute it.

Of all places in Greece Delphi was considered the most sacred. The situation of the town was very beautiful. It lay at the foot of Parnassus, a mountain dedicated peculiarly to the gods, which was covered at its base with myrtles, laurels, and olive trees, and contained numerous caves, glens, and romantic ravines supposed to be visited by nymphs and goddesses. The buildings of the town sloped one above another, in a semicircle, something like a theatre; and at the highest point was the temple of Apollo, which the Alcmæonids had so splendidly built of Parian marble. In the centre of this temple was a small opening, from whence a vapour issued at times, which made any person who leant over it dizzy. When the priestess of Apollo held her head over this vapour, and became, as it were, intoxicated by it, the words which she spoke were supposed to be the inspiration of the god; and were carefully written down by the priests, and afterwards repeated in verse to the person who came to consult the Oracle. The fountain of Castalia, which it was imagined gave the persons who drank of it the power of becoming poets, flowed very near Delphi; and other places in the neighbourhood were considered sacred also; so that the approach of the Persians must have seemed quite a profanation of all which the Greeks were accustomed to revere. The people of Delphi fled away when they heard that their enemies were approaching. But when they asked of the Oracle what should be done with the sacred treasures, they were told not to touch them, for the god would be able to guard his own. The city therefore was left without defence, and the Persians drew nearer and nearer; but, strange to say, as they came quite close, a sudden fear seized them, and instead of obeying the orders given them, they suddenly turned back and fled; and, being pursued by the Delphians, many of them were killed. It is impossible to tell now what was the exact cause of their fears; probably they had an impression that the place was sacred, and that they were doing wrong in trying to plunder it, for its fame was spread far beyond Greece.

Some writers say that a fearful thunderstorm burst upon them, and that portions of the great rocks and cliffs near the city fell upon them and crushed them. The Persians themselves declared that they saw two giant warriors foremost in pursuing them; and these the Delphians said must be two of their native heroes. But all these stories cannot of course be believed, and the only fact we can be quite certain about is, that the Persians, in consequence of their fears, left Delphi untouched.

Xerxes and his army then moved on to Athens, plundering the country through which they passed, and burning the towns and villages. They found Athens deserted; only the few old people, who had refused to go with their fellow citizens, remained; and these shut themselves up in the citadel, and built a wooden wall round the top of the rock, and when the Persians tried to clamber up, threw down heavy stones upon them, and crushed them.

The great Persian king was almost baffled by these few poor people; but after some time a way was found of climbing up the north side of the

Acropolis, whilst the little body of Athenians were defending the western side; and so the Persian soldiers at last entered the citadel. Some of the Athenians threw themselves over the rock; others took refuge in the temple of Athene. But the Persians had no compassion upon them. They were all killed, and the soldiers then plundered the temple, and set fire to the citadel.

The light of the flames spread far and wide. It reached the Grecian fleet, anchored at Salamis, and told the sad news that Athens was taken. The Greek commanders were at that moment assembled at Salamis, in council, and were deliberating at what place it would be best to wait for the approach of the enemy. When the fate of Athens was known, some instantly retired to make preparations for a retreat; the others proposed to give battle near the Isthmus of Corinth. The discussions lasted till midnight. All then went on board their ships, prepared to sail the next morning for the Isthmus.

Themistocles was amongst the number; he was not the chief on this occasion, as Eurybiades, the Spartan, had the command at sea; and though he disapproved of the plan, he could not prevent it. Upon his return to his vessel, he was met by one of his countrymen, a man of very superior judgment, somewhat older than himself, who inquired what had been resolved upon. Themistocles told him. "Then," replied his friend, "all is lost. The fleet will disperse, and Eurybiades will be unable to retain them. Go, and, if you can, make him stay and fight here."

This advice quite agreed with the ideas of Themistocles himself: he felt sure that if once the Peloponnesian allies were in sight of their own shores, they would be only anxious to save themselves and their cities, and would directly leave the fleet. After hearing his friend's opinion, he went on board the ship of Eurybiades, to tell him what they feared, and persuade him to go on shore again, and call another council. Eurybiades, when he had heard all that was to be said, consented, and the council was again assembled.

Themistocles, in his impatience, would not wait for Eurybiades to propose his plan, but began himself to explain his views, and endeavour to persuade the assembly that he was right. "Themistocles," said Adeimantus, the Corinthian admiral, "those who rise in the games before their time are flogged." "Yes," replied Themistocles, "but those who loiter are not crowned;" and then, turning to Eurybiades, he made a speech, setting forth the advantages of remaining where they then were. The real motive of his proposal (his fears that the Peloponnesian allies would desert) he was of course obliged to conceal. Adeimantus still objected. He was probably afraid that Corinth, his own city, would be exposed to danger, if the fleet continued at Salamis. He called on Eurybiades not to listen to a man who had no country. The ungenerous taunt roused the anger of Themistocles. "The Athenians, who have manned 200 vessels," he replied, "have more land than the Corinthians, and there is not a people in Greece who can resist their attack." Once more appealing to Eurybiades, he declared his final determination. "If," he said, "the plan of remaining where they were was not agreed to, the Athenians would at once take their families on board their ships, set sail for Italy, and leave Greece to defend itself." This threat determined the question. The commander yielded, and it was resolved to remain and fight at Salamis.

Six days after the Grecian fleet had retired from Artemisium, the Persian fleet anchored in the bay of Phalerum, on the coast of Attica, and therefore not far from Salamis. Xerxes, with his chief commander, Mardonius, came from Athens, and went on board one of the ships, and then summoned a council, to deliberate on the question, whether or not they should at once risk a battle with the Greeks. All present were inclined for it, with the exception of one person, a woman, — Artemisia, queen of Caria, in Asia Minor, who had sent vessels to aid Xerxes, because her country was tributary to Persia, and who actually commanded her subjects in person. Her advice was to delay. The Greeks, she thought, must soon be driven from Salamis by the want of provisions; and if they then retired near to the Isthmus, they would be likely to have dissensions amongst themselves, and to disperse, when, of course, they would be more easily conquered. Xerxes was not displeased with Artemisia for her boldness in differing from him, but he did not take her advice, and a battle was resolved upon. That very day he ordered his fleet to sail towards Salamis, and by nightfall the ships were formed in line of battle.

The Greeks were as much alarmed when they saw their enemies' fleet made ready for action, as they were when they heard of the taking of Athens. The Peloponnesians, especially, were loud in their complaint. They knew that a large body of Peloponnesian allies had been assembled at the Isthmus of Corinth, and that the army had worked night and day to raise a wall of stone, brick, wood, and sand across the isthmus. They could not but think it much safer and better to be near their friends, within the reach of help, than to be obliged to oppose the Persians by themselves at Salamis.

Themistocles saw that arguments were thrown away. A meeting was called, in which all except the Athenians and the people of Ægina and Megara protested loudly against the folly of remaining near a country which was already in the power of the Persians. If some step were not immediately taken to force them to fight, all the plans and hopes of Themistocles would, he knew, be disappointed. Whilst the commanders were still talking angrily, he left the council without being observed, and sending for a slave, who had the charge of his children, and who, having been brought from the East, could speak the Persian language, he despatched him secretly to the Persian admiral with the following message: "Themistocles, the general of the Athenians, wishes well to the king, and desires to see his cause prevail; therefore he has sent, without the knowledge of the Greeks, to say that they are panic-struck and bent on flight. If you prevent their escape, you insure a complete and easy victory. Already divided among themselves, they will no sooner see themselves pent in by your ships, than they will begin to turn their arms against one another." The slave departed on his errand, and Themistocles returned to the council.

The commanders were still engaged in discussion, and Themistocles had no wish to stop them; every minute's delay gave time for the Persians to approach, and when once Salamis was surrounded, it would be in vain for the Greeks to think of removing to the Isthmus. They would have no hope then but in instant battle. So the night was wearing on, when Themistocles was called out of the room, and told that a stranger wished to speak to him. He obeyed the summons. But it was no stranger whom he was to meet; it was Aristides, once his rival, who for three years had been in exile, but whose love for his country had overcome every petty personal feeling of enmity. He had crossed over from Ægina, making his way, under cover of the darkness, through the midst of the Persian fleet. "Themistocles," he said, "let us still be rivals, but let our strife be which can best serve our country. I come to say that you are wasting words in debating whether you shall sail away from Salamis. We are encircled, and can only escape by cutting a passage through the enemy's fleet."

Themistocles wished for no better intelligence. He did not hesitate to confess to Aristides that it was he himself who had induced the Persians to approach; and having thus gained his point, he took Aristides with him to the council-chamber, that he might declare to the assembled commanders the pressing danger which threatened them. At first they refused to believe it, but the information was soon confirmed by other persons, and dispute being now at an end, the Greeks prepared bravely to meet their foes.

It must have been a splendid sight which presented itself to the eyes of the Persian monarch, when, in the month of September, in the year B.C. 480, he stationed himself on the southern slope of a mountain that overlooked the gulf and the island of Salamis, to watch the event of the coming battle. Dressed in his royal robes, he sat upon a throne of gold supported by silver feet; around him were his princes and courtiers, and on each side stood his secretaries, with tablets in their hands, on which to note down the names of the Persian warriors who might distinguish themselves in the conflict.

His immense fleet was drawn up in three lines in the straits below him; the ships from every quarter of his vast dominions decked out with splendour, and the men collected from his numberless tributary states appearing with every variety of dress, but all looking forward eagerly to the battle, as believing themselves certain of victory.

Opposite to them, lining the eastern coast of the Island of Salamis, lay the joint fleet of Athens, Sparta, and Ægina. Aristides remained on the shore, watching for what would happen; but after the battle began, he crossed with a body of men to a little islet at the entrance of the straits, where Xerxes had placed troops to prevent the escape of the Greeks, and by defeating them proved a great help to Themistocles. He was far too noble to allow any feeling of envy to interfere with his duty, and fought for his country as bravely as if he had not known that all the praise would be given to Themistocles.

The Greeks had 378 ships. The Persians more than 1200. But as it has been said* "Xerxes sat and encouraged the Persians; Themistocles fought and commanded the Greeks." The example thus given by a leader whom all admired, inspired the Greeks with courage, whilst they were also cheered by the hope that the gods were assisting them; since they had especially sent to Ægina to pray for the assistance of the peculiar deities of that island and of Salamis.

Before embarking to begin the battle, Themistocles addressed the assembled Greeks. "All that was noble and good in the Grecian character," he said, "depended on the event of the day. Virtue, honour, prosperity, and happiness, must all be lost if they became subject to the barbarians:" and earnestly he exhorted them "to choose and hold fast the good." When he ceased speaking, the troops took their stations in the different vessels, and the war song burst forth, echoing amongst the island rocks,

* See Wordsworth's Pictorial Greece.

and followed by the splash of oars beating in regular order, as the navy moved onward in a close body; the Greeks cheering each other with one heart and one tongue to free their country, their children, their wives, the temples of their gods, and the tombs of their ancestors; for all these were now at stake.*

The straits between Salamis and Attica are not more than a quarter of a mile wide in the narrowest part; and here it was that the Greeks awaited the approach of the Persians. It was a wise arrangement, for in consequence only a few of their enemies' ships could approach them at a time. The Persians fought with great valour, knowing that their king was watching them; but those who were behind, wishing to distinguish themselves, pressed forward too eagerly, and so caused confusion. They were also distressed by a strong breeze, which blew up the channel every day at a certain hour. Themistocles is said to have foreseen that this would be a difficulty in their way, and to have delayed the battle in consequence.

But one of the greatest disadvantages of all was that there was no real union amongst the Persians. Their forces were composed of so many different nations, that they had very little concern for what happened to each other. Artemisia, queen of Caria, for instance, being much pressed by the Corinthian admiral, and finding a vessel belonging to one of the Persian allies in her way, made no scruple of running against it, and sinking it, so that not one of the crew escaped. Of course the Greek commander, supposed he had been pursuing a friend, and turned away.

All these causes united, spread terror and confusion amongst the Persian ships. After a long

* See Wordsworth's Pictorial Greece.

struggle they were dispersed; and on the evening of the same day on which Xerxes from his golden throne had surveyed his fleet in hope and triumph, he saw the surface of the sea and the shore covered with the wreck of his vessels and the dead bodies of his men; whilst the troops which had been sent against Aristides, and which are supposed to have been a band of his Immortals, were also completely defeated. Unable to endure the sight, he groaned deeply, rent his clothes, and rushed from his throne in an agony of disappointment and despair. From that moment he must have begun seriously to dread that his hopes of conquering Greece were vain.

The battle of Salamis was important not only to the Persians and Greeks, but to the whole world. If Xerxes had gained the victory, he would probably have been able to subdue all Greece; the habits and customs of the East would have been introduced amongst the nations of the West; and instead of becoming more and more civilised and free, they would by degrees, have sunk into mere slaves to their princes, caring only for pleasure and ease. The Greeks were more admired and imitated than any other people, and from them, learning and taste, and a knowledge of the fine arts, have spread over the world, and have been brought down to our own days. We may well therefore be thankful for the Providence which prevented their falling under the power of the Persians, and so ordered events, that the general good of mankind should be provided for, by what must have seemed, at the time, merely a succession of accidental circumstances.

The person who, next to Xerxes, felt the most grieved at the loss of the battle of Salamis, was Mardonius, his cousin and the chief commander of his armies. It was Mardonius who had especially urged the Persian monarch to undertake the expe-

dition against Greece, and now he began to feel that
he should be reproached for its failure. He did not,
however, confess his regret openly, but knowing the
king's disposition, and being quite sure that Xerxes
would only be too willing to have an excuse for returning to Persia, since he had been so humbled in
Greece, he went to him and entreated him not to let
his spirits be cast down by the loss of a few ships.
"The Persians," he said, "were not used to rely on frail
planks, but on men and horses for victory. Their
arms were still as irresistible as ever on their proper
element. Let the king but make the trial by advancing into Peloponnesus, and he would see that
the Greek sailors, however proud they were of their
triumph, would none of them dare to land and meet
him. If, however, he was satisfied with the display
he had made of his power, and thought it time to return to Persia, Mardonius himself, if he were permitted to select 300,000 troops from the army, would
undertake to complete the conquest of Greece."
Xerxes was much pleased at the proposal. He pretended to consult with Artemisia, queen of Caria,
though it is probable he would not have listened to her,
if she had given him advice against his wishes; but,
as it happened, she quite agreed with his views, and
the plans were soon arranged. The children of
Xerxes were entrusted to the charge of Artemisia,
who immediately set sail for Ephesus; and orders
were given to the fleet to make its way to the Hellespont with all speed, and guard the bridges till the
king's arrival.

Xerxes himself set out on his return by land; his
movements being much hastened by a secret message
sent him by Themistocles, to warn him that the
Greeks had a plan of sailing themselves to the
Hellespont, and destroying the bridges, and so to cut
off his retreat. The fact was, that the idea had been

suggested, but was laid aside, as it was thought better not to drive the Persian king to desperation, and force him to remain in Greece, when he was evidently anxious to leave it.

Mardonius accompanied Xerxes to Thessaly. There he was to take up his winter quarters, and in the spring the war was to be renewed.

The retreat of Xerxes was a miserable contrast to the proud grandeur of his first setting forth. Instead of a glittering host of soldiers, marching boldly forward and certain of success, his followers were, in appearance, a crowd without order, weakened by want and illness. No one had been careful to keep up the supplies for the magazines, at the places through which they had passed when they entered Greece; so that there was a great lack of provisions; the inhabitants of the towns and villages were quite unable to feed such a multitude, and the unhappy Persians were at last obliged to eat the grass in the fields, and the bark and leaves of trees. Such unwholesome food naturally brought on dreadful diseases, and numbers were obliged to be left behind, to be taken care of by the people of the country. Very many also perished by a terrible accident which happened upon the river Strymon, in Thrace. The river was frozen over when they reached it: those who came first, at night, crossed it easily; but the next morning the heat of the sun began to melt the ice, and when the soldiers ventured upon it, it suddenly gave way, and multitudes perished in the waters.

It took Xerxes forty-five days to travel from Thessaly, where he had left Mardonius, to the Hellespont. He found on his arrival that a storm had broken up the bridges, but his fleet was in readiness to carry the troops over to Abydos, and there they enjoyed rest and plenty. The change, however, was not of as much service as might have been expected. The poor famished people, by eating too eagerly, did themselves a great deal of harm; and when at length the army reached Sardis, it could be called nothing but a wreck or fragment of the vast host which had set forth to conquer Greece.

CHAP. XIV.

THE BATTLE OF PLATÆA.

B.C. 479.

THEMISTOCLES and the fleet pursued the Persians by sea a little way, the day after the battle of Salamis; but being unable to approach near, they gave up the attempt to overtake them, and contented themselves with going to some of the Greek islands which were known to have given assistance to the enemy, and forcing them to pay considerable sums of money as a punishment for their offence. Andros was one of these islands. When Themistocles demanded a contribution from the inhabitants, he told them that the Athenians had brought two powerful Deities to second their demand,—Persuasion and Force. The Andrians however replied, that they also had a pair of ill-conditioned Deities, who would not leave their island, or let them comply with the will of the Athenians,—Poverty and Inability. The Greeks in consequence laid siege to Andros, but they were not able to take it; so Poverty and Inability proved in the end too strong for Persuasion and Force.

Themistocles was now in the highest favour with every one. It was allowed by all that his foresight and prudence had been the chief causes of success, next to the favour of the gods. The best of the spoils which had been taken from the enemy were dedicated to the temple at Delphi, or at least their value was given in the form of an immense statue larger than life. When this was done, the Greek commanders met in the temple of Poseidon, or Neptune, on the Isthmus, to settle who amongst them had distinguished himself the most. Not one of them was noble enough to give up the claim of the first rank for himself; but almost every one agreed that Themistocles ought to be placed second, which of course was really owning his superiority to all. Shortly afterwards Themistocles went to Sparta, where he was presented with an olive crown for his wisdom, whilst Eurybiades received another for his bravery. The Spartans also gave Themistocles the best chariot in the city, and sent 300 knights to escort him to the frontiers of their state on his return.

These, however, were affairs which concerned only a few persons. That which was of the most consequence to the common people, was the task of resettling themselves in their homes, and recovering, if possible, from the effects of the terrible invasion. The Athenians went back to Athens shortly after the battle of Salamis, hoping they might now be permitted to repair their houses, and cultivate their fields; but they were, as yet, by no means safe.

Mardonius and his army were in Thessaly; and although no attempt was made to renew the war during the winter, yet when the spring came, they were obliged again to prepare for meeting their deadly enemy.

Their first trial, however, was to resist a tempting proposal for peace. Early in the season, an ambassador arrived at Athens from the Persian general, bearing a proposal which Xerxes himself had commanded Mardonius to make. "The Persian king," he said, " was ready to forget past offences, to secure the Athenians in the unmolested possession of their territory, and to add to it any other they might covet. He would also undertake to rebuild all the temples which he had burnt in their city; and in return, he desired only that the Athenians should be his friends. He did not wish them to be his subjects, but his allies."

The tidings of this embassy to Athens soon reached the ears of the other Grecian states. The Spartans, especially, were alarmed at it. If Athens sided with Persia, the inhabitants of Peloponnesus could not long hope to be free.

An ambassador was instantly despatched to Athens, to remind the Athenians of the duty they owed to Greece, and recall to their minds the glory they had gained in the late war. "The Spartans," said the envoy, "felt for the distress which the Athenians had suffered from the Persian invasion, and would do their utmost to help them for the future. They would maintain the families of the Athenians, as long as the war lasted, at their own expense; and Athens would do wrongly in preferring the hollow promises of the barbarians to those of friends and natural allies."

The reply given to this advice at once satisfied the Spartans, and showed the ambassador of Mardonius that it was in vain to try and bribe the Athenians to desert the cause of Greece. "So long as the sun held his course, Athens," it was said, "would never come to terms with Xerxes. Enormous as his power was, she would continue to defy it, relying on the gods and the heroes whose temples and images he had burnt and defaced."

With regard to the offer of assistance made by the Spartans, the Athenians were grateful, but declined to accept it. They had no wish to be a burden, and it was not the kind of aid which they needed. They begged, however, that the Spartans would put their forces in motion without delay, to meet Mardonius in Bœotia, as on receiving the answer just given, he would probably, immediately invade Attica.

The Spartan ambassadors departed; but if the Athenians really wanted to obtain help from Sparta, they must have been grievously disappointed. Mardonius set out on his march as soon as he received their proud message. He entered Bœotia, and found no one to oppose him. The Bœotians were his friends, and readily welcomed him. The Spartans, caring only for themselves, set to work to build fortifications across the Isthmus of Corinth, but never thought of sending troops beyond it; and the Athenians, at last, knowing themselves to be far too weak to oppose Mardonius without aid from the other states, once more fled from Athens, and took refuge in the island of Salamis.

Ten months after the taking of Athens by Xerxes, the city was again in the hands of the Persians under Mardonius. The Persian commander sent directly to Salamis to offer the same terms of peace which had been proposed before; but even then, in such great peril, the Athenians were not to be moved from their resolution. Only one man in the council dared to propose that they should yield, and he was terribly punished for his weakness. When he quitted the house where the council was assembled, the common people gathered round him, and in their fury stoned him to death; and, what was far more shocking, the Athenian women rushed in a body to his house, and murdered his innocent wife and children.

It is not to be imagined that the Athenians would allow the Spartans to continue their selfish conduct without complaint. They sent an embassy to Sparta, in which the people of Megara and Platæa joined, to reproach the Spartans with their neglect, and to beg them once more to assist in driving the barbarians from Attica. The ambassadors, on their arrival, found the Spartans engaged in celebrating a great public festival as quietly and easily as if nothing was amiss. The Ephors, who were the persons chiefly to decide these questions of war, declined giving them an answer till the morrow, and when the morrow came, they still put it off, on pretence that they were engaged with the festival. So it went on for ten days, till the Athenian ambassadors were quite weary; but, at length, when they began to threaten that Athens would become the ally of Persia, and give up the cause of Greece, if some help was not afforded, they were told that an army had been sent out secretly, and had probably, by that time, reached Arcadia.

This was actually the case, and the envoys, as soon as they were convinced of it, followed in all haste, accompanied by 5000 soldiers from amongst the best of the Lacedæmonian troops.

Mardonius soon heard of the forces which were advancing against him. Upon consideration, it seemed better not to wait for them in Attica, but to return to Bœotia, where the people were all his friends. He accordingly left Athens; but before his departure, he allowed his soldiers to plunder, ravage, and destroy everything which came in their way. Up to that time, he had still fancied it might be possible to bring over the Athenians to his side, and therefore had forbidden his men to do any injury to their houses or lands, thinking that the hope of saving their property might be an inducement to the citizens to agree to his terms.

The Persian army retreated quickly from Attica,

followed by the Spartans and their allies, under the command of Pausanias, a nephew of Leonidas, and the guardian of his son, the young king of Sparta. On entering Bœotia, Mardonius found every one friendly to him, but he was not so confident of victory now, as not to guard against a defeat. On the contrary, he enclosed his treasures within a high wooden wall guarded by towers; and this kind of fortification he intended also to serve as a refuge, in case the Greek army should prove superior to his own. Whilst this work was going on, one of the principal men at Thebes, in order to show his kind feeling for the Persians, invited Mardonius and fifty of his chief officers to a great entertainment in the city of Thebes. Fifty Thebans were invited to meet them; and as it was the custom of the Greeks, as well as of the Romans, to lie upon couches when they took their meals, it was arranged that one of each nation, a Persian and a Theban together, should share every couch. This was to prove their friendliness; and certainly they do not seem to have had any distrust of each other; for Herodotus, a famous Greek historian, afterwards met one of the Thebans who had been invited to the entertainment and was told by him, that the Persian who shared his couch on that occasion, talked to him privately of the battle that was likely soon to take place, and confessed that he looked forward to it with the greatest anxiety, fearing that the Spartans and their allies would gain the victory.

Yet the Persians were still three times more in number than the Greeks, and ought properly, therefore, to have had no fears. They had been taught, however, by this time, that valour and determined resolution have more to do with victory than mere numbers; and the next engagement with the Greeks proved the same fact still more strongly.

The Greeks and Persians met at the foot of Cithæron, a rugged mountain in Bœotia, where an engagement took place between the Spartan horsemen and some of the Persians, in which the Spartans had the advantage, and one of the Persian commanders, a particularly fine, handsome officer, was killed. His horse was wounded by an arrow, and reared and threw him. The Athenians, who were assisting the Spartans, rushed forward to slay him, but he wore a gold scale corselet or body-piece, which protected him, and he might perhaps have escaped, if some one had not pierced his eye, and so destroyed him.

The whole Persian army paid him funeral honours. They not only shaved their own heads, but cut off the tails of their horses and beasts of burden; and, Herodotus says, that their wailing resounded throughout all Bœotia. Yet they could not get possession of his body, which was carried off by the Greeks; and being afterwards placed in a cart, was drawn along the lines, whilst the men ran out from their ranks, to gaze upon the gigantic barbarian.

Pausanias, after this victory, moved his forces to the banks of a river, at about two miles distance from the town of Platæa, where he thought that he should be better supplied with water than in his former position. Mardonius and the Persians encamped on the opposite banks, but neither army was willing to begin a regular battle. The Spartan soothsayers declared that the gods were not yet favourable, and the Greek soothsayers, on the Persian side, said the same. It is strange to hear of a Persian general listening to a Greek diviner, but the Persians seem to have had a great belief in the Greek superstitions. One of these diviners had been induced to come over to their side, partly because of a bribe which had been offered him, and partly because he hated the Spartans, who had once thrown him into a dungeon, and put his feet into stocks. He escaped, but only by cutting off the fore part of his own foot, and, in spite of the wound, breaking through the prison wall, and travelling by night, and hiding himself in woods by day, till he reached a place of safety.

Ten days passed, and still no favourable omen could be obtained, and Mardonius then resolved to follow his own judgment. He told his intention to Artabazus, one of the other commanders, but Artabazus tried to dissuade him from it, saying, "that he had much better go back to Thebes, instead of risking a battle. There were magazines at Thebes, to supply the soldiers, and if Mardonius would give large presents to the leading men in the Grecian cities, no doubt they would soon be induced to join him." Mardonius was a very eager, impetuous person, and would not listen to this advice. He called a council of the Persian officers and those of his Greek allies, and tried to persuade them that the gods would not be unfavourable to the Persians, because they had spared the temple at Delphi; then, bidding them dismiss all scruples, he told them to prepare cheerfully for battle the next day.

In the dead of the following night, a horseman rode up to the outposts of the Greek camp, and desired to speak with the Athenian generals. On being admitted, he discovered himself to be the ambassador who had before been sent by Mardonius to ask for the alliance of Athens. He was a Macedonian prince, an old friend of the Athenians, and now he was come to warn them of their danger, at the risk of his own life. "Mardonius," he said, "was determined to give them battle the next morning, notwithstanding the unfavourable omens. It was possible, however, that the engagement would be delayed, in which case he exhorted them still to keep their ground, as the Persians had only a few days' provisions left, and would soon be obliged to retire." In return for this information, the Macedonian prince prayed them to remember his good will if the cause of Greece triumphed, and then rode away.

The next day went by, and the Persians gave no signs of being ready for a general battle, though they made an attack upon the Spartans, and took possession of a spring of water. The loss of this fountain was a serious misfortune, for the Persian horsemen prevented the Greeks from procuring water from the river, and Pausanias found it would be impossible to remain in such a position any longer. Having consulted with the other generals, it was agreed that they must move as soon as possible; and, accordingly, when night came, the greater part marched to Platæa, and posted themselves close to the town. Pausanias, and his fellow commanders were detained; for a Spartan, named Amompharetus, who had not been present at the council, had fancied that this movement was intended for flight, and, considering it a disgrace, steadily refused to go, though Pausanias urged him most earnestly to consent, knowing that he and his soldiers must be killed if they remained behind. The Athenians, being surprised at the delay, sent to learn the cause of it, and to ask what they had better do themselves, as they were waiting to go with the Spartans. Their messenger came up just whilst the dispute was going on. Amompharetus was still quite determined, and taking up a large stone with both hands, he flung it down at the feet of Pausanias, exclaiming, "There is my vote against flying before the strangers." Pausanias called him a madman, and sent back a message to the Athenians, ordering them to bring up their forces and follow him; but nothing that he could say had any effect upon Amompharetus, and at last, in despair, Pausanias was obliged to leave him. After marching about a mile, however, Pausanias stopped, hoping that Amompharetus would change his mind when he found himself left alone with his small body of troops. And so it really happened. After a little while, they saw him coming slowly after them; but, in consequence of the delay, some of the Persian horsemen were able to overtake them, and trouble them, as they had done before, with skirmishes and slight attacks.

A battle was now very near at hand. When Mardonius heard that the Greeks had retreated during the night, he scoffed at the notion of their bravery, and declared that Xerxes should be told of the cowardly counsel of Artabazus, who had advised him to retire before such men; and he lost no time in crossing the river with his whole army, and following the road which the Greeks had taken.

The Spartans were the first whom he came up with, and they were, in consequence, the first to be attacked. The Athenians could not give any assistance, though Pausanias sent a horseman forward to tell them what was going on; for just about the same time, some of the Greek allies of the Persians were approaching them, and they were obliged to defend themselves. Even then the Spartans would not begin to fight without being told by the soothsayers that the gods were favourable to them. Animals were sacrificed, and the diviners began to examine them, as was their custom, to see if they could discover, by their appearance after death, what would be considered a favourable omen.

Whilst this was being done, Pausanias ordered his men to seat themselves on the ground, and, holding their long shields before them, to wait till the gods should give the signal for battle. The Persians came nearer and nearer, till at last they were within bowshot. Then they fixed the wicker shields which they used into the ground, so as to form a sort of screen for themselves, and shot their arrows at the Spartans. Not one of the Spartans moved. One man particularly famed for his beauty was amongst them, but he, as well as his companions, steadily faced the shower of arrows, and at length died, lamenting only that he had not been able to raise his arm in the defence of his country.

Pausanias was in great distress; but at length the soothsayers pronounced that the favourable omen had been discovered, and the Spartans sprang up and rushed forward. The Persians fought bravely, but they were unable to resist the strength of the Spartan arms. Mardonius, mounted on a stately white charger, and distinguished by his glittering armour, was foremost in the fight; a thousand chosen men, a portion of the royal guards, surrounded him, but no valour and no protection could save him. Whilst the victory was yet doubtful, a Spartan soldier attacked him, wounded him mortally, and the event of the battle was decided. The Persians fled when they knew that their commander was slain. They took refuge in the fortified camp which Mardonius had prepared, barred the gates, and manned the towers and the walls; but they were followed closely by the Greeks, who, after some difficulty, forced away the wooden defences and entered the camp. The Persians were now enclosed within a narrow space, like sheep crowded into a sheepfold. They had neither spirit nor power to defend themselves, and the Greeks, maddened by the recollection of their own losses, killed them without mercy. It is supposed that only 3,000 of those who had retreated to the camp escaped; but a large body of 40,000 men, under Artabazus, who had not arrived at the field of battle till the victory was lost, saved themselves by taking the road to Phocis, and then retreating, with the utmost possible haste, to the Hellespont. The treasures found in the Persian camp were of immense value; the furniture of the tents glittered with gold and silver, and even the common vessels, used every day, were made of the same precious metals. The bracelets, collars, and rich suits of armour were innumerable; and, amongst other things, the Greeks took possession of the manger of Xerxes' horse, which was made of brass, curiously wrought. We are told that when Pausanias entered the tent of Mardonius, and saw the rich curtains, and soft carpets and couches, and the tables covered with vessels of gold and silver, he ordered some Persian slaves to prepare a banquet, such as they would have made ready for their own masters. As soon as it was ready, he commanded his own Helots to set by its side the simple food to which he was himself accustomed; and summoning the Greek officers, bade them mark the folly of the barbarian, who, when he had already such great wealth, and was able to enjoy so much luxury, thought it worth while to come and rob the Greeks of their simple store.

Thus was Greece at last delivered from her powerful enemies. Artabazus, indeed, reached Asia in safety, but a part of his army perished on the road from hunger, and from the attacks of the barbarous Thracian tribes, through whose country they were obliged to pass. To complete the triumph of the Greeks, a great victory was gained over the Persians by the Greek colonies in Asia Minor, on the very same day that the battle of Platæa took place, B.C. 479. These colonies had been obliged to assist Xerxes in his expedition; but the people were in their hearts Greeks, and not Persians, and there was always reason to doubt whether they would be thoroughly faithful to the Persian king. During the time of the war, the European Greeks had tried to bring the Asiatic Greeks over to their side. For instance, after the battle by sea, at Artemisium, when the Greek fleet retired, Themistocles ordered sentences to be engraved upon a rock near, calling upon the Ionians in the Persian army to leave the Persians and support the people from whom they originally came. The Ionians remained steadfast at that time; but when Xerxes was defeated at Salamis, there seemed a good opportunity for some of the Asiatic Greeks, and the people of the Greek islands, who were subject to Persia, to free themselves from the Persian yoke. They were encouraged in this notion by the presence of a Greek fleet, commanded by one of the Spartan kings, which was stationed near the coasts, and would, they were sure, be willing to help them. The Ionians did not openly revolt, but the people of the island of Samos did, and the Spartans assisted them, and afterwards sailed to Ionia, hoping that the inhabitants of that colony would join them. A Persian army was ready to oppose them there, and amongst the forces were many Ionians. The Spartan king, wishing, like Themistocles, to make the Ionians declare themselves on the Greek side, addressed a proclamation to them by a herald, calling upon them to remember the liberty of their country. Soon afterwards, a battle took place at Mycale, and the Ionians, seeing that the Greeks were gaining the victory, deserted to them, and assisted in completely defeating the Persians. This was the victory which was gained on the same day that the battle of Platæa was fought.

The islands of the Ægean Sea were now entirely united to Greece, and permitted to join in a union or confederacy of the Greek states; but the Ionians were left to make their peace with Persia as they could, for there was no way of protecting them, except by keeping an army in their country, which was impossible. The Grecian fleet divided after the victory at Mycale; the Spartans went home, but the Athenians made up their minds to try and recover what had once been the dominions of Miltiades, in the Chersonesus. They accordingly laid siege to Sestos; and, after spending all the winter in endeavouring to take it, at last succeeded.

We must now return to the Greeks at Platæa, whose chief thought, when they found themselves delivered from their enemies, was to show their thankfulness to the gods, whom they believed had aided them in the struggle. A tenth part of the spoils was set apart for the temple at Delphi, and was formed into a golden tripod. There were several kinds of tripods used by the Greeks; some were employed for common purposes, and were merely tables, supported by three legs; others were pots, resting upon three feet, used for boiling meat; but the tripods given to the temples were often employed as moveable altars.

There was one tripod, especially famous, at Delphi, on which the priestess stood when she delivered the oracles of the god. The tripod, which was presented to the temple by the Greeks after the battle of Platæa, was in the form of a golden ball, supported by a three-headed bronze serpent. It was preserved for a great number of years, and as late

as A. D. 1675,—in the reign of our Charles II.—
the bronze serpent is said to have been seen by a
traveller at Constantinople. The bowl had been
removed from it. The serpent was fourteen or
fifteen feet high.

Another portion of the Persian spoils was given to
the great temple of Zeus at Olympia. This was in
the form of an enormous statue of the god, on the
base of which were engraved the names of the cities
whose inhabitants had shared in the contest. A statue was also given to the temple of Poseidon on the
Isthmus, and a large sum was reserved to enable the
Platæans to build a temple to Athene; for whatever
was the ignorance and superstition of the Greeks
they still were wise enough to know that there was
a power mightier than their own watching over and
defending them; and they would have scorned to
receive great benefits, and not to show their gratitude for them to the utmost of their power. Neither
were they forgetful of those who had died in defence of their country. Barrows or mounds were
raised over them, and this was considered such a
distinction, that even the cities which had not lost
men in the battle raised mounds, by the side of
those who had actually fallen, to commemorate their
share in the victory. Amongst those slain at
Platæa, was the Spartan who escaped from Thermopylæ. He fought dauntlessly, and fell as he
had wished, making amends for his former weakness. But the Spartans could not forget that he
sought death because he had once loved life too
dearly, and they paid no honours to his memory.
The Thebans, having assisted the Persians, were
obliged to give up the chief persons who had encouraged them to do so, and the offenders were put
to death.

Pausanias received, as his reward, ten samples of every thing that was most valuable amongst the spoils. He showed a noble spirit after the victory; for, when it was suggested to him to impale the dead body of Mardonius, because Xerxes had insulted that of Leonidas at Thermopylæ, he indignantly rejected the proposal, saying, "that victims enough had fallen to appease the shades of Leonidas and the heroes of Thermopylæ."

But although much praise is doubtless due to the Spartan general, and the brave soldiers, there was one person present at Platæa to whom perhaps more real credit is due than to any one else. This was Aristides, whose moderation, unselfishness, and excellent temper had great influence over the Athenians, and induced them to behave in the most admirable manner in the midst of all their difficulties and hardships; for they showed no jealousy of the Spartans, but seemed quite to forget themselves, and only to be desirous of doing what would be best for all. Before the army broke up Aristides took advantage of the good feeling which at such a moment prevailed, to persuade the Greek leaders to unite together more closely than they had ever done before. They agreed to keep up an army of 10,000 men-at-arms, and 1000 horsemen, besides a fleet of 100 galleys, to prosecute the war against the barbarians. It was settled that deputies should be sent every year to Platæa, from the different states, to consult about public affairs, and to celebrate the anniversary of the battle of Platæa with religious rites; and every fifth year a festival was to be held there, called the Feast of Liberty. It was also agreed to erect an altar on the spot to Zeus, under the title of the Deliverer; but before the first sacrifice was offered on it, the

Delphic oracle commanded that all the fires in the
country should be put out, as having been polluted
by the presence of the barbarians; and that they
should be re-lighted from what was considered the
national hearth at Delphi. In obedience to this
command, a Platæan ran from the camp to Delphi,
a distance of sixty miles, to fetch the sacred fire,
and returned with it the same day; but he had
scarcely time to deliver it, before he fell down dead.
He was buried in a consecrated place, and an inscription near his grave told what he had done.

The Platæans undertook to offer the sacrifices
which were instituted in remembrance of the deliverance of Greece, and also to pay respect to the
memory of the brave men who had fallen in the
battle: and, as long as they did this, their land
was to be considered sacred. Many years afterwards, about the time of the Roman emperor Nero,
Plutarch, the biographer, a native of Bœotia, who
wrote the lives of many of the most celebrated persons of ancient days, described the ceremonies
which were still used in honour of the heroes of
the battle of Platæa. A martial procession marched,
he says, at break of day to the sound of trumpet,
through the midst of the city, followed by waggons, filled with myrtle boughs and chaplets; then
came the black bull which was to be sacrificed, and
a number of young men, freemen (for no slaves
were allowed to bear a part in these ceremonies),
carrying the vessels which held the libations or
drink offerings for the dead. Last of all came the
chief magistrate, the archon, dressed in a purple
tunic, and carrying a sword in his hand; though at
other times he always wore white, and was not allowed to touch a weapon. The archon bore an urn
which was kept especially for this occasion. When
the procession reached the burial ground, the ar-

chon washed and anointed the tombstones, and then sacrificed the victim, and poured out the libation; and, having prayed to the gods who were supposed to watch over the dead, he solemnly invited the brave men who had fallen in defence of their country to share the banquet which, as a mark of gratitude, had been provided for them. This was according to the idea which the Greeks had of a future state. They had no notion of a life different from that of this world, and all their talents and learning were of no use in teaching them the truths which it most concerned their happiness to know.

CHAP. XV.

THE REBUILDING AND FORTIFICATION OF ATHENS.

B.C. 478.

WHEN the Athenians returned to their homes they found their lands wasted, and their houses in ruins, with the exception of a few which had been occupied by the principal Persians. They immediately set to work to restore them, but, as every person was allowed to follow his own wishes, there was no regularity in the streets; and the houses were small and mean, and built with such ugly and inconvenient projections, that, after a time, Themistocles and Aristides prevailed upon the Court of Areopagus to insist upon their being altered. Even then, Athens could not be made a handsome city. The temples which had been destroyed were still left in ruins, as Aristides and Themistocles, who were the persons of greatest influence in the state, were anxious to fortify the city before they did anything else. But the temple of Athene, in the

Acropolis, was still safe; and in it was placed the silver-footed throne, on which Xerxes sat when he watched the battle of Salamis, together with a golden poignard taken from Mardonius at the battle of Platæa.

The Spartans, who were always jealous of the power of Athens, no sooner understood that the Athenians were rebuilding their walls strongly, and enclosing a larger space than before, than they began to take alarm. Ambassadors were sent to Athens with a message which sounded very friendly, but which in reality was full of envy. "Instead of raising new walls," said the Spartans, "which would only serve to shelter the barbarians in a fresh invasion, the Athenians would do much better in assisting to throw down all the walls north of the Isthmus; for they might be sure of a refuge at any time in the Peloponnesus."

The Athenians were too quick to be deceived by this pretence of kindness. They saw at once that Sparta wished to become chief herself, and did not like anything which would tend to make Athens strong.

Themistocles undertook to go himself to Sparta, and carry back an answer, and the envoys were dismissed.

Themistocles set out on his journey; but, on his arrival at Sparta, he delayed asking an audience of the ephors so long that they sent to know the cause. "I am waiting," replied Themistocles, "for my colleagues, whom I left behind to despatch some very urgent business; but I expect them daily, and hoped to have seen them before." This excuse satisfied the Spartans, till they were told that all this time the Athenians were actually at work at the walls, which were rising rapidly. Themistocles begged them not to listen to reports so easily, but to send messengers themselves to discover if they were true. Some of the gravest and most trustworthy Spartans were accordingly sent to Athens; but they were not allowed to return, for Themistocles gave a secret message at the same time, bidding the Athenians quietly to detain them, till he should go back to Athens himself. Whilst all this was passing, men, women, and children were at work at Athens rebuilding the walls, which were soon high enough to stand a siege. The report of their progress was forwarded to Themistocles by Aristides and another ambassador; and Themistocles then begged for an audience of the Spartan governors, and after telling them that the fortifications were too far advanced to be stopped, advised them, when next they sent ambassadors to Athens, to deal with the Athenians as with reasonable men, who knew what was necessary for their own safety, and for the interests of Greece. The Athenians, he said, "had not needed the counsels of the Spartans when they left their city, and committed themselves to their ships; and they thought they might now trust their own judgment in rebuilding their walls."

The Spartans were very clever in concealing their feelings. So they only expressed their regret that the Athenians should have misunderstood the motive of their suggestions; and the ambassadors on both sides returned home, without any further complaints or reproaches. The city walls were quietly completed, but any person who examined them could see how hastily and strangely they had been put together; for the Athenians, in their eagerness, had pulled down houses and sacred buildings, and everything which could be used for materials, without considering whether what they destroyed was beautiful, or useful, or valuable. A traveller

in Greece, in 1850, describes the remains of these
walls as still existing, and says that they are made
of fragments of temples, houses, &c.*

The next object of Themistocles was to fortify
the ports and harbours near the town, for he began to see that the chief power and safety of the
Athenians would be found in their ships. Before
this time there had been only one small harbour,
called Phalerum, but Themistocles now proposed to
fortify three. Piræus was the chief; it was not
quite so close to Athens as Phalerum, but it soon
grew to be of great importance, and became a
town in itself. Themistocles caused a large space
round it to be enclosed by a strong wall, and sent
for an architect to plan out the streets; and soon
there were temples built in it, and a market-place,
and a theatre; and at last it was a much handsomer
town than Athens, and became the great resort of
foreigners, and of all persons whose business connected them with the sea. From Piræus to Phalerum there was another strong wall built along the
sea shore; and this helped also to guard the third
port, Munychia, by which it passed. The wall was
sixty feet high, and broad enough to allow of two
waggons standing on it a-breast of each other. It
was the great wish of Themistocles to make the
Athenians depend on their sea forces; and he is said
to have changed the seats on the hill, where the
people held their public assemblies, in order that
they might look towards the sea and the harbour
instead of the land and the rock of the Acropolis;
and so might be accustomed to think of the power
of their navy rather than of their armies. And now
the time was come when a trial of power was to be
made between the two great Grecian states, Athens

* Picturesque Sketches in Greece, by Aubrey de Vere.

and Sparta. Their strength seemed about equal: for, although Themistocles and the Athenians had first distinguished themselves in defeating the Persians at Salamis, Pausanias, the victorious general at Platæa, and the regent of Sparta, was the man who seemed to have had the greatest share in finally freeing Greece from her invaders. It was to him that the command of the allied fleet was given, when it was again sent out to carry on the war against the Persians on their own shores. This was in the year after the expedition made by the Athenians to recover the dominion of Miltiades in the Chersonesus. Thirty Athenian vessels formed part of the fleet, and these were commanded by Aristides, and by Cimon, the son of Miltiades, who was celebrated for his talents and virtues.

The Greeks sailed to Cyprus, which belonged to Persia, and conquered the greater part of the island; and then they laid siege to Byzantium, now Constantinople, and soon took it. Whilst the allied Greeks remained near this place, they began to perceive a great change in the character of Pausanias; or rather, they discovered the faults which no doubt he had before, but which there had not been much opportunity to display. Instead of being gentle and courteous, he became haughty and disagreeable, and treated his allies as if they were his subjects; whilst he took pains to follow the customs of the Persians, as if he despised those of his own nation. He had shown something of this disposition before, after the battle of Platæa; for he was then vain enough to have his own name inscribed upon the tripod which was given to the temple at Delphi, together with some verses, which attributed the victory and the offering to himself. The Spartans caused the inscription to be effaced, and the names of the cities whose soldiers had assisted them engraved in its stead; yet this did not do away with the folly and conceit of such an action. It was evident now that Pausanias was tired of being chief only in a small Grecian state; and people began to suspect that he was inclined to make friends with the Persian king, in the hope of obtaining some government under him, which might give him greater riches and grandeur. In Sparta he would, in a few years, become a private person, because he was only regent and the guardian of the young king; and this was an idea which he was too proud and ambitious to be likely to bear patiently. But if his discontent was natural, considering his great ambition, his want of caution was very surprising. By the help of some prisoners of rank whom he had taken at Byzantium, he sent messages to Xerxes, offering to make the Persian monarch Lord of Greece, if he would only give him his daughter in marriage. Xerxes seemed inclined to listen to the proposals. Pausanias then threw off all disguise, and took upon himself the pomp and state of a Persian nobleman, wore a Persian dress, ate and drank in the same way, and with the same luxury, as the Persians, and at length actually travelled through Thrace, escorted by a guard of Persians and Egyptians. Such conduct, as might well have been anticipated, was exceedingly irritating to the Greeks, and especially to the colonies in Asia Minor, who had just thrown off the Persian yoke, but who now found that Pausanias was likely to be quite as severe a master as Xerxes.

They bore with him as long as they could, but they could not help thinking that it would be much happier for every one, if Aristides, who was so mild and just, or Cimon, who was remarkable for his generosity and gentleness, were to be their governors infiend of Pausanias, and in the end they proposed that the change should be made.

Aristides was careful to ascertain that the idea was not a hasty resolution, but well planned and considered; and when he was certain upon this point, he did not hesitate to take upon himself the position that every one wished him to hold. He was made the head of the confederacy, the object of which was to protect the Greeks in the islands, and on the coasts of the Ægean Sea, and to humble the barbarians. His judgment and moderation were now particularly valuable; for when it was necessary to settle how many ships and how much money each state was to contribute, he managed to arrange the business in such a way as to satisfy all parties; since no one for an instant suspected him of having any view to his own advantage, whatever he might propose. The total sum to be raised yearly was fixed at 115,000 pounds, and the island of Delos was chosen as the treasury.

Complaints of the conduct of Pausanias soon reached Sparta, and the ephors immediately sent another commander to take his place, and ordered him to return home. But it was too late for Sparta to regain the place she had lost, as the head of the Grecian confederacy. It was given to Athens; and the Spartans, not choosing to be second, withdrew their forces from the allies. Pausanias, on his return to Sparta, was obliged to undergo a very strict examination; but, though many charges were brought against him, none could exactly be proved. Still, he found himself in a very uncomfortable position. He was looked upon with suspicion, and was no longer a person of any consequence. This made him so restless and wretched, that he left Sparta without asking the consent of the ephors, as he ought to have done

M

according to the laws; and went again to Byzantium, where he renewed his treasonable plans with the Persians. Again, however, the Spartans heard what he was doing; and they sent for him a second time. Pausanias did not venture to disobey, because he was not quite sure of having help from the Persians if he did so. He therefore went back to Sparta, and was directly thrown into prison; probably as a punishment for having gone abroad without leave. He was soon, however, set free, as there was still not sufficient evidence of his being a traitor to his country to allow of his being publicly accused. He might have remained at peace, if he had not been foolish and wicked enough to try to excite an insurrection amongst the Helots; whilst he still kept up a correspondence with Persia. His plots were betrayed to the ephors, probably by some of the Helots themselves, who knew that they could not succeed, and must bring all concerned in them to ruin. But the ephors took no notice, until a circumstance occurred which gave them the means of obtaining the fullest evidence upon the subject.

As is usually the case, Pausanias had been led on from one crime to another, till he did not know where to stop. Knowing himself to be a traitor to his country, he was so afraid of being found out, that he had recourse to the most cruel means in order to conceal his guilt. Whenever he sent a letter to the Persian governor who managed all the secret business with him, he used the precaution of desiring that the bearer of his letter should be put to death. One of the messengers, having observed that those who had been sent from Pausanias before never returned, suspected that some order of this kind was given, and therefore opened the letter which was entrusted to his charge. His anger was roused to the utmost, when he found that his suspicions were true. Pausanias, who professed himself to be his friend, had in this letter given directions that he should be killed as soon as he had executed the commission he was charged with. The Spartan messenger lost no time in revealing all the secrets of Pausanias to the ephors; and, together, they formed a plan by which the ephors would have the opportunity of learning the guilt of Pausanias from his own mouth.

The Spartan messenger set out for the temple of Poseidon, on the borders of Laconia, which being a sacred place would, he knew, protect him from any danger. Here he waited for Pausanias, who, he was sure, would seek him, and enquire why he had neglected to execute his commands. Some of the ephors went to the same place, and hid themselves where they could hear all that passed. Pausanias came, and the messenger began to reproach him with the treachery which he had discovered; and instead of denying the truth of the complaint, Pausanias acknowledged it all, and only tried to pacify the Spartan by assuring him that if he would still carry his letters he should run no risk of losing his life. This, of course, was quite sufficient evidence for the ephors; and as soon as they went back to Sparta they took measures for arresting Pausanias.

As he was walking along one of the streets of the city, the ephors went up to him in a body, intending to take him; but one of them, who had a friendly feeling for him, gave him a sign to escape, and he fled for safety to a building which stood on some ground belonging to the temple of Athene. This place being considered sacred, no one dared to drag him from it; but, in order to prevent his escape, the ephors placed guards around the building, unroofed it, and blocked up the entrance. His aged

mother is said to have been among the first to lay a
stone at the doorway, for the purpose of immuring
him. A lingering death was all that Pausanias had
now to expect. The ephors waited till he was on
the point of expiring, and when he was too weak to
make any resistance — which would have profaned
the sacredness of the place — they caused him to be
taken out of the consecrated ground, to save it from
the pollution of his death. The unhappy Pausanias
breathed his last as soon as he had crossed the
bounds of the temple.

It was a sad end to his ambition; and as time
went on, people began to forget his treachery, and
to remember the services which he had first rendered
to his country. The Delphic oracle declared
that the temple of Athene had been profaned, and
ordered two persons to be given up to the goddess,
in the room of him who had sought refuge in her
temple, and had not found it. The Spartans, therefore,
caused two brazen statues of Pausanias to be
made for the sanctuary of Athene; but this was not
considered, by many persons, to be acting up to the
commands of the oracle, and their enemies still reproached
them that their land was not freed from
the guilt of sacrilege.

Pausanias was, certainly, a great general; but a
much more distinguished person than he suffered
for his faults. Some letters which the ephors discovered
when searching out the plot, gave them
reason to believe that Themistocles was acquainted
with the plans of Pausanias, and was inclined to
assist in them. They sent to Athens to accuse
him, and to insist that he, as well as Pausanias,
should be punished with death. Themistocles was
then living at Argos, in exile; for, notwithstanding
his past services, he had excited the ill-will of his
fellow citizens by his pride and covetousness; and,

like Aristides, he had been condemned to exile for a time, by the sentence of ostracism.

Proud, no doubt, Themistocles was. It is said that he took pleasure in reminding the Athenians of their vast obligations to him — asking them, on one occasion, where they would have been without him; and on another, comparing himself to a spreading tree, under which they had taken shelter in the storm of the Persian invasion — and it is certain, also, that he did not scruple to enrich himself by every possible means, and contrived to become very wealthy when he had the care of the public money; yet, with all these great faults, there seems no reason to believe that he ever was so rash or so wicked as to join in the plans of Pausanias. It appears that Pausanias told him of them, but this was all. Themistocles must have considered them the schemes of a madman; and he might not think it necessary or right to betray them. The mere fact, however, of his being acquainted with them, was a sufficient reason for many persons to deem him guilty. He was not a favourite with the people as he had once been; and as, before, they had forgotten all his services and exiled him, so now they were willing to have him put to death upon an unproved accusation.

Themistocles knew how greatly the general feeling was against him, and as he did not choose to trust himself to be tried at Athens, he fled from Argos, where he was living, and took shelter at Corcyra. From thence he crossed over to Epirus.

The Molossians, the most powerful people of Epirus, were then ruled by a king named Admetus, who was said to be descended from the Greeks, and who was certainly more civilised than his barbarian subjects. Themistocles had once opposed Admetus in a favour which he asked of the Athenians, and he had no reason, now, to expect kindness from him. But he was in great danger, and had no time for consideration; and as he intended to pass over into Asia, and his way led through the dominions of the Molossian king, it seemed best to trust to his generosity.

When Themistocles arrived at the palace of Admetus, the king was absent; and he therefore made himself known to the queen, and implored her compassion. The wife of Admetus had no revengeful feelings against her husband's enemy, now that he was in distress. Instead of bidding him find a refuge elsewhere, she gave him her infant child, and told him to seat himself by the hearth, holding the child in his arms, till the king should arrive. This was the most solemn mode of supplication among the Molossians, and it touched the heart of Admetus. When he returned home, and saw his once powerful enemy so humbled, he forgot every cause of anger, received him as his guest, and though the Athenians and Lacedæmonians sent to demand him, refused to give him up.

It was not safe, however, for Themistocles to remain in Epirus; for Admetus was not sufficiently powerful to guard him, and he determined, as soon as possible, to go to Asia, and place himself under the protection of Xerxes. Admetus gave him every assistance for his journey, and after many risks Themistocles arrived safely at Ephesus, where his family met him, and where he also received some of his property, which his friends had been able to secure for him.

A few months after Themistocles reached Asia, Xerxes was murdered, and his son Artaxerxes succeeded him. Themistocles, having a powerful friend to protect him, ventured to proceed to the court of the young prince. But before presenting himself in person, he wrote a letter to Artaxerxes, owning that he had done injury to Persia in the defence of his country, but adding, as a fact in his favour, that it was he who had given Xerxes warning of the intention of the Greeks to cut away the bridge of boats across the Hellespont; and who, indeed, had prevented them from attempting it. His present misfortunes, he said, were owing to his zeal for the king of Persia's interests; and he assured Artaxerxes that he was willing to show his attachment yet more, if he might only be allowed a year to enable him to learn the Persian language, and so to discover his plans to the king himself.

Artaxerxes granted his request without hesitation; and Themistocles immediately began to study the language and manners of the country; and became so great a favourite with the king, that the courtiers all envied him. After a while, he was sent to live near the sea-coast, and a pension was given him for his support; not in money, however, as would be the case with us, but according to the Eastern custom. Three large cities were obliged to provide for his maintenance. Magnesia, in the south-west of Lydia, provided him and his family and followers with bread; Lampsacus, in Mysia, with wine; and Myus, in Caria, with meat and other provisions. It was at Magnesia that he lived, almost like a prince, with every kind of splendour and luxury; and it was there he died,—some suppose from poison, which he took himself, others from vexation. But almost all agree that his death was hastened by the knowledge that he had made promises to the king of Persia which he was quite unable to perform. His feelings seem to the last to have clung to his country, for he desired that his bones might be privately conveyed to Attica; and a tomb within the port of Piræus is said to have contained them: though a splendid monument was raised to him in Magnesia.

There is a pleasure in turning from the fate of the selfish and ambitious Themistocles, — living in luxury, but dying wretchedly in a foreign land, under the protection of his country's enemy, — to that of Aristides the Just, who died the year after Themistocles was banished. There are very few amongst the distinguished men of those ancient days, whom we can think of with so much pleasure.

The chief work of Aristides was that of uniting the Greeks together for their common defence; but he is also said to have introduced great changes in the government of Athens, by which all persons in the state, however low their birth might be, were allowed to hold the highest offices, if they were fitted for them. Aristides was universally respected during his lifetime, and was more honoured by his poverty when he died, than he could have been by wealth. The great offices which he had held had been no source of riches to him, for he spent everything for others, and laid by nothing for himself; and though, as has already been said, he left behind him scarcely sufficient to pay the expenses of his funeral; yet his monument was built at the public charge, his children were provided for by the public money, and his name has been handed down through hundreds of years, as an honour to his country, and an example to mankind.

CHAP. XVI.

CIMON BANISHED FROM ATHENS.

B.C. 461.

CIMON, the son of Miltiades, is the next person whom we hear of as greatly distinguishing himself in the events connected with the history of Greece. As a boy Cimon did not appear very clever; and, indeed, we are told, that he was not even as accomplished as the Athenian gentlemen usually were. But he quite made up for any deficiencies when he grew up to be a man, though he had not the gift of eloquence, and therefore, could not gain favour with the people by fair words, as some of his rivals did.

When his father Miltiades died, Cimon was left with a very small fortune, and had great difficulty in paying the sum of money which, it may be remembered, was required of Miltiades for an offence against the state. The money was paid at last, by the help of a rich Athenian, who agreed to discharge the penalty, if Cimon's sister, a very beautiful, but a very wicked woman, would consent to be his wife.

The first time that Cimon attracted particular notice, was on the occasion of the Athenians leaving their city on the approach of Xerxes, when he was the foremost to hang up a bridle in the Acropolis, as a sign that from thenceforth, they must not hope to find safety by land. He also fought bravely at Salamis; and Aristides, perceiving that he was a person of talent and honour, agreed that he should be joined with himself afterwards in the command of the Athenian fleet. So Cimon advanced more and more in the public favour, and when the power of Themistocles was declining, persons looked to him as the leader who was most likely to advance the glory of the state. He kept up this general good opinion by a series of successful enterprises against the Persians in Asia Minor; and also by subduing a race of pirates who inhabited the isle of Scyros. Besides which, he contrived to gain great power for his native city, by obliging several small states and islands which did not choose that Athens should be the head of the Greek confederacy, and be considered superior to them, to submit as if they were subjects. The assistance which these little states had formerly given by sending ships and men to aid Athens in her wars, was now exchanged for a fixed sum of money; and by this means the small states became unwarlike, and so were not able in the least to resist the increasing power of Athens, whilst the money was of the greatest use in enabling the Athenians to fit out their vessels, and keep up their navy, upon which they so much depended.

All this was going on whilst Pausanias was carrying on his schemes at Sparta, and Themistocles was living in exile at Argos; and about the time that Themistocles was obliged to flee for his life, Cimon sailed over to the coast of Asia, and gained so great a victory over the Persian fleet, which was stationed at the mouth of the Eurymedon, a small river of Pamphylia, in Asia Minor, that it may be considered as the complete termination of the war between Persia and Greece. Soon after, Xerxes died; and then, there was such confusion at the court of Persia, that the Greeks were left to themselves. But whilst Cimon was thus gaining such renown abroad, he had a rival at home, who was trying to supplant him in the favour of the people; and whose notions of government were so entirely different from his, that it was clear the time must come, sooner or later, when serious disputes would arise between them.

This rival was Pericles, the son of the same person who had brought forward the accusation which caused the ruin of Miltiades. The enmity seems thus almost to have descended from father to son on both sides.

Pericles was a man of high birth, for he was one of the Alcmæonids. From his early youth he had been admitted into the best society, and had entered with the greatest delight into all kinds of deep studies and researches. Unlike Cimon, he was extremely eloquent; and thus, whilst Cimon sought for honour in his wars abroad, Pericles gained the favour of the people at home by his splendid speech, and his care for their general interests.

His appearance, too, was very much in his favour. He was an extremely majestic, graceful person; though some of the comic writers of the day, used to laugh at him for the extraordinary length of his head. The old men of Athens declared he was very like Pisistratus, and had just the same sweet voice and quick manner of speaking.

Cimon belonged to what may be called the aristocratic party, or the party of the nobles; and Pericles to the democratic, or the party of the people. Cimon thought it best that the state should be ruled by a few persons of rank and wealth; Pericles was willing that every one who had sufficient talent should have a share in the government. This, we may recollect, was the idea that Aristides seems to have had, when he proposed that persons of the lowest rank might be made archons if they were fit for the office. With regard to foreign affairs also, Cimon and Pericles had different opinions. It was the wish of Cimon and his friends, to keep all the states of Greece about equal in power and importance; and, for this reason, they carried on the war with Persia vigorously; thinking, that whilst the Greeks had a foreign enemy to fight against, they would not have time to quarrel amongst themselves as to which should be the greatest. Pericles, on the contrary, had a great desire to make Athens the head of Greece, and did everything he possibly could to render her more powerful than the other states.

The difference in these two men was to be seen

in everything they did. Cimon, though a poor man originally, had become rich by the spoils taken from the Persians, and also by having recovered some of the property which his father had lost in the Chersonesus. Being naturally very liberal, he made a generous use of his wealth, for he assisted in building walls round the citadel, and from the town to the harbours of Phalerum and Piræus. The latter were called the Long Walls. They were quite the pride of the Athenians, from their strength and usefulness. Cimon also planted trees in the city; and, by the means of water-works, changed a barren waste, about two miles to the north of Athens, into a beautiful grove. This grove was called the Academy; and there the philosophers and grave persons of the state used to walk up and down, and meditate, and the young ones to amuse themselves with games and exercises.

But besides these expenses for the public good, Cimon indulged in others, which were not by any means so useful. Though his principles led him to side with the party of the nobles, yet, in order to gain favour with the common people, he threw down the fences round his fields and orchards, and allowed all who chose to go in and eat as much as they pleased; and he also feasted the people continually. When he went into the streets, he was generally attended by a number of well-dressed persons, who, if they met an elderly citizen, scantily clothed, would insist upon taking off their own warm garments, and exchanging them for the threadbare mantle of the poor man. Others of his followers were ordered silently and respectfully to offer money to any poor citizen of good character, whom they might see in the market place. If all this had been done from really kind motives, there would have been great cause to admire the goodness of Cimon's disposition;

but although he was undoubtedly a generous and amiable person, it seems too probable that his intention in these extraordinary attentions to the poor, was only to gain their favour for himself and his friends.

Pericles, it appears, had suspicions of this kind; for all his endeavours, when he had power in the state, were used to undo the effects of Cimon's profuse extravagance to the lower orders. He, also, was thoughtful about the poor; but instead of making them dependent upon himself, he tried to introduce laws by which they might be provided for at the public expense.

His own fortune was not as large as Cimon's, and he was very economical and careful; knowing that extravagance constantly leads people to dishonesty. His habits of life were retired. He declined all entertainments, and was only once known to break through his rule, — in order to honour the wedding of a relation. His friends were very select, and his time was entirely given up to public business. Indeed, he never was to be seen out of doors, but on the way from his own house to the place of council. He was particularly attentive to prepare his speech beforehand, when he knew that he should be called upon to make one; and he used to say himself, that he never began one without praying that no inappropriate word might drop from his lips. This quietness and dignity of character and manners gave great effect to all he said; and as he did not think it desirable to show himself very often to the people, his appearance, when he did come forward on any occasion, was thought a great deal of. He never allowed himself to be ruffled by anything which was said, and never forgot to be courteous to all persons. There is a story told of him, that one day as he was transacting business in public, a man began to abuse him, and, after railing at him a long time, followed him home in the dusk, still using the same rude language. Pericles did not stop him till he reached his own door, and then, without making any complaint, calmly ordered one of his servants to take a light and conduct the man home.

It seems strange that so grave and dignified a person should have exerted himself to diminish the power of the ancient judges of Athens; yet this was really the case, and one of the greatest changes which Pericles tried to bring about was with regard to the power of the court of Areopagus. His object in this must have been, according to his principles, to give greater authority to the people in general than to the few who were Areopagites. The measures which he proposed in order to diminish the authority of this court were just about to be discussed, when, a few years after the last defeat of the Persians by Cimon, an embassy was sent from Sparta to request the assistance of the Athenians, in a war which they were carrying on against the Helots and Messenians. These people had long before been conquered by the Spartans, but had now seized the opportunity of a tremendous earthquake, which destroyed the whole city of Sparta, with the exception of five houses, to rise in rebellion, and fortify themselves in the ancient stronghold of Ithome.

Cimon was at this time in Athens, and had only just escaped a great danger. After the battle of Eurymedon, he carried on a war with the people of the island of Thasos, who had taken possession of some gold mines in Thrace, which the Athenians said belonged to them; and then he received instructions to make an expedition against some tribes on the borders of Macedonia, who had done great injury to the Athenian colonists settled in their neighbourhood. These instructions, however, Cimon did not obey; and when he came back to Athens, a public accusation was brought against him, and some people said he had been bribed by the Macedonians. Pericles was appointed to be one of the public accusers; but before the day of trial, Cimon's beautiful sister came to his house, and begged so earnestly that he would not do an injury to her brother, that Pericles was induced to consent. Instead of making an oration against Cimon, he merely said the few words which were required, for form's sake, and Cimon was pronounced "Not guilty." But the accusation was a very serious one, and might have cost him his life.

On the occasion of the embassy from Sparta, the two parties of Cimon and Pericles took opposite sides. Cimon was a great admirer of the Spartan laws, and liked the character of the people, and had named one of his own sons, Lacedæmonius, as a proof of this partiality. When it was now proposed that the Spartans should not be assisted, because it was not wise to raise up a fallen enemy, Cimon's reply was, "Let us not permit Greece to be lamed, nor Athens to lose her yoke-fellow."

His counsel was followed, and he was sent with a large force to assist the Spartans at the siege of Ithome. The Spartans had hoped that the Athenians, who were particularly skilful in sieges, would very soon take the place; but a long time passed, and Ithome was still unconquered. They then began to suspect that the Athenians were not really trying to help them, and dismissed their troops without giving any sufficient reason for such conduct. The Athenians were extremely angry, and determined at once to break off all friendship with

the Spartans, and to enter into an alliance with the
state of Argos, which, from the earliest times, had
been at constant variance with Sparta; so much so,
indeed, that the jealousy between the two states was
the cause of the Argives refusing to assist in the
defence of Greece during the Persian war.

The party of Pericles were very pleased at this
turn of affairs. They were able, now, to find fault
with Cimon for having insisted upon the expedition
against Ithome; and, as he and his friends seemed
to be quite out of favour, it appeared a good opportunity to carry on the scheme for diminishing the
power of the court of Areopagus, which Cimon upheld. It is not known what were the exact changes
that Pericles and his friends wished to make in
this court. Some persons say that they desired to
prevent trials for murder being brought before it;
and others, that they disliked the power which its
members had of making decrees about the education
and conduct of the citizens; but, however this might
be, it is certain that Cimon opposed their wishes,
and was supported in his own views by Æschylus,
a great poet, and one of the most celebrated persons
of either ancient or modern times. Æschylus was
a warrior, as well as an author. He had fought
nobly, both at Marathon and Salamis; but he is
most distinguished for his tragedies, which not only
contain most beautiful poetry, but are also full of
the noblest sentiments that it seems possible for a
heathen to have had. The tragedies of Æschylus
were particularly interesting to the Greeks, because
they were generally composed from subjects connected with their religion or their history. After
the battle of Salamis, he wrote one upon the flight
of Xerxes; and now, when it was proposed to alter
the court of Areopagus, he brought forward another called "The Eumenides," or "The Furies," in

which he declared that Athene and the Furies were the peculiar guardians of the court of Areopagus, and that it would be profane to make alterations in it.

But, although the tragedy of "The Eumenides" is one of the finest that was ever written, it did not answer the purpose for which it was composed. Pericles and his friends gained their point, and a law was passed which took away a great deal of the power of the Areopagus, and, almost directly afterwards, Cimon was exiled by the sentence of ostracism. This was done, probably, not so much because the people were angry with them, but because the most sober judging persons in the city thought that if he was absent for some time, there would be less likelihood of disturbances, and complaints of the changes which had been made.

Cimon remained between five and six years in exile. During this time the Athenians were carrying on wars both at home and abroad; but they were not so successful as they had been when he was their commander. After their quarrel with the Spartans, for sending back their troops from Ithome, it naturally happened that any small state which also took offence at Sparta looked to Athens for assistance; and in this way the Athenians were mixed up with endless disputes.

The people of Megara, being at enmity with the Corinthians, and thinking that the Spartans, who professed to be their friends, did not help them as they ought, sought to ally themselves to the Athenians instead; and Athens was then obliged to be at war with Corinth. About the same time she was called upon to assist an African prince, subject to the king of Persia, who had excited an insurrection amongst his people in order to throw off the Persian yoke. It was quite natural for the Athenians to oppose the Persians, wherever they might be; and their fleet, which was then lying off Cyprus, was immediately sent to Africa.

It is wonderful that so small a state should have been able to carry on several wars at the same time; and the Athenians themselves seem to have been aware that their power was very surprising; for there is an inscription still preserved in the Louvre, at Paris, which records that in the same year, B.C. 457, their slain fell in Cyprus, in Egypt, in Phœnicia, at Haliæ, in Ægina, and in Megara. Those who fell at Haliæ, Ægina, and Megara, were engaged in the Corinthian war; and those in Cyprus, Egypt, and Phœnicia, in the African war. Haliæ was a town in Argolis.

The enmity of Sparta and Athens led at last to the defeat of the Athenians, in a battle in which Pericles himself was engaged. The Phocians had invaded Doris, which was the parent state of Sparta, — for Peloponnesus, we may remember, was chiefly peopled by Dorian tribes. The Spartans went to the aid of the Dorians, and compelled the Phocians to give up the towns they had taken. As they were returning home, the Athenians stopped them, and a battle took place at Tanagra, in Bœotia, on the borders of Attica. Cimon, who was living in the neighbourhood, came to the Athenian camp, and requested leave to join in the battle; but the Athenian generals refused, and Cimon was obliged to retire, leaving his armour with his friends, and exhorting them to refute by their deeds the accusation which had sometimes been brought against them, of preferring Sparta to their own country. The armour was placed in the ranks, and Cimon's friends fought round it desperately, till they fell, each one at his own post. Pericles also distinguished himself by extraordinary bravery; but, in spite of all these efforts, the battle was lost, owing to the treachery of some Thessalians, who professed themselves the allies of Athens, but went over to the Spartans after the battle had begun.

War continued in this way for about two years longer, and then Cimon was recalled from exile. Pericles himself proposed his return, and the Athenians were very willing to consent. Their troops which had been sent to Egypt, met, about this time, with a great defeat, and they had also been unsuccessful on several occasions at home. It was not difficult for Cimon's friends to contrast these misfortunes with the great victories which Cimon had so-often gained over the Persians; and to convince the people that it would be wise to recall him, and to make peace with Sparta. Pericles was probably anxious that he should be at Athens again, in order to restrain the bad conduct of his own party, who began to be so turbulent that it was difficult to keep them in order. Cimon, therefore, was restored, and his return was followed by a peace of several years between the two great Grecian states.

Cimon's rest at Athens did not continue long. His last expedition, like that which had first rendered him famous, was directed against the power of Persia. He took the command of a fleet which was sent to Egypt to assist in the war that was still going on there, and in that undertaking met with his death.

He died of an illness caused, it has been sometimes said, by a wound which he received whilst besieging a town in Cyprus.

CHAP. XVII.

THE BUILDING OF THE PARTHENON, THE PROPYLÆA, ETC.

B.C. 438.

THE truce which had been concluded with Sparta, soon after Cimon's return from exile, continued for a few years after his death; and then, after a slight renewal of the old quarrel, it was proposed to be settled for thirty years more. The terms agreed upon, when the arrangement was made, were not very much to the advantage of the Athenians; but it was extremely desirable for them to have a time of rest; and peace made them in reality much more prosperous than even their successful wars.

Though the Athenians professed the utmost love of freedom themselves, yet they took care that the small states which were in alliance with them should have very little of it. Cimon had done a great deal towards making these states subjects instead of allies, by causing them to pay tribute, and rendering them unwarlike; but when Cimon was dead, and Pericles had no one to oppose his wishes, he carried out these beginnings a great deal further; and the small states were kept under such subjection, that they were not even allowed to settle their law cases for themselves, but were obliged to go to Athens, to have them decided, unless they were of a very trifling nature.

This hard usage was very nearly the cause of the breaking up of the thirty years truce, — for some of the inhabitants of the island of Samos tried on one occasion to throw off the Athenian yoke, and the question was publicly discussed amongst the other Grecian states whether they might not assist them. It was, however, determined in the end, that the Samians were to be considered as rebels, and they were left to the vengeance of Athens. Pericles undertook the command of the fleet which was sent out against them, and subdued them, though not without difficulty.

Both sides behaved disgracefully to the prisoners who were taken. The Athenians branded theirs with the figure of a peculiar kind of Samian merchant ship; and the Samians marked theirs with the figure of an owl, the favourite bird of Athene, the goddess of Athens. Pericles was received with great honour by his fellow citizens when he returned home; and the women showered upon him chaplets and wreaths as he was pronouncing the funeral speech over the dead who had fallen; but Cimon's beautiful sister refused to join in the public applause, for she remembered her brother's victories over the Persians, and thought it nobler to triumph over the barbarians than to conquer a Grecian city.

Besides thus keeping the allies in subjection, the power of Athens was now much increased by the colonies which Pericles caused to be planted in several of the neighbouring countries. The colonists were still considered Athenian citizens, so that they took the greatest interest in the parent state, and did all they could to make it prosperous.

And with all this care for the public honour, and the government of the country, Pericles gave a great deal of his time and attention to the improvement of the city, and the encouragement of learning and the arts. The temples, which had been destroyed by the Persians, were now rebuilt in the most splendid manner. The summit of the Acropolis was covered with sacred buildings, statues, and monuments; and the Parthenon, a temple of Athene, was built with such exquisite taste, that even its ruins cause delight and admiration to all who see them. It was of marble, and supported by rows of magnificent columns, and the ornaments of leaves and flowers were painted in the most brilliant colours. This was also the case with the sculptures on the top, which must have looked like splendid pictures set in marble frames. Within was the colossal statue of the goddess, composed of ivory and gold, and the work of Phidias, the most celebrated sculptor of antiquity. The entrance to the Acropolis was through a building called the Propylæa, which was also supported by columns, and richly painted. There was a portico to the Propylæa, wide enough to admit of a road passing through it. On the occasion of the great festivals, long processions used to go under this portico, and through a corridor or passage, leading from it, with columns on each side, till they came in front of five great bronze doors, which, being thrown open, discovered all the beautiful buildings, the statues, and columns, and brilliant colours of the interior of the Acropolis. The Parthenon was the largest and finest temple of Athene within the Acropolis; but there was another more venerated, because it contained a statue of Athene, made of olive wood, which the Greeks believed to have originally fallen from heaven. The throne of Xerxes and the sword of Mardonius were placed in this latter temple, which is sometimes called the Erectheum,—from Erectheus, one of the earliest Athenian kings, whose tomb was within it.*

There was a porch to the Erectheum, which, instead of being supported by pillars, was upheld by the figures of six women, dressed according to the fashion of the virgins, who took part in one of the great processions which have before been mentioned. These figures were called Caryatides. One

* The Erectheum existed in very early days, but was rebuilt about the time of Pericles.

of them was brought to England some years ago, and the modern Athenians being dreadfully grieved at its loss, declared, — and many of them believe at this day, — that the other five figures moaned and lamented with tears and sobbings all night long for the departure of their sister, and were only comforted when the sun rose in the morning, and dried the tears upon their stony faces.*

There is a large church in London, St. Pancras', part of which is supported by figures, resembling the Caryatides. The architect seems to have forgotten how very unfitting such heathen images must always be for a Christian church.

The most interesting part of ancient Athens now remaining is the Acropolis, full as it is of the remains of the great works, ordered by Pericles and executed by Phidias; and we might well wonder how persons of so much taste, and such wisdom as regarded the things of this world, could have been so senseless and superstitious in their religion, if we did not see daily, ourselves, that even in Christian countries, the cleverest men are often the most ignorant and careless as regards the knowledge of heaven.

The erection of so many beautiful buildings employed a great number of persons, and thus became of general use; and the Athenians were extremely proud of them, and never grudged the money that was spent upon them. On one occasion the question was discussed, publicly, whether marble or ivory should be employed for the statue of Athene, which was to be placed in the Parthenon. Phidias recommended marble, because it was the cheaper material; but when the assembly heard this, they immediately decided that it should be ivory. Athens

* See "Picturesque Sketches in Greece and Turkey," by Aubrey De Vere.

seems also to have made a sudden advance in learning and poetry, about this time, as well as in works of art. Before, she could boast of no poets or artists at all equal to those of some of the other states; but now, besides Phidias, the sculptor, and Æschylus, there were several other Athenians whose names and writings have come down to the present day. Sophocles is one of them. He was younger than Æschylus, but became his rival as a poet and a writer of tragedies; and on the first occasion when there was a trial of their talents, in the public theatre, he was considered to surpass him. This was a great vexation to Æschylus, who was so annoyed that he left Greece, and went to Sicily. Sophocles was afterwards honoured in a way which seems strange to us. He was made a general, and accompanied Pericles in the expedition before mentioned against the island of Samos. In the end, however, Sophocles had to bear the same disappointment as Æschylus, for before his death a new poet had sprung up, Euripides, whom the Athenians preferred to himself.

Æschylus is said to have written seventy tragedies, but only seven have been preserved. They are all of a solemn character, and relating chiefly to the gods. The tragedies of Sophocles and Euripides are of a lighter kind, and more concern the actions of human beings.

The labours of Pericles for what he considered the public benefit, though they were very great, did not prevent him from gaining ill-will. He had provided work for those who were in want of it, caused the building of splendid temples, encouraged painting and sculpture, and afforded to the poor the means of frequenting public amusements, of which the Athenians were extremely fond; and yet there were persons to find fault with him and be jealous

of him. They could not, indeed, discover much to
say against his public government, but they tried to
raise a suspicion against him, by bringing accusations against his friend, Phidias the sculptor. They
declared that Phidias had taken possession, for
himself, of some of the gold which had been given
for the statue of Athene in the Parthenon. If this
charge had been proved, every one would have supposed it probable that Pericles, who knew all which
Phidias did in his public works, had some share in
the fraud. The accusation, however, was shown to
be entirely false, and the enemies of Pericles then
made another attempt against his friend, by asserting that Phidias, in painting the shield of Athene,
had introduced amongst the figures his own portrait
and that of Pericles. This was considered a profane act; and though the charge was not properly
proved, Phidias was thrown into prison and died
there.

After the success of this attempt, the persons
who so hated Pericles were induced to try a new
charge, which they knew would be more distressing
to him than any other. There was a foreign lady
living in Athens, extremely clever and fascinating,
to whom Pericles was exceedingly attached. This
lady, whose name was Aspasia, was accustomed to receive at her house a number of the most learned and
clever men of the age, with whom she discussed very
deep and difficult subjects; and the meetings were
attended also by many of the Athenian ladies.
Aspasia was a foreigner, and therefore did not care
about the manners of the Athenians; but as it was
not usually the custom for ladies to attend meetings
of this kind, many persons thought it very wrong in
them to go; and by degrees it was reported that the
subjects which were talked of were irreligious and
wrong. At last a public accusation was brought

against Aspasia, for encouraging such bad practices, and at the same time Pericles was called upon to account for the money which he had spent on the public works, as it was said that he had taken some for his own use.

This was the most trying situation in which Pericles had ever been placed, but he was far more distressed for Aspasia than for himself. He pleaded her cause even with tears and entreaties, and in the end he was successful. The charge against her was dropped, and so also were the accusations against himself, and after this time he became more powerful than ever. Anaxagoras, a celebrated philosopher, and a friend of Pericles and Aspasia, was accused with them of teaching wrong doctrines about religion, and was severely punished; but it is uncertain whether he was condemned to death, and managed to escape from prison; or whether he was only banished.

CHAP. XVIII.

THE BEGINNING OF THE PELOPONNESIAN WAR.

B.C. 431.

THE thirty years truce between Athens and Sparta was broken after it had lasted fifteen years. Many things happened beforehand which showed that war was at hand, in the same way as the constant bickerings of two persons who dislike each other, give reason to believe that they will soon have a decided quarrel. There were two events which served especially to increase the enmity of the great rival states. The first was a dispute between Athens and Corinth. The Corinthians were engaged in a war with the people of Corcyra, respecting a

colony from that island, which had been founded on
the coast of Illyria. Some of these colonists in
Illyria had, from various causes, separated from
Corcyra, and put themselves under the protection
of Corinth. The Corcyræans would not allow the
persons, who were in a manner their subjects, to
seek protection from any but themselves; and when
they found that the Corinthians took part with
the colonists of Illyria, they declared war against
Corinth, and sent to Athens to beg for her assistance. The Athenians would not agree to give the
Corcyræans help openly; but only said that they
would make an alliance with them, and defend
them if their territories were attacked. This show
of keeping aloof did not last very long. Ten vessels
were sent by the Athenians to Corcyra, with orders
not to join in any battle unless the territory of
Corcyra should be attacked; but in the first sea-
fight, the Corcyræans were nearly defeated, and
then the Athenians, whose ships were stationed
near, were tempted to assist them, and so became
openly engaged in the war.

About this same time a war was going on in
Macedonia, between Perdiccas, the king of that
country, and Philip his brother. The Athenians
took the part of Philip, and Perdiccas did all he
could to gain the support of some of the other
Grecian states, particularly Corinth and Sparta.
He also tried to make several towns in Macedonia,
which were subject to Athens, revolt. We must
remember that Athens had many subject towns in
different countries: and though now, in Europe,
which is so thickly peopled, and where all the
kingdoms and governments are fixed, we cannot so
well understand how this should be; yet, in India,
the same thing has been done in later days; and
the Portuguese have had towns in one place, and

the Dutch in another, whilst the English have been masters of the greater part of the country.

The town of Potidæa, in the south of Macedonia, was one of those which Perdiccas tried to make revolt. It was originally a colony from Corinth, and was still governed by Corinthian magistrates, though it had been forced to become tributary to Athens. Now that Athens and Corinth were at war, and that Perdiccas, king of Macedon, was trying to gain the support of the Corinthians, the Athenians did not choose that a town which was tributary to them, should have anything to do with their enemies. So they ordered the Potidæans to send away their Corinthian magistrates, and to pull down their fortifications. The order was not complied with, for the Potidæans knew that, if they were attacked, not only the Corinthians, but the Spartans also, would come to their assistance. They rebelled; and several other towns near, which were likewise tributary to Athens, were persuaded by Perdiccas to do the same.

The Athenians immediately besieged Potidæa; and, notwithstanding the efforts of the Corinthians, and of King Perdiccas, who joined to defend it, there seemed every probability that the town would be taken. The Corinthians were now extremely angry, and anxious above all things to engage the Spartans in their quarrel; and as they knew that many of the other states had the same dislike to the power of Athens which they had themselves, they invited deputies from all quarters to meet at Sparta, and make their complaints; the Spartans being very willing to hear them. The question of peace or war with Athens was then to be discussed.

The meeting was accordingly held; all who had wrongs to complain of stated them; and when every one else had spoken, the Corinthian deputy came forward to urge the Spartans to decide against Athens, and to join in the war.

"Sparta," he said, "had trusted too much to the good faith of Athens, and suffered her to act tyrannically without interfering. If this went on, the ambition and insolence of Athens would know no bounds." "You seem," he added, "never to have reflected how wide a difference there is between you and the people with whom you have to contend. They are ever forming new projects; you are content to keep what you have, without aiming at more. They are prompt and eager for foreign expeditions: you are loth to stir from home. Whatever they may gain they account little in comparison with what remains to be won. They make a pastime of business, and prefer laborious occupation to indolent repose." And having thus described the character of the Athenians, the Corinthian deputy ended his speech, by hinting, that if the Spartans did not comply with the demand now made, the Corinthians would be obliged to seek a new alliance by which was meant an alliance with Argos, a state always at enmity with Sparta.

It happened that there were present in the assembly, some Athenian envoys who had been sent to Sparta on business, not regarding the war. They had obtained leave to attend the meeting; and after the speech of the Corinthian deputy, one of them addressed the assembly, and in a long harangue endeavoured to set forth the moderation of the Athenians, and their gentle government, which he asserted was much greater than that of Sparta. "All that they had done," he said, "was only from necessity; and if the Spartans were determined upon war, they would do well to remember, that it was very uncertain, and that it might be much better to settle their differences quietly."

When the strangers had been heard, they were
desired to withdraw, and the Spartans were left to
discuss the question amongst themselves.

Archidamus, the elder of the two kings, was one
of those most inclined for peace, or at least for
delay. "They were not then in a condition," he
said, "to bear a war. They had no navy. It would
be better to wait two or three years, and endeavour
in the meantime to arrange their disputes by ne-
gotiations. If these failed, they would have time to
prepare for war by making alliances with other
nations, who might be able to furnish them with
the aid they most wanted—money and ships."

But this advice did not suit the wishes of the
assembly. The presiding ephor rose up, and spoke
very differently. "He could not understand," he
said, "what the long speeches of the Athenians
meant. They had said much in praise of themselves, but not a word to prove that they had not
injured Sparta and her allies; and the better their
conduct had been in past times, the more they
deserved to suffer for having acted differently now.
Other states were strong in ships, and horses, and
gold; but Sparta was strong in her allies, and she
ought not to desert them."

"Let us not listen," be concluded, "to those who
recommend deliberation, which becomes persons who
are about to commit an injury, rather than those
who have received one; but vote, as befits the dignity of Sparta, for war."

He then put the question to the vote. The
greater number were for war; and war was decided
on; not however immediately. The Delphic oracle
was to be consulted, and another general meeting
of the allies was to be held, and preparations were
to be made, both at Sparta and in the other Peloponnesian states, and so a whole year passed away,

before the army was actually ready to invade Attica.

Even then the Spartans were anxious to find some more decided reason for going to war than had yet been brought forward; and envoys were sent to Athens to make demands which it was well known could not possibly be complied with. The charge against the family of the Alcmæonids was revived again. The goddess Athene, it was said, still demanded vengeance against them, and it was necessary they should be banished for the insult which had been offered her so many years before, when Megacles, the archon, killed the prisoners who had placed themselves under the protection of the goddess. This demand was made expressly for the purpose of obtaining the banishment of Pericles, whose mother was an Alcmæonid.

The Athenians, however, were able to retort the same kind of charge upon the Spartans; and on their side they demanded that amends should be made for the murder of Pausanias, who was killed whilst taking refuge in a temple of Athene at Sparta.

Both parties, in fact, were trying to bring forward old complaints, in order to have an excuse for war. The Spartans indeed protested that they wished for peace, but they insisted so strongly upon the Athenians giving up the siege of Potidæa, and granting greater freedom to their allies, that it was evident they would never be brought to agree: for the Athenians, at that time, were full of pride and self-confidence, and did not choose to yield in the smallest degree; still less, to confess that they had ever been in the wrong.

Pericles, especially, was urgent for war. When the last assembly was held at Athens for the purpose of giving a final answer to Sparta, he entreated his fellow citizens not to yield. "Athens," he said, "had nothing to fear from Sparta and her allies, either by sea or land. Their navy could not rival hers; and though they might invade Attica, and even occupy a fortress there, yet the Athenians could retaliate by ravaging their coasts. When Sparta would make her allies independent, then Athens would do the same with hers." "Yet," he declared to the Spartan envoys, "Athens was still willing to have all differences decided by an impartial judge, and would not begin the war, but only keep herself in readiness to repel an attack."

With this answer the ambassadors returned to Sparta.

Still there was a pause, and war had not openly been declared; but early in the following spring, B.C. 431, in the fifteenth year of the thirty years truce, an event took place which increased the anger of all parties, and hastened the evil that had so long been threatened.

The city of Platæa was at that time in alliance with Athens. The alliance was disliked by a few of the inhabitants, and they secretly invited the Thebans to come and take possession of the city. The Thebans, feeling that a general war was near at hand, were very well inclined to strengthen themselves, and in the dead of the night a body of three hundred men marched to Platæa; and, the gates being left unguarded, were admitted into the town by one of their friends. They proceeded to the market-place and made a proclamation, inviting all persons who were anxious that Platæa should be one of the cities in alliance with Thebes, to join them. The Platæans, at first, believing the Thebans to be numerous, entered into a parley with them; but, when they discovered what a small body they really were, they began to think it possible to overcome them.

During the night, they formed their plans, and a little before daybreak they fell upon the unfortunate Thebans, and fought with them in the streets, whilst the women and slaves showered stones and tiles upon them from the tops of the houses. The Thebans fled, but they could not find their way in the dark, through a strange town. Some mounted the walls, and threw themselves down on the outside; and a few contrived to reach one of the gates, in a lone quarter, and made a woman give them an axe to beat the gate to pieces, and so escaped.

The largest body which kept together entered a great building, fancying its gates were those of the city, and were shut in. The Platæans thought of setting fire to the building, but they gave up the idea, and the Thebans surrendered, and were all afterwards killed. This circumstance of the murder of the prisoners we shall find afterwards brought great trouble upon the Platæans; for it was contrary to a promise made to a body of Thebans, who came in the morning, thinking to support their countrymen in their attempt, and who were induced to retire upon being told that, if they did, all their friends who were taken prisoners should be saved.

Naturally enough the Athenians considered this attack upon Platæa to be an insult to themselves. They determined to revenge the Platæans; and the Spartans offered to assist the Thebans; and then at last the great Peloponnesian war broke out.

As this war is one of the most important in Grecian history, and concerned the whole nation, it may be as well fully to understand what was the condition of the two states with regard to their allies.

On the side of Sparta were all the Peloponnesian

states, except Argos, which remained neutral. Beyond the Isthmus their allies were Megara, Phocis, Locris, and Bœotia. The Ætolians also were friendly to them, and they were supported by three Corinthian colonies in Acarnania; and as they wished still further to strengthen themselves, they sent ambassadors to Persia to beg for the help of the Persian king; and entreated for ships and money from the Greeks who had settled in Italy and Sicily.

The Athenians could reckon upon greater foreign support than the Spartans. The islands of Zacynthus and Corcyra, and all those lying between Peloponnesus and Crete; the Cyclades, except Melos and Thera; Caria, Doris, and Ionia, in Asia Minor; the countries near the Hellespont and along the coast of Thrace, were all either in alliance with or tributary to them: and though, in Greece itself, the Platæans were their chief support, yet Thessaly and the greater part of Acarnania were favourable to them. From one town in Locris also the Athenians could look for assistance;— Naupactus, which was peopled by the Messenians, who we may remember rebelled against Sparta in the time of Cimon, and sought refuge in the fortress of Ithome.

When the Spartans took Ithome, which they did after a great deal of difficulty,— they allowed the Messenians to quit Peloponnesus, on condition of being made slaves if they returned. The Athenians, having just at that time obtained possession of the town of Naupactus, gave it to these poor exiles; and of course, ever after, the Messenians of Naupactus were devoted to their cause.

Archidamus, the king of Sparta, who had so strongly urged the delay of the war, was the person who first took the command of the Peloponnesian army. Even to the last he had hopes of peace; and, when his forces were actually collected together on the Isthmus of Corinth, he sent a last ambassador to Athens. But the envoy was not even admitted within the walls; for Pericles had persuaded the people to decree that no embassy should be received from the Spartans whilst they were under arms. The ambassador was ordered to quit Attica that very day, and persons were appointed to travel with him to the frontiers, to prevent his holding communication with any one by the way. He parted from his conductors exclaiming, "This day will be the beginning of great evils to Greece."

And so indeed it proved. The very first step that was taken was a sad one, at least for the Athenians, whose pride and ambition had in such a great measure caused the war.

It was according to the advice of Pericles. Rich indeed they were, as he told them, in gold and silver, and strong in their ships and their forces; but it would not be well to expose themselves to the invasion of an enemy by remaining scattered in the country. Athens must be their refuge, and thither all must remove with their families and property. This counsel was followed, but not without great grief. Since the Persian invasion Athens had become very prosperous; and the Athenians had not only learnt to take pleasure in country pursuits, but many rich persons had elegant villas, in which they delighted to spend a great portion of their time. These they could no longer enjoy; and, to the poor husbandmen, the thought of giving up their quiet, peaceful homes, with all the pleasant sights and the fresh air of the open fields, for the narrow, crowded streets of a great city, was a trial scarcely to be borne.

Nothing else, however, was to be done; the flocks

and cattle were removed to Eubœa, and the islands near; and all other things that could be carried away,—even the timbers of the houses,—were taken with their owners into Athens. The city was not large enough, suddenly to receive so many persons. A few had friends or relations who gave them shelter, but the greater part were obliged to find refuge in the temples, or to live in the towers on the walls, or to build little huts for themselves in any vacant spot they could find. Such hardships would have been enough to damp the spirits of any other people; but the Athenians were not to be soon discouraged. They did indeed think that extraordinary events were going to happen; and reports were spread of prodigies being seen, and of an earthquake having taken place in the holy island of Delos, supposed to be safe from such calamities,—all of which caused a great deal of expectation and wonder; but, upon the whole, the Athenians were full of hope, and awaited cheerfully and bravely the advance of the Peloponnesian army.

It was not difficult to remain quiet whilst the enemy's forces were at a distance; but the Athenians soon beheld a sight which roused their anger and their energy to the utmost. Archidamus, on the return of the Spartan envoy from Athens, having assembled his officers, and warned them to proceed cautiously, and to keep their troops carefully in order, set forth on his road to Attica. He advanced slowly, but it was only that he might inflict greater evils in the end. The harvest was near; the corn just ripe; and as the army approached one of the most fertile districts of Attica, only seven or eight miles from Athens, the unfortunate Athenians saw the troops wasting their rich lands, whilst they were pent up within the walls of the city, unable to raise an arm for their defence. In grief and indignation they reproached Pericles for his advice, but Pericles was immovable. "Trees cut down," he said, "might shoot again, but men were not to be replaced." He could not be induced either to lead an army into the field, or to call an assembly to consult upon the subject. All he would do was to provide for the defence of the walls, and to send out horsemen to protect the neighbourhood of the city. In the end, his decision was proved to be a wise one. Archidamus, finding that he could not bring the Athenians to a battle, and knowing that the provisions for his army were nearly consumed, thought it better to retreat; and, after travelling through the country, destroying every thing that came in his way, he returned home and disbanded his forces.

Archidamus had not left Attica before the Athenian fleets set sail to revenge the injuries he had inflicted. One fleet ravaged the coast of Peloponnesus, another wasted the lands of Locris; whilst the people of Ægina, who had made special complaints against Athens before the war began, were driven from their homes, and sent to wander in exile, and were only saved by the Lacedæmonians, who gave them permission to settle on the borders of Laconia. Besides these successes, the island of Cephallenia surrendered to the Athenians, and they were offered the support and friendship of a powerful king of Thrace, and of Perdiccas of Macedon, who was formerly their enemy.

So far all seemed prosperous; but success in a war carried on in Greece against Grecians, was very different from success when the Persians were repelled. Though Athens prospered, other states suffered; and this was especially the case with Megara, a small state, one of the foremost to make complaints against Athens, and the inhabitants of which had incurred the vengeance of the Athe-

P

nians some time before, by having caused the death of an Athenian herald. As the war went on, the Spartans and Peloponnesians entered Attica once every year, whilst the Athenians ravaged Megara twice. The hatred of the Athenians against the Megarians was indeed so great, that part of the oath taken by the ten generals who commanded the Athenian armies was, to invade Megara twice a year

CHAP. XIX.

THE PLAGUE AT ATHENS.

B.C. 430.

In the winter of the first year of the Peloponnesian war, when both the Athenians and the Spartans were obliged, from the season, to cease from hostilities, Pericles, according to the custom of his country, pronounced a funeral oration over those who had fallen in battle.

He spoke of the glory of Athens, her laws, her freedom, the extent of her commerce, the reverence shown to the gods, the enjoyments provided for the poor, the education bestowed upon the young, the taste and learning which gave her a right to be called the School of Greece. But something very different from glory and greatness was then present to him. For at that moment there lay before him ten coffins of cypress wood, — one for each of the tribes into which the citizens of Athens were divided; and within the coffins were the remains of the dead, — the victims to the pride and ambition of their country, — about to be laid to their rest amidst the trees and shrubs in the beautiful burying ground of the Ceramicus.

They were the first of a vast number who died in those terrible wars. But the Athenians had not then learnt to regret the wilfulness with which they had urged on the quarrel with the Spartans. When the funeral procession of citizens and strangers, mourning friends and wailing women, followed the dead to their graves, no one, probably, considered whether the cause for which those they lamented had died was a right one. They were comforted by the thought that their friends had fought bravely, and perished honourably, that their names would be remembered with gratitude, and their sons educated at the public expense.

It is only when we trace the history of Greece to its end, that we can understand the miserable consequences of the Peloponnesian war, and see the difference between a people fighting for the defence of their country against a foreign enemy, as the Athenians fought at Marathon and Salamis; and the same people giving way to a love of power, and a wish for conquest, and engaging in wars with those who ought to have been their firmest allies.

In the one case war, in spite of its miseries, produced unselfish actions, and high principles, and brought lasting honour upon the nation;— in the other it began in jealousy, tyranny, and suspicion, and ended in ruin.

And so, we might almost be inclined to think that the anger of Heaven against those who engaged wrongfully in war, was shown in the fearful plague which the next year visited Attica. It broke out early in the spring, just as Archidamus had returned with his armies to invade the country. The winter had been uncommonly wet, and the summer was singularly hot, whilst there were none of those refreshing sea breezes which usually made the warmth endurable. The city of Athens was crowded to excess;—not only every house was filled, but the huts which had been built up to receive the country people, still remained standing, and the close little rooms in the towers on the walls were all occupied. The disease first broke out in Piræus, and many thought that the Spartans had poisoned the waters; but as it spread wider and wider they became convinced that it was a calamity not brought upon them by man. The open streets, the public buildings, even the temples of the gods, were strewn with the bodies of the dead; whilst around the walls and cisterns lay crowds of the suffering and the dying, who had rushed from their homes in the eagerness of an unquenchable thirst, longing only to plunge into the waters, though death was to be the certain consequence. For men in such terrible seasons seldom think that of which will come after death. Even in Christian countries, when visited by a like calamity, the very greatness of the suffering and the danger has been known to make evil persons more hardened in their crimes; and in Athens, amongst a heathen people, the wickedness of those days of terror must have been something too dreadful to think upon. Because men knew they might in all probability die the next day, they gave way to every sinful inclination of the present hour; and so great was the general selfishness, that the few persons who ventured to attend upon their dying relations were considered to show extraordinary virtue. In that respect, indeed, they were very different from Christians, who have continually risked their lives in cases of equal danger, not only for their friends, but for the poorest and most wretched of their fellow creatures.

Whilst the Athenians were thus suffering from the plague, it was not difficult for Pericles to persuade them that it was better to keep within the walls of Athens, as they had done the year before, and not to try and stop the Lacedæmonians when they were invading the country. After a time, however, he agreed to sail to the coasts of Peloponnesus and ravage them, but the expedition was unsuccessful, for the plague broke out in the fleet, and obliged him to return home.

The people of Athens now began to complain both of the war and of Pericles, who had induced them to undertake it. They even insisted upon sending an embassy to Sparta to propose peace, but the Spartans would not listen to them, for they knew that it was only because the Athenians were weak and frightened that they had thought about it. Pericles alone was hopeful. He called together an assembly, and made a long speech to cheer them, begging them not to be cast down by their calamities, and to think only of the honour of their country. "Their empire," he said, "was not confined to the territories of their present subjects, but might be extended wherever they chose to turn their arms; for the sea was all their own, and, in comparison with the conquests they might make by that means, Attica itself ought no more to be valued than a little flower pot, the trifling ornament of a rich man's estate.

These flattering words soothed the Athenians, who were always pleased to be told that they were a great people, and they consented to continue the war. But they were still rather angry with Pericles, and some persons made charges against him as to the way in which he had commanded the armies when he was their general. He was brought to trial and obliged to pay some money as a fine; but when the Athenians had thus indulged their spite, they were satisfied, and Pericles was restored to his office, and ruled every one just as he had done before. But the time was drawing near when all the great projects and ambitious thoughts of this celebrated man were to end. The war had been carried on for two years and a half, and the pestilence still raged in Athens. It had come very near to Pericles. His sister, some of his most valued relatives and friends, and two of his sons, had perished by it. The elder son was worthless and extravagant, and had caused his father much sorrow; but the younger was a boy of much promise, and all the hopes of Pericles were fixed upon him. The great Athenian had borne many trials in his life,— false accusations, anxieties, disappointments, the loss of those he loved, and nothing had been able to move him from his usual calmness; but when, according to the custom of the Greeks, he approached the dead body of his favourite child to place a garland of flowers upon the lifeless head, the agony of his grief overcame all self command, and bursting into tears, he sobbed aloud.

It was his last and most grievous trial, and his own death followed in the autumn of the year, B. C. 429. The illness which seized him was a lingering one, though it seems in some respects to have resembled the pestilence. He retained his senses to the last. The women who attended him hung a charm round his neck, under the idea that it would be of service; but Pericles had no belief in such superstition, and smiled as he showed the charm to one of his friends, saying, "that it was a proof to what a pass illness had brought him, when he could submit to such trifling." As he grew worse and worse his friends collected round his bed, and tried to relieve their grief by recalling all his brave actions, and the trophies of victory he had raised, but Pericles, who had before appeared insensible, roused himself, and interrupted them. "They had omitted," he said, "the most glorious praise which he could claim. Other generals had been as fortunate, but he had never caused an Athenian to put on mourning." This was indeed a singular boast from the man who had urged the Athenians to engage in the Peloponnesian war. But so it is that the wisest of mankind deceive themselves.

CHAP. XX.

THE SIEGE OF PLATÆA.

BEGUN B.C. 429.

THE situation of the Athenians after the death of Pericles was not by any means to be envied. There was no one at all able to take his place. On the contrary, the person who soon made himself the most remarkable, was a cruel coarse minded man named Cleon, a tanner by trade, not very clever, and in no way fit to rule; but who gained the notice of the common people by speaking out boldly, making complaints of the rich, and pretending to be very anxious for the interests of the poor. Cleon had been one of the foremost to find fault with Pericles during his lifetime, and the last years of Pericles had been rendered anxious and unhappy by the efforts made by his enemy to disturb the minds of the people, and excite them to murmur against his government. No two persons, indeed, could have been more unlike than Pericles and Cleon. In their manner of addressing the people in public speeches, the difference was especially remarkable. Pericles, as we have already said, was calm and dignified. His expressions were lofty, and his words well chosen, and he seldom moved from his position. But Cleon, when he spoke, cast aside his upper garment, clasped his thigh, and rushed from one side of the speaker's stand to the other; and this eagerness caught the attention of the common people, and so gave him influence over them.

It was not, however, just at first after the death of Pericles, that Cleon had so much power. Two persons, one a dealer in flour, and the other a cattle dealer, who married Aspasia, brought themselves into notice for a little time; but the dealer in flour was soon surpassed by Cleon, and the cattle dealer died, and then Cleon was for a time left alone without any one to be his rival.

It was very unfortunate for the Athenians to be left in such bad hands, for there was much to be done which required talent abroad, and upright conduct in the management of affairs at home. The Peloponnesian war still went on, and brought suffering and ruin upon many. The Potidæans who, we may remember, had been besieged by the Athenians before it actually broke out, defended themselves till they were reduced to such dreadful misery by the want of provisions, that they were forced to live upon human flesh. Then they yielded, and the Athenians took possession of the town, and allowed the Potidæans to go away wherever they liked. But such a permission could have been little better than death, since their homes were destroyed, and their friends had perished.

The siege of Platæa was yet more memorable than that of Potidæa. It was begun in the year B. C. 429, the same year in which Pericles died. In the beginning of that year king Archidamus of Sparta crossed the isthmus with his armies, as he had so often done before; but instead of proceeding to Attica, he directed his course to Platæa, which

was in alliance with Athens. The Platæans sent
envoys to remonstrate with him, reminding him of
all they had done for the defence of Greece at the
time of the Persian invasion; and that after the
battle of Platæa their state had been declared independent,
and the other Grecian states were
bound to protect it. Archidamus did not deny
this, but he insisted that the Platæans should be
neutral in the war, and that if they would not assist
Sparta they should also refuse to help Athens.
To this, however, the Platæans could not venture
to agree. Their wives and children were then
at Athens, and might suffer if they offended the
Athenians. The siege accordingly began. There
were only 400 Platæans in the city, 80 Athenians,
and 110 women, who had remained behind to
prepare food for the men. Yet this small force
was able to resist the united efforts of a large army
for two years. Archidamus did his very utmost to
take the town. He was engaged for seventy days
and nights in trying to raise a strong mound before
it, made of earth and rubbish, wood and stones:
and if he had succeeded he might easily have gained
possession of the city. The Platæans knew this,
and they used to creep out at night through an
opening made in their wall, and scoop out and
carry away large quantities of earth from the lower
part of the mound. The Peloponnesians continued
to repair these breaches; and then the Platæans
dug a deep hole, or shaft, as it is called, within the
city, and when they had sunk it very low, they
worked an underground passage from it to the
bottom of the mound, so as to undermine the mound.
Besides this they built up an inner wall to protect
themselves in case their enemies should break down
the outer one. Archidamus began at last to despair
of ever taking the city, but he resolved to make

one more attempt. He caused all the hollow space between the mound and the wall, and even on the other side as far as the Peloponnesians could reach, to be filled with faggots which had been steeped in pitch and sulphur. These faggots were then set on fire. The blaze was something quite extraordinary. One of the Greek historians says that it was like a burning forest, and if the wind had carried the flames towards the houses in the town, no doubt the whole place would have been burnt. But it so happened that the wind did not set that way, and though the Platæans were terribly frightened their town was saved. Archidamus now resolved to give up all idea of taking the town by force, and instead, he dug ditches, and built walls with towers, all round it, and set soldiers to guard them, so that no one could go into the city nor come out of it without being discovered. He then returned himself to Sparta, leaving the Bœotians and the other allies to watch Platæa, and feeling sure that in the end they must gain possession of the place. Even if they were not successful in any other way, it was certain that the poor people not being able to provide themselves with fresh food, would be obliged to yield when all which they had within the walls was gone.

After a defence of two years the Platæans became so weak from want of food that they were quite desperate. Some one at length proposed that they should try and escape through the midst of their enemies: and the very moment the plan was mentioned it was agreed to. A certain time was fixed upon for making the attempt, but as it drew near, half of the men were frightened, and only two hundred and twenty were bold enough to carry out the undertaking. It was then the depth of winter, and on a dark stormy night, a small party, very

lightly armed, and having their right feet bare, to
keep them from slipping in the mud, crossed the
ditch that Archidamus had dug round the town,
and planted ladders, made for the purpose, against
the enemy's walls. No one heard them, for the
howling of the wind drowned the noise of their
movements, and the soldiers, who ought to have
watched from the battlements, had taken shelter
in the towers. The Platæans mounted the ladders,
one by one, as cautiously as possible. But one
of them unfortunately, in laying hold of a brick
on the battlements, dislodged it, and as it fell, the
nearest sentinel was alarmed. The besiegers were
called to the walls, but no one knew what was to
be done, or where he was to go; and just then
the party of Platæans who had remained in the city
sallied out, according to an agreement made beforehand, on the side of the town opposite to that by
which their companions had escaped, and thus
greatly increased the confusion. There were, however, a body of three hundred men amongst the
besiegers, who were always kept in readiness to
march at a moment's notice, and these immediately set forth in search of the place from
whence the alarm had arisen. Before they could discover it, some of the fugitives had made themselves
masters of two towers on the wall which they had
scaled; and after killing the sentinels, had mounted
to the roofs, and by discharging their arrows at
their enemies, prevented them from drawing near,
whilst the rest of their friends were climbing the
ladders and escaping. When all were safe on the
other side of the wall, the men came down from
the towers. But their difficulties were not over.
Another ditch was in their way, very deep, and
only thinly covered by a crust of ice. The greater
number had crossed, and the last of their body were

preparing to follow, when the three hundred besiegers came up with their torches. This, however, was not so great a danger as it seemed, for the Platæans being in the dark could not well be discovered, whilst their enemies were plainly seen, and, by discharging arrows at them, the Platæans kept them at a distance, and so moved away in good order.

The besiegers no sooner found out what had happened than they made signals by fire from the walls, in order to give notice to the Thebans; for Thebes was only a few miles from Platæa, and the inhabitants of the two cities had long been enemies. The Platæans were prepared for this, and in order to prevent the Thebans from understanding what was meant, they also lighted fire signals on their own walls, by which means the Thebans were quite confused. The fugitives in the meanwhile proceeded for some little distance on the road to Thebes in order to mislead their enemies, but when they saw by the light of the torches which their pursuers carried, that they were following in a wrong direction, they turned into a road leading to Athens, and soon afterwards arrived safely, and had a joyful meeting with their wives and children. One poor man, however, amongst the two hundred and twenty who had escaped, fell into the enemy's hands after he had crossed the outer ditch; and seven turned back in a fright, and reported that all their companions had been killed. The Platæans in the city, in consequence of this report sent a message to the besiegers in the morning begging to have the bodies of their friends restored to them, and then to their great delight heard the joyful news of their safety. No doubt many then wished that they also had been bold enough to escape, and the wish must have been sadly increased afterwards, for they had fatal reasons to regret their fears, from the events

which in the end took place. For a considerable
time they continued still to hold out against their
enemies, but being at length nearly starved, they
were forced to yield. No promises of safety were
made them, and five judges were sent from Sparta
to try them for their offences.

The only question which the judges asked was
whether during the war the Platæans had done any
service to Sparta and her allies. This question
was quite sufficient to show the unfortunate Platæans
that their enemies were determined to be revenged
upon them. They tried in the most touching way
to move the Spartans to pity, and recalled all that
they had ever done in former days to help them,
ending with an entreaty that they might not be
given over to the Thebans, since they would rather
die by hunger, the most fearful of all deaths, than
fall into the hands of such bitter enemies. The
Spartans were moved by this mournful appeal, but
the cruel Thebans, who were standing by, spoke
next, and endeavoured to harden their hearts again.
They said that the Platæans were the friends of the
Athenians, and therefore enemies to the liberty of
Greece; and they reproached them for having, a
few years before, murdered the body of Thebans
who had been invited to take possession of Platæa,
by some of the principal inhabitants. For these
offences they demanded vengeance.

The Spartan judges granted it. One by one the
Platæans were brought forward, and each was
again asked whether he had aided Sparta and her
allies in the war. The answer could only be No;
and the sentence of death was then passed.

Two hundred Platæans and twenty Athenians
perished on this occasion, and the women were
made slaves. From that time the state of Platæa
ceased to exist. The city was given over to the

Thebans, and a year afterwards razed to the ground.

Whilst the siege of Platæa was going on, the Peloponnesians and the Athenians carried on the war in different places; sometimes one side being successful, and sometimes the other. The Athenians had a large fleet, and a skilful admiral, and were upon the whole victorious by sea. But on the other hand, the Spartans planned an attack upon Pirœus, which frightened the Athenians extremely, and although they did not carry it out, as they at first intended, yet they did succeed in plundering the island of Salamis which was very near it.

Besides other disasters the Athenians also lost at this period the friendship of the island of Lesbos, famed for its wealth and its navy. The inhabitants were tired of being subject to Athens, and having fortified their chief city, Mitylene, they determined to revolt and join the Spartans.

It was on the occasion of this revolt that the cruel character of Cleon, the Athenian, was first remarkably shown. Pachés, one of the Athenian generals, having besieged and taken Mitylene, sent some of the leaders of the revolt prisoners to Athens; at the same time begging to know what was to be done with the city and its inhabitants.

The question was discussed in the public Assembly. Cleon urged strongly that the Mitylenœans should be severely punished. "If the Athenians," he said, "did not at once make an example of such rebels, there would be no end to the dangers and contests which they would bring upon themselves, since their other allies would think that they too might revolt whenever they pleased. He therefore proposed that all the men in Mitylene should be put to death, and all the women and children made slaves. Cleon's eagerness gained his point. The decree was passed, and the very next day the order was despatched to Paches at Mitylene. But the Athenians, though they were harsh when excited, soon began to repent. They felt that they had acted hastily, and some Mitylenæan envoys then in Athens easily persuaded the magistrates to call another Assembly, and consider the question again. Cleon repeated his arguments, and the friends of the Mitylenæans said all they could against him; and this time the Athenians decided for mercy. A vessel was instantly made ready which was to bear orders to Paches contrary to those that had been determined on the day before. The Mitylenæan envoys put wine and bread on board, and promised to reward the crew largely if they should arrive in time to save their countrymen; and the vessel set sail. The men rowed night and day, sleeping in turn, and eating bread dipped in wine and oil, whilst they worked at the oars. They met with no contrary winds, and as the crew of the first vessel had not been in any haste to perform their disagreeable errand, they arrived very soon after them. Paches had just read the cruel decree, and was about to execute it. But the counter orders stopped him, and the unfortunate Mitylenæans were saved. The next intelligence, however, which reached them from Athens must have saddened all their hearts. Cleon had persuaded the Athenians to put to death all the prisoners who had been sent to Athens, without allowing them any trial; and orders were now given that the walls of Mitylene should be pulled down, the ships belonging to it seized, and nearly the whole of the island of Lesbos be given over to Athenian colonists.

CHAP. XXI.

PYLOS TAKEN AND FORTIFIED.

B.C. 425.

MANY dreadful events, worse than those which have been already described, happened during the course of the Peloponnesian war, for men were everywhere full of deadly anger and distrust. In almost every city in Greece there were two parties; the nobles, who wished to side with the Lacedæmonians; and the people, who were inclined to take part with the Athenians. No person was allowed to remain quiet, without saying which of the two he preferred; or if he tried to do so he was considered an enemy by both. This disagreement spread amongst private families, so that husbands and wives, parents and children, were opposed to each other. Persons who had once been friends were now suspicious and revengeful. Those who were the most violent and reckless, led on their companions to commit all kinds of cruelty; and piety, benevolence, justice, and all right and honourable feelings, seemed at times entirely forgotten. Yet neither the Athenians nor the Spartans were without some superior men who, it might have been supposed, would have been able to guide them right. Cleon, indeed, had a great deal of influence at Athens, but there were two other generals, Nicias and Demosthenes, who were of a very different disposition — prudent, and sincere, and really brave; whereas Cleon only made a pretence of courage.

The Spartans also had a general on their side, of exceedingly high character, Brasidas, who distinguished himself very early in the war, and was their chief hero for many years. The great Greek historian, Thucydides, who lived about this time, and wrote an account of the Peloponnesian war, praises this Spartan general far more than any other commander of his age. He says that the kindness of Brasidas, and his gentleness of manner, did more harm to the cause of the Athenians than even his great skill and bravery in battle; for that he gained the hearts of his enemies, and so won them over to the Spartan side.

But even such men as these were not able to prevent the evils of the long war, and, indeed, having once taken part in it, as they were obliged to do, they thought it their duty to carry it on boldly, and to obtain as much power for their several states as they possibly could.

It was not till the seventh year of the war that either side began to think of peace, and then it was Sparta who proposed it, in consequence of some serious losses, which are now to be related. Demosthenes, the Athenian general, had, a short time before, obtained the permission of his fellow citizens to sail over to Peloponnesus, land on the coast, and make any conquests he could. There was some discussion between him and the commanders of the fleet, in which he and his men sailed, as to where it would be best to go, but, a storm coming on, they were obliged to land at Pylos, in Messenia, which was just what Demosthenes wished. Pylos was a rocky headland, very difficult to be reached by land, and the plan of Demosthenes was to fortify it, so as to give the Athenians a fortress of their own in their enemy's country. The commanders of the fleet laughed at the notion, and thought it merely an idle fancy; but as the storm continued for several days, and they were obliged to remain there, the men began to build up a wall just for the sake of passing away the time. There were plenty of stones near, which they put together as they best could, filling up the vacant spaces with mud, and as they had no masons' tools with them they were obliged to do all the work with their hands. Pylos was only fifty miles from Sparta, and of course the Spartans soon heard what Demosthenes was doing. They did not, however, trouble themselves much about it at first, for they were engaged in celebrating one of their festivals, and felt quite sure that they should be able to dislodge the Athenians at the first attack.

The rough wall was finished in about six days, and then, as the storm was over, the commanders of the Athenian fleet sailed off with all their vessels except five, which were left, together with a small body of men, under the command of Demosthenes. The Spartan forces were at that time in Attica, but when intelligence arrived that Demosthenes was building a fortress in Peloponnesus, they set out for Pylos, and orders were given to the Spartan fleet to join them there. On their arrival they took possession of the little island of Sphacteria, which was just in front of Pylos, and prepared to overwhelm the Athenians by attacking their fortress on all sides.

This, however, was a plan much more easily formed than executed. Demosthenes and his men defended themselves so skilfully, that although the Spartans were much more numerous, and were commanded by the celebrated Brasidas, the Athenians were the more successful of the two; and when their fleet soon afterwards came up to their assistance, they gained a complete victory. The body of Spartans who had been placed in the island of Sphacteria were now completely enclosed by their enemies. Some of the noblest and most distinguished persons in the state were amongst them, and there was little hope of rescuing then.

This it was which made the Spartans so suddenly desirous of peace. Envoys were sent to Athens, and terms were proposed, to which it seemed likely the Athenians would agree. But, to their surprise, they found their offers refused. The Athenians were prouder than ever, and Cleon urged them to continue the war; and when the Spartan ambassadors saw that they could not obtain peace without giving up what they thought was their country's honour, they broke off the treaty and returned to Pylos. After this the sieges of Pylos by the Spartans, and of Sphacteria by the Athenians were carried on for a considerable time. The Spartans in Sphacteria were well supplied with provisions, for the Spartan government promised freedom to the Helots, and great rewards to all other persons, who would carry them any. The Helots in consequence did their very utmost. Sometimes they would sail to the back of the island in the night, especially if it happened to be stormy, and they knew that the Athenian ships would not be likely to keep their stations near. Sometimes they contrived to dive under the water, carrying with them a mixture of bruised seeds and honey for the soldiers; and by these and other means they managed to escape the watchfulness of their enemies. The Athenians on the contrary, had great difficulty in obtaining food, and suffered exceedingly from the want of water; there was only one small spring in the fortress, and many of the soldiers were obliged to drink the bad brackish water which they procured by digging into the beach. Then their ships were crowded into a very small space, and the landing was very difficult; and yet the crews of the different vessels were obliged to go on shore by turns for their meals; which caused great inconvenience.

The Athenians began at last to fear that after all they should never succeed in taking Sphacteria, and that it would have been wiser to listen to the Spartans when they proposed peace. Cleon was now blamed for having given his advice against peace; and, in order to pacify his fellow citizens, he declared that the accounts brought them of what was going on at Pylos were not true. This, however, did not satisfy the people, and Cleon then changed his tone, and began to find fault with the Athenian generals. "If," he said, "they had been any better than women, they would not have suffered such an easy conquest as that of Sphacteria to be so long delayed. Had he been in office, it would have been already finished." Nicias was one of the generals for the year, and every one knew that this taunt was aimed at him, for Cleon had a great dislike to him. Cleon's boast, however, only provoked the people, and they began to laugh at him, and to whisper amongst themselves that, if he did think it so easy to take Sphacteria, he might as well try. Nicias himself, who was present, hearing what was said, caught at the idea, and rose up in the assembly to propose gravely that Cleon should collect any force he might think necessary, and make the attempt. "Full permission," he said, "was given him by the generals." Cleon was extremely perplexed. He had not the least idea of being taken at his word, and did not know enough about war to venture upon such an expedition. The people quite enjoyed his annoyance, and insisted upon it that he should be forced to go. It might seem strange at first that they should have been willing to run such a risk, but in fact they knew, and so did Cleon, that it was the plan of Demosthenes, the general at Pylos, to make an attack himself upon the Spartans at Sphacteria; and of course with the help of such an able general, there was not so much to be feared from Cleon's ignorance. The Athenians, too, were not at all sorry to put Cleon in a situation of danger, for they were beginning to be tired of him; and they pleased themselves by thinking that if they did not conquer the Spartans they might at any rate be rid of him, since he might be killed, or, if he failed, all his influence would be gone.

Cleon set out for Pylos, and, when he arrived, found that Demosthenes was already preparing to attack the Spartans in their island. He would have done so long before if he had known well how many Spartans there were in Sphacteria; but it was uninhabited, and covered by thick woods, which hid them, and gave them a great advantage over their enemies. A little while before, however, a party of Athenians, having landed on a corner of the island to dine, lighted a fire, which caught the wood near. The wind was blowing, and the flames spread in consequence, and very soon nearly the whole of the island was left bare. This made a great difference to Demosthenes; and when Cleon arrived with additional forces the Athenians lost no time in attacking the island, having first, however, sent offers of peace to the Spartans, which were refused. Some of the Athenians landed in two divisions on opposite sides of the island, a little before daybreak,—and others followed soon afterwards.

The plan of Demosthenes was to begin the attack from a distance by showers of arrows, javelins, and stones; and this was much more trying to the Spartans than a close combat. After a brave defence their strength began to be spent, and their spirits to flag,—and when the Athenians drew nearer, the Spartans were not only distressed by the broken shafts of the weapons which had been showered upon them, and had pierced their armour, but were also nearly blinded and choked by a cloud of dust which rose under the trampling of the soldiers from the ashes of the burnt woods. So the conflict continued till the day was wearing on, and the Athenians were growing faint with thirst and fatigue. A suggestion was then made which quickly decided the victory. The commander of some of the Athenian allies offered to take a small body of men, and make his way to a spot behind the Spartans, so as to attack them in two places at once. It was a difficult undertaking, for the soldiers had to march along the foot of some cliffs, and then to mount to the top by an ascent which was so steep that it had been thought quite secure, and had therefore been left unguarded. They succeeded, however, and the Spartans had no chance of escape. It was not the wish of the Athenians to kill them, but to take them prisoners to Athens. A herald therefore was sent, calling upon them to yield, and after some delay the summons was accepted, and the Spartans were made prisoners. Twenty days after Cleon had set out from Athens, he returned—as he had said he would—victorious; but how little of the merit was due to himself may easily be imagined.

The Spartans were quite overwhelmed by their defeat, and the other Grecian states could scarcely believe the intelligence to be true. That Spartans should surrender, whilst they had arms in their hands and provisions for their support, was something unheard of before. But no courage could have saved them under such difficult circumstances. An Athenian asked insultingly, "Whether those who had fallen were of the true Spartan blood." "Remember," replied the Spartan, to whom the question was addressed, "that we died, not in close combat, but as the dart or the arrow happened to speed."

CHAP. XXII.

THE PEACE OF NICIAS.

B.C. 421.

THE disasters of Sphacteria made Sparta again think of peace, but Athens was haughtier than ever, and as it was impossible to comply with the demand she made, the war went on as before. For another year the Athenians were the conquerors, but after that their usual success seemed to forsake them. A vast plan which they had formed against Bœotia failed, and this, joined with the victories of Brasidas, the Spartan, in Thrace and Chalcidice, where the Athenians had several subject cities, at length humbled them so much that they agreed for a year's truce. Even this, however, was not lasting. Both sides found causes for disagreement before the truce was actually settled, and it was not till the war had been carried on for eleven years, that a peace for fifty years, generally called the peace of Nicias, was concluded.

This peace was confirmed at Athens, on the 4th of April, B.C. 421. It is called the peace of Nicias, because it was chiefly brought about by the exertions of Nicias. All parties, indeed, had by this time suffered enough to make them wish for it; but, probably, one great cause of its being actually agreed upon, was that Cleon, the Athenian, and Brasidas the Spartan who were the chief supporters of the war, had died not long before. They were killed in the same battle, at Amphipolis, in Macedonia,

Brasidas was wounded whilst boldly rushing against his enemies, but lived long enough to hear that his army was victorious. Cleon was killed in the act of retreating.

Both these men had been urgent for war from different motives. Brasidas had the heathen love of glory in which he had never been taught to see that there was anything wrong; but Cleon's only object was to engage the Athenians in foreign contests, in order that he might be able to carry on his own evil designs without observation.

Brasidas was a very great loss to the Spartans. The people of Amphipolis allowed him to be buried within their walls, which was an extraordinary honour in a Greek city; the whole army attended his magnificent funeral, and sacrifices even were offered to him as if he were almost a god. He was especially beloved in that neighbourhood, for the kindness and prudence he had shown in bringing over the Athenian cities to the side of the Spartans, and for years afterwards his name was remembered and honoured.

Thucydides, the Athenian historian, who wrote the history of the Peloponnesian war, was at one time engaged as a commander against Brasidas. The expedition which he undertook was not successful, although he showed great skill in it, and the Athenians brought him to trial, and it is supposed, that he was condemned to death, and to save himself, went into exile. At any rate, it is certain, that he was absent from his country for twenty years, and during that time wrote the history which has made his name famous for ages. He was a very great as well as a very clever man, and so free from any feeling of revenge against those who had unjustly punished him, that in his writings he says nothing against them, and only mentions his misfortunes as giving him the opportunity of collecting the information necessary for his history.

The Athenians and Spartans kept the peace which had been agreed upon for about seven years; that is to say, they did not invade each other's territories during that time; but the war cannot properly be said to have been at an end, for neither party strictly observed the terms agreed upon, and the smaller states, especially Corinth and Argos, being jealous of both, tried to form a league independent of them, of which Argos was to be the head. These circumstances caused much suspicion and ill feeling; and it was easy to perceive that the contest would after a while be renewed.

It seems, indeed, that there were never wanting persons at Athens who preferred war to peace. Now that Cleon was dead, another man rose up, whose whole advice and desire was, that the alliance between Sparta and Athens might again be broken. This person was Alcibiades, a young man of high birth, of the family of the Alcmæonids, and a relation of Pericles. The father of Alcibiades was killed in battle when his son was about eight years old, and Alcibiades was then put under the care of Pericles, who being very prudent in all money arrangements, managed his affairs extremely well. Alcibiades inherited from his father one of the largest fortunes in Athens, and from the wise care of Pericles, this was so much increased, that when he grew up to be a man, he came into possession of immense riches. He was besides exceedingly handsome, and very quick and clever, and all these seeming advantages gave him distinction from his childhood. But they were not really blessings; they helped to encourage his natural faults, and in the end brought him to ruin. His temper was extremely hasty, and so determined was he upon having his own way that nothing could stop him. As an instance of this disposition, it is said that, when he was one day playing as a child in a narrow street, a waggon came up, which would have interrupted him, and in order to hinder it from advancing he laid himself down before the wheels. He was also both vain and proud. At one moment he would flatter the people of Athens absurdly, and the next provoke them by an insult. But that which was worse than any thing else, he was not sincere. Instead of gaining his object, whatever it might be, in a straightforward way, he always had some scheme in hand which might be very clever, but was certainly cunning, and unworthy of an honourable man. His habits of life were selfish, extravagant, and luxurious, and he not only spent great sums of money at Athens, in order to gain the good will of the people, but also endeavoured to dazzle all Greece by his splendour.

At the Olympic games he displayed greater magnificence than kings and princes. At one time he had seven chariots to contend in the same race, and won the first, second, and either the third or the fourth crown, and afterwards feasted all the spectators.

On this occasion the states and cities subject to Athens paid him such homage as had never been shown to anybody before. One pitched a splendid Persian tent for him; another furnished food for his horses; a third provided the victims which were to be sacrificed by him to the gods; and a fourth gave the wine and other things necessary for the banquet.

On his return home he engaged Euripides, the first poet in Greece, to celebrate his victories, and caused two pictures to be painted to commemorate them, in one of which he was represented as the most exquisitely beautiful person that could be imagined.

Of course all these whims and follies excited a good deal of notice; and sensible persons began to think that they were not suitable in a state like Athens, where the general principle was that men ought to be as much as possible on an equality, or at least only distinguished by the services which they rendered to their country.

But Alcibiades took delight in showing that he considered himself a privileged person, and beyond the reach of the laws; and the people in general humoured him. For instance, it was the fashion amongst the young Athenians, in those days, to carry a tame quail under their cloaks. One day, at a public meeting, Alcibiades suffered his to escape, and the business of the whole assembly was stopped, till the bird was caught and given back to him. The favour thus shown him naturally made him still more conceited, and his rudeness and presumption were often quite intolerable.

A character like that of Alcibiades, could not, we might imagine, in any way, be attractive to good and wise men. Yet this was not the case. There was one person in Athens, Socrates, the philosopher, who saw much in Alcibiades to love, and who yet was himself so nearly perfect, that his character, when we read of it, seems more like that of a Christian saint than of a virtuous heathen. It was in fact the very goodness of Socrates which made him so merciful to the faults of another, and caused him to take so much pains to convert the headstrong, violent, careless Alcibiades, into a soberminded, honourable, unselfish Athenian citizen.

Socrates was much older than Alcibiades. At the time of the peace of Nicias he must have been about forty-six years of age. Alcibiades was then not more than twenty-eight, and, as it has been remarked, exceedingly handsome; whilst Socrates was

singularly plain,—for he had a flat nose, thick lips,
prominent eyes, and a very awkward figure. His
temper was by nature extremely violent: indeed
it is said that when he did at any time give way to
it, it was actually terrible; but in general it was
kept under the strictest control. He had a very
strong constitution, and was able to endure great
hardships. His habits of life were of the plainest
kind. He wore scanty clothing, went about with
bare feet, and allowed himself only the simplest
species of food. He was not of noble birth, for his
father was a statuary, and he himself at one time
gained his livelihood in the same way. His cleverness, however, drew the attention of some of the
chief persons in Athens, who took pains with his
education; and the celebrated Aspasia herself, it is
said, instructed him in many kinds of knowledge.
Like every other Athenian, he took part in the
wars of the times. His strong constitution enabled
him to bear hardships particularly well, and when
many of his comrades sank under them he was still
full of vigour and energy. Yet his peculiar habits
followed him wherever he went. A story is told,
that on one occasion, whilst in the camp at Potidæa,
he fell into a reverie early one summer morning,
and stood perfectly motionless, without paying the
least attention to any one who spoke to him. So he
continued, not only for an hour or two, but for the
whole day. When evening drew on, the soldiers,
from curiosity, came and sat down by his side, and
ate their evening meal; but still without apparently
disturbing him. At last some of them actually
brought out their beds, that they might lie there
and watch him. Socrates took not the least notice
of them. He remained in the same posture all
through the night, and only woke up from his trance
when the sun rose over Mount Athos the following

morning. Then he started, offered a prayer to Apollo, the god of the sun, and went away.

Such a man must have been a strange companion in daily life; but he was not allowed to follow his own way much in his own home, for his wife Xantippe was excessively cross, and was always scolding him when he did anything she did not like; and sometimes, when she thought he had been talking too long in public, she would rush after him and force him to go home with her. Socrates bore her temper with the greatest meekness, thinking it afforded him opportunities for conquering his own. Now and then he and Xantippe differed as to the manner of entertaining their visitors. Xantippe liked to have a handsome dinner prepared, but Socrates thought it right that the persons who came to see him should be contented with the same fare he had himself. He used to say, that "if they were wise and worthy people they would not care for luxuries; and if they were not he would rather not receive them."

Yet, with all his peculiarities, Socrates was not a person to live apart from other men. It was the custom for the philosophers in those days to take money for the lessons which they gave; or, at any rate, to teach their pupils in private houses; but Socrates did nothing of this kind. Sometimes he would seat himself under the shade of a plane tree, or beneath the rocks near the river Ilissus, to enjoy the quietness and coolness of a country scene; but he was more often to be met with in the dusty road between the Long Walls that joined Athens and Piræus; or in the busy bustling port itself. When he appeared, a crowd generally gathered round him, attracted by his strange appearance, so different from the brilliant Athenians, with their gay, coloured dresses, and polished manners. At first, perhaps,

Socrates would talk with the drovers, and tanners, and artizans, who were at work near him, and make them laugh at his jokes; but by degrees he became more serious, and then, as his wonderfully sweet voice deepened into earnestness, and he discoursed of all that was good and right, and tried to prove the blessedness of virtue and the misery of vice, his hearers felt as if transfixed by a magic spell. Their hearts beat quickly, tears rushed to their eyes, and for the moment, doubtless, they felt —as many Christians also have felt, when listening to a far higher teaching—that the ways of goodness, like those of religion, "are ways of pleasantness, and all her paths are peace."

Like Christians also, many turned away and forgot. Amongst these was Alcibiades. It was impossible not to admire the eloquence and genius of the great philosopher, and Alcibiades long listened to him willingly, for they were friends not only in Athens, but also amidst the scenes of war, where they were thrown together under circumstances which naturally encouraged a kindly feeling for each other. Alcibiades was once severely wounded, and was saved from falling into the hands of his enemies by the valour of Socrates. The reward of a crown, given for distinguished courage, was afterwards due to Socrates; and though it was bestowed upon Alcibiades instead, the philosopher was not in the least jealous, but said every thing he could in praise of his friend. Alcibiades, on this occasion, was equally generous, for he openly proclaimed the superior merit of Socrates; and afterwards we are told that he was enabled to protect Socrates from his enemies, as he had been saved himself. If Socrates had been contented with merely exciting admiration when he spoke, Alcibiades would have been his willing disciple always. But the philo-

sopher desired to teach the rich young Athenian to
govern his temper, to correct his evil inclinations,
and to live a strict and virtuous life for the good of
his country; and the warnings and instructions
which he gave were too severe for Alcibiades to
bear. He turned away from Socrates, and listened
to the teaching of other philosophers, the Sophists,
as they were called, — men, who did not allow that
there was any real difference between right and
wrong, and who encouraged him in indolence and
presumption. The consequences of this teaching
we shall see as the history proceeds.

The conceit of Alcibiades had been much hurt
when the peace of Nicias was concluded. At that
time the Spartans took no notice of him, although
he was a public man, but preferred rather to
transact their business with the prudent intelligent
Nicias; and for this insult he resolved to take revenge.
Every effort was made by him to break the
peace; and having such an object in view he encouraged
the Athenians to enter into a treaty of alliance
with Argos, the constant enemy of Sparta, which
in the end caused them to assist the Argives in a
quarrel with the Lacedæmonians. These smaller
contests were in fact always going on; and thus,
although the peace between Athens and Sparta was
still formally kept, yet the miseries of war continued.

CHAP. XXIII.
COMMENCEMENT OF THE SICILIAN WAR.
B.C. 415.

WHILST Greece was in this jealous unsettled condition
the attention of the Athenians was directed

to a fresh object of conquest; which, however, chiefly tended to the carrying on of the Peloponnesian war, since Sparta and her allies were induced to take part against them.

This object was the conquest of Sicily. Even in the time of Pericles the Athenians had formed designs against that island; and since then they had often interfered in its affairs; for, as there were several Greek settlements on the coasts, it was natural for the inhabitants to call upon the Greeks to assist them whenever they had quarrels, either amongst themselves, or with the Sicels, the natives of the island.

It was an appeal of this kind which induced the Athenians to enter upon a Sicilian war. A dispute having broken out between the towns of Selinus and Segesta in Sicily, the Selinuntians sought for help from Syracuse, the most powerful city in the island; and the Segestans sent ambassadors to Athens. The Segestans had good reason for expecting a favourable hearing. Syracuse, the city which opposed them, had been founded by Dorians. The Syracusans, therefore, claimed kindred with the Spartans, who, we may remember, were a Dorian race, and were likely at any moment to help them in the event of a war. This was in itself a sufficient inducement to the Athenians to do all they could to lessen the power of Syracuse; and when it is considered besides, that the city was wealthy, and that the Athenians were restless, and longing for a decided war, it can scarcely be wondered at if such powerful temptations proved too strong for their prudence and their better feelings.

The help asked for was granted, and a fleet fitted out to be placed under the command of Nicias, Alcibiades, and Lamachus,—the last being a brave and honourable man, who was held in much esteem, though he had not before been employed in any very important service.

The delight of Alcibiades was unbounded. To be the chief of such an expedition was all that he most earnestly desired. But the prudent Nicias neither desired the command nor approved of the undertaking. He was in ill health, and little able to undergo the hardships of a war; and perhaps his prejudices against Alcibiades made him view the scheme on the dark side. Yet there was certainly much to be said against it, and Nicias did not fail to show the Athenians clearly the danger which he dreaded. Even when the decree was passed, he begged them to consider it again, and to revoke it; and whilst he made the request he reminded them that no one had a better right than himself to be heard upon such a subject, since he was speaking against his own interests,—no one having more honour to gain by the expedition than himself. "They must not fancy," he said, "that when they sailed to a foreign land they would leave peace at home. Their enemies in Greece would doubtless take the first opportunity of falling upon them, whilst their forces were divided; for, even at that moment, when they were setting out to found a new empire, many of their old subjects were in open revolt. It would surely be time enough to send assistance to strangers when they had provided for the safety of their own dominions. And neither ought they to listen to the counsels of their own citizens, when they were known to be recklessly ambitious. One there was, especially, who cared not in what danger he might involve his country, so that he might have a brilliant command, which would afford him the means of supporting his extravagance and of repairing the breaches it had made in his private fortune."

Alcibiades rose to reply. "The extravagance which Nicias had censured was, in fact," he said, "a wise liberality. Even the magnificence which he had shortly before displayed at the Olympic games had reflected lustre upon Athens, and raised the credit of the state at a moment when persons supposed it was exhausted by war. But prosperity, he knew, was always attended by envy, and he was not surprised, therefore, that he had given offence. With regard to the Sicilian war, the dangers of which Nicias had spoken were exaggerated. The enemies whom they would leave behind were never less disposed to attack them; and, if they were, the naval forces that remained would be sufficient to prevent any great damage. But, in fact, the spirit shown by the Athenians in invading Sicily, would cow the spirits of the Peloponnesians. Success in a distant island would probably make them masters of Greece; whilst failure would be attended with no danger, since their fleet would enable them to stay as long as they thought fit, and to retire whenever they chose." He ended by observing, "that the eagerness of youth was no less needed in their public counsels than the sobriety of age; and warned them that the high position which they had already attained could only be preserved by an uninterrupted series of brave enterprises."

These arguments agreed with the wishes of the people, and the counsels of Nicias were set aside. The prudent general made one more effort to alarm them. He reminded them of the immense forces which would be required, and of the enormous quantity of supplies which must be provided; since they were likely to be detained at sea by contrary winds, or to be kept in places where food could not be had; whilst the land they were going to was so distant that it might take four months before news from the army could reach Athens. But these difficulties only served to rouse the spirit of the Athenians. They silenced Nicias by saying that the generals should have all the forces they might require; and the preparations for the expedition immediately began.

The news spread rapidly throughout Greece, and the Athenians themselves were in a state of the greatest possible excitement. Every old soldier who happened to have taken part before in the Sicilian quarrels was called upon to tell what he knew of the country; and the sports and exercises of the young were interrupted, whilst they drew the form of the island of Sicily on the ground, and tried to settle what its position was with regard to Carthage and Africa, — a point much more difficult to decide than we can imagine, who have maps to refer to whenever we are in doubt.

It was a time, too, when people were full of omens and prophecies, many of which were evil. Nicias was peculiarly superstitious. It is said that he kept a private soothsayer, whom he consulted in cases of difficulty; and, as it was well known that he disapproved of the war, it is probable that the Athenian priests announced as many bad omens as they could, in order to please him. Alcibiades, on his side, had friendly diviners, who declared that they had found some ancient predictions which foretold that the Greeks were to gain great renown in Sicily; and this, together with the favourable answers received from two oracles which he consulted, kept up the spirits of the people. The Oracle of Delphi, however, was against him.

But further difficulties were still to be thrown in the way of the expedition. The preparations for the voyage were nearly completed, when one morning it was discovered that several of the stone busts of Hermes, or Mercury, the messenger of the gods, which adorned the streets of Athens, had been broken and injured during the night. This might only have been a frolic of some idle persons; but the Athenians, who looked upon such an act as an insult to the gods, and therefore a great crime, could not pass it over lightly. Persons were appointed to inquire into the affair, and great rewards were offered to any one who would discover the offenders. At the same time all Athenians of every rank were called to reveal any other acts of impiety which they knew to have been committed. This command was secretly meant to do injury to Alcibiades, who had before been suspected of irreverent behaviour; and now a person came forward to charge him with a still greater offence, — the profanation of what were called the Eleusinian mysteries.

These mysteries consisted of ceremonies and religious acts which took place in the temple of Demeter or Ceres, the goddess of the earth, at Eleusis, in Attica; and had been introduced amongst the Greeks from the earliest ages. It is said that they were first known and practised by the Egyptians. Some of the ceremonies might be witnessed by all persons, but the mysteries were secrets which were told only to a few, who were forbidden on any account to reveal them.

Alcibiades was accused of having divulged these mysteries by imitating the Eleusinian ceremonies in a private house; and hints were also given that he and some other persons were forming plots against the state. It was a very heavy charge against an Athenian general, and, if proved, would certainly be the means of removing him from his command. What Alcibiades, therefore, most desired was that it should be inquired into at once, whilst he was on the spot to defend himself. His enemies, however, knew that he would very probably be acquitted at that time, whether he were innocent or guilty, because the people were partial to him, and wished him to undertake the command of the Sicilian expedition; and they contrived therefore to delay the trial, so that Alcibiades was obliged to set out on his great undertaking with a serious charge hanging over him, which might at any moment cause his ruin.

This circumstance alone may, doubtless, in a great measure have depressed his spirits; but, when at length the day arrived on which the fleet was to sail, all other fears and hopes must have been forgotten in the feelings excited by the departure. When the Athenian forces came down to embark at Piræus, nearly the whole of the population of Athens, both citizens and foreigners, accompanied them to the water-side, and lined the shores of the harbour. Many were the mournful partings between dear friends and near relations; and even the sight of the immense fleet, and the number and splendour of the troops, which had never been surpassed in any former wars, could not, at that instant, have cheered them. For, how much that was precious to themselves and valuable to the state, was now about to be risked in the dangers of a long voyage and a distant war! All was at length ready. By the sound of a trumpet silence was proclaimed; and, after a pause, a solemn prayer, offered as with one mouth, from the mighty host, rose up to heaven. The voices of the multitudes who stood gazing from the shore, joined in the chorus of entreaty; drink offerings to the gods were poured forth from every ship, from vessels of gold and silver; and when the pæan, or hymn of hope and triumph, had been sung, the fleet moved slowly out of the harbour.

s

CHAP. XXIV.

CONTINUATION OF THE SICILIAN WAR.

WHEN the news of the preparations made by the Athenians for the Sicilian war reached Syracuse, the inhabitants of that city could with difficulty be persuaded to believe it. It was well known that Sparta and the other Peloponnesian states were at that very time enemies of Athens; and it seemed exceedingly unlikely that the Athenians should venture upon a distant and dangerous expedition, and interfere with the quarrels of other people, whilst they were so likely to be invaded themselves. Hermocrates, however, one of the chief persons in Syracuse, who had before exerted himself much to promote peace amongst the Greek towns in Sicily, declared that he had received the intelligence on the best authority; and that it would be very unwise to neglect taking every possible precaution for their safety. He therefore recommended them to strengthen and repair the defences of the city, to procure assistance from the native tribes, and to send embassies to the other Greek towns, both in Sicily and in Italy, to prevent them from joining with the Athenians. He also urged that no time should be lost in dispatching ambassadors to Sparta and Corinth, urging those states to renew the war with Athens. The advice of Hermocrates was at first listened to with doubt and hesitation. It was supposed that he had some secret reasons for endeavouring to frighten the people; but the next information which reached Syracuse proved the truth of his words, and the inhabitants then set themselves vigorously to work to defend their city from the expected attack.

The Athenian fleet, in the meantime, had sailed to Corcyra, where it was joined by the vessels and forces of the states and cities in alliance with Athens. From thence all proceeded along the coast of Italy, hoping that the inhabitants of the Greek colonies in that country would join them. But this hope was vain. Not one of the cities would open its gates to the troops; and only one, Rhegium,—the inhabitants of which had always before been friendly to Athens,—gave them the opportunity of buying provisions. Even there, the soldiers were kept without the walls, whilst the market was brought to them; and the people seemed quite disinclined in any way to assist the expedition.

This disappointment was severely felt by the Athenians, but there was a still greater vexation in store for them. One of their chief inducements to begin a war with Syracuse was the hope of the wealth they should gain from it, and the idea that their Sicilian allies would be both able and willing to bear a large share of the expense. They had even sent envoys to Segesta, the city which begged for their alliance, to inquire into the amount of its treasures; and these envoys brought back wonderful reports of the wealth of the citizens, and the quantity of gold and silver plate which they had seen on the sideboards of the chief persons who entertained them. But now, when the Athenians dispatched messengers from Rhegium, where they were stationed, to Segesta, to concert plans for their further proceedings, and to bring back word how much the Segestans could contribute towards the expenses of the war, it was discovered that all the wealth they were supposed to possess was a delusion. The gold and silver plate, which had been so much admired and coveted, had been borrowed from some neighbouring cities, and lent in turn to the different citizens who gave entertainments; and the sum which the Segestans were really able to give was a mere trifle in comparison with that which was expected from them.

The sudden end of such dazzling expectations exceedingly depressed the spirits of the Athenian generals, — though it surprised Nicias much less than it did his colleagues. Consultations were immediately held as to what ought to be done, and Nicias gave his advice, as usual, very prudently. "It would be desirable," he said, "that they should call upon the Segestans to supply payment for as many ships as they had asked for, and they might afterwards sail to Selinus, the city at enmity with Segesta, and compel the people to come to some agreement with the Segestans. The Athenians would then have done as much as they had offered; and he should recommend that, after coasting along the island of Sicily, to show the strength of their fleet, they should all return home, and not put the state to any more cost or risk."

It was not to be supposed that this very cautious advice could be approved by the other generals. Lamachus wished to make an immediate attack on Syracuse; and Alcibiades declared it would be disgraceful to retire without having done more with their great armament, and proposed a scheme for winning over the Sicilian towns to their side, and then attacking Selinus and Syracuse. This plan was adopted, — for it suited Lamachus much better than the prudent advice of Nicias; and as he could not have his own way, he thought it better to agree to that which came the nearest to it.

Sixty vessels accordingly were sent over to Sicily, under the command of Alcibiades and Lamachus, to hold communications with the several towns which, it might be supposed, would be favourable to the Athenians. The rest remained at Rhegium. The success of Alcibiades and his colleague was not quite what they had hoped for. In one or two places they found friends, but into others they were not allowed to enter; and before they could return to Rhegium, an event happened which entirely altered their plans.

The enemies of Alcibiades had worked unceasingly to injure him since he left Greece. They had encouraged all who chose to bring information against him; and the accusations being of a serious nature, a state galley was sent to Sicily, with orders to convey him and several other persons who were serving with the army, to Athens, to take their trial on the charge of profanation and irreverence to the gods. What was strictly meant by these charges it is not very easy to discover, for the people of Athens had worked themselves up into such a pitch of anger and suspicion, that they had mixed up with it all kinds of accusations. But that which they mostly appear to have imagined was, that the mutilation of the busts of Hermes had some connection with a plot against the government and the liberty of the people. The assertions made were very vague, and some must have been false. One man declared that he knew quite well who the persons were that had mutilated the busts, for that on the same night on which the offence was committed he happened to be in a street by the theatre, and as he was standing behind a pillar, he saw nearly three hundred persons enter the place where the musicians usually sat, and remain there for a time, fifteen or twenty together. "There was a full moon," he said, "and it shone full upon their faces, so that he was able to observe the features of almost all. He did not know at the time what they were met for, but when he heard the next day of the injury done to the busts of Hermes he was sure they must be the guilty persons; and since then some of them had given him money to say nothing about it." It happened that on the night on which this man professed to have seen three hundred persons by the light of the full moon, there was no moon visible. His account, therefore, must have been untrue; but no one thought of remarking this, or, in consequence, stopping the accusations that were going on. The people listened eagerly to all that was told them; and the general belief was that a great conspiracy had been formed to upset the government, in which Alcibiades also was concerned; and a decree was therefore passed to recall him.

He was not made a prisoner,—for that, it was feared, would excite the anger of his troops. He was only ordered to return to Athens in the ship which had been sent for him, and this he did not refuse to do. But Alcibiades had no honourable principles, to guide him under such circumstances. He was willing to serve his country, as long as it suited his own purposes, but when his country turned against him, he saw no harm in revenge. The ship in which he sailed delayed off the coast of Italy, and he and his companions landed, hid themselves till it had sailed again, and then crossed in a merchant vessel to Peloponnesus; from whence Alcibiades proceeded to Sparta, to join himself with the enemies of his native city, and devote his talents and his energy to the injury of Athens. When his escape was made known at Athens he was sentenced to death, his property was given to the state, and the priests and priestesses were ordered to curse him, according to an ancient custom, with their faces turned to the west, and waving red banners in the air.

Alcibiades being gone, Nicias had less difficulty in persuading Lamachus to agree to his plans for carrying on the war; for Lamachus held him in great respect, and was willing to submit to his authority.

But Nicias had now given up the idea of ending the war quickly, and after sailing to two or three places in order to find out what help might really be expected from the people of the island, he prepared to besiege Syracuse.

The fears of the Syracusans were much lessened by this time; and even when the Athenians encamped round their city, the Syracusan horsemen were so bold, that they used to ride up to their camp and ask what they were come for. A battle, however, that soon afterwards took place, in which they were defeated, changed their ideas, and they began to perceive that it would be necessary to exert themselves vigorously.

The winter was now coming on, and the war was as usual suspended. The Athenians moved away from Syracuse to the island of Naxos, and sent a vessel to Athens to ask for a supply of money, and troops of cavalry; and the Syracusans, by the advice of Hermocrates, took measures to fortify their town, and sent ambassadors to obtain assistance from Corinth and Sparta.

The petition of the Syracusans was strengthened by the advice of Alcibiades, who did not fail to use the utmost efforts to persuade the Spartans to join in the war. The very arguments which he had brought forward at Athens to induce his fellow citizens to begin the Sicilian expedition, he now turned into what might be called accusations against them. "The invasion of Sicily," he said, "was but the beginning of the ambitious designs of the Athenians. When they had conquered that island, they would turn their arms against the Greeks in Italy, and would afterwards attack Carthage; and in the end Peloponnesus would be invaded, and the whole of Greece made subject to them. No time therefore was to be lost in sending a body of troops to Sicily, but especially a Spartan commander to direct them." He also advised that Attica should be invaded, so that the Athenian forces might be engaged at the same time both at home and abroad.

The Spartan government had before this planned the invasion of Attica, and now they began to see that it might be well to hasten their movements. Gylippus, one of their chief generals, was also ordered to sail to Sicily, with as many ships and men as he could raise immediately. Some Corinthian forces were also to accompany him; and a further supply of troops was to be sent as soon as possible.

When the spring returned, Syracuse was again besieged. The inhabitants had worked well at the fortifications during the winter, but they had neglected one very important hill called Epipolæ, or, as we should say, "Overton," or "Overtown," from its overlooking the town. This omission they discovered before the siege was actually renewed; but whilst they were preparing to guard the hill, the Athenians, who were more quicksighted and expeditious, perceived what a good place it would be for their camp, and by mounting to the top at full speed took possession of it for themselves.

The possession of this hill gave them a great advantage; and their first attacks against the Syracusans were so successful, that many of the Sicels, or natives, were induced to take part with them. Provisions also arrived from several places, so that they were full of confidence, whilst the spirits of the poor people in the besieged city sank, and their hopes grew less and less. As is often the case with persons in difficulty, they became unjust, and caused Hermocrates and two other generals to be thrown into prison, fancying that they were the cause of their misfortunes; and they were just beginning to think of making peace with the Athenians, when fresh vigour was given them by the happy intelligence that Gylippus and the Spartans had landed in the island, and were marching to their assistance

CHAP. XXV.
CONCLUSION OF THE SICILIAN WAR.
B. C. 413.

The inhabitants of Syracuse assembled in arms, and went forth to meet Gylippus when he drew near the city, and to welcome him as their deliverer. And they had indeed great reason to rejoice. From the moment of his arrival, the whole prospect of their affairs was changed. His vigour and talents gave them confidence; and though Nicias opposed him bravely, it was soon evident that the position of the Athenians was becoming very dangerous. The possession of the hill of Epipolæ had been their greatest advantage, as it had enabled them to begin building a wall round the city; but Gylippus contrived to stop this work, by building another wall which interfered with it; and then Nicias saw that he could not carry out his first plans, and thought it would be better to remove his army to the opposite side of the harbour.

The Syracusans at the same time began to man their fleet, so that they might be able to resist their enemies at sea, where the Athenians were generally victorious; and all these circumstances united made

Nicias think so badly of his own prospects, that he wrote letters to the people of Athens to be read in the Assembly, describing his distress and dangers. Before this he had only sent messages by word of mouth, for letters were not written every day then as they are now. "The Syracusans," he said, "still expected more succours, and would soon attack him both by land and sea. His ships and their crews were no longer in a flourishing state; the ships, having been so long at sea, were growing leaky, and the number of the men was much diminished. It would be quite necessary, therefore, to send more forces and more money; and he must also beg for a new commander to take his place, as he was suffering from a very painful disorder, and was really unfit to bear the burthen of his office. If these suggestions were not agreed to, the army must be recalled; but whatever they might resolve, something must be done as soon as the spring came." This was very gloomy news for the Athenians to receive, but it did not overcome their proud spirit. A new armament, under the command of Demosthenes (the same who had distinguished himself at Pylos), and another general named Eurymedon, was made ready and sent forth, as Nicias had desired, early in the spring. They would not consent that Nicias should give up the command, but it was hoped that Demosthenes would be a great assistance to him. These fresh forces were collected at the time when the Spartans, following the advice of Alcibiades, had invaded Attica, and approached so near Athens, that it was quite like a besieged city. Money was becoming every day more scarce, provisions were only to be obtained with difficulty, and it seems quite wonderful that they should in any way have been able to carry on a distant war.

Gylippus had not been idle whilst Nicias was

sending for help from Athens. He had collected allies from the people of Sicily, and sent envoys to procure more forces from Sparta and Corinth; and when Demosthenes set sail from Athens, he was just about to attack the Athenians at Syracuse with increased vigour.

His great object was to persuade the Syracusans to man their ships, and engage in a sea-fight. If they were successful there, he knew that it would give them great confidence, and very much alarm the Athenians, who fancied that by sea they were invincible.

The Syracusans were not very easily persuaded, but they did consent at last, and several sea-fights took place, in which the Athenians were by no means as victorious as they had expected to be, though they cannot exactly be said to have been defeated.

The hopes of the Syracusans were now much raised, and they were looking forward to a complete triumph both by sea and land, when the Athenian fleet, commanded by Demosthenes, sailed proudly into the great harbour to the sound of martial music. Eight thousand men were on board, all gallantly equipped and ready for battle.

The astonishment and dismay of the Syracusans were excessive. Athens, they knew, was suffering from the invading army of the Spartans; how, then, could such a force have been spared?

Their terrors, however, were greater than the hopes of the Athenians at the arrival of the fleet; for when Demosthenes began to enquire into the state of affairs, he perceived that it was exceedingly doubtful whether even now Syracuse could be taken. One thing was certain, that Nicias ought to have attacked the Syracusans, and thoroughly frightened them, before they had time to call in the help of their friends. His slow measures had been the cause of great evil, and all that Demosthenes could now do was to reattempt some great thing at once. He therefore proposed that they should try to recover possession of Epipolæ, so that they might be able to complete the wall round the town.

There seemed no chance of being able to ascend the hill in the daytime, as it was closely watched by the enemy's troops. It was determined, therefore, to make the attempt by night. The soldiers were told to provide themselves with food enough for five days, and the masons and carpenters were to be in readiness with their tools; in short, every necessary preparation was made for taking possession of the hill, and afterwards building the wall.

Nicias, being very infirm from illness, was to remain in the camp; but in the dead of the night the other generals set forth. The first attack they made succeeded, and they reached the cross wall which had been built by the Syracusans, and began to pull it down. By that time Gylippus and some of the Syracusan troops had sallied forth against them, and the Athenians, who were pressing forward hastily, were thrown into confusion. There was a bright moonlight, but it served rather to perplex than to help them, for it was not strong enough to enable them clearly to distinguish their friends from their foes. The space in which they were all fighting was very narrow, and the noise of the battle prevented any questions and answers being heard. The Spartans and Syracusans also found out the particular pass word which the Athenians used, when they wanted to know each other, and managed to perplex them very much by repeating it themselves; whilst some of the Athenian allies, being of the same race as the Spartans, were accustomed to the same war cry, which sounded to the Athenians like

that of their enemies. All these circumstances
caused such excessive confusion, that no one scarcely
knew whom he was fighting with, or what he ought
to do; and several times the Athenians, by mistake,
fought with each other. The Athenians at length
were driven back towards a narrow way by which
they had ascended the hill; and as there was not
space enough in it for them all, many were forced
over a cliff at the side, and dashed to pieces. Between two and three thousand are said to have
perished on this night; and so great a loss entirely
destroyed their hopes of finally taking Syracuse.

When a council was held after the battle to settle
what was to be done, Demosthenes gave his opinion
most strongly and decidedly for a retreat. "Sickness was spreading," he said, "amongst the men;
and if they did not at once return to Attica where
they might be really useful to their country, he
feared that the Spartans and Syracusans would
attack their fleet, and so completely ruin them."

To the surprise of every one, Nicias was the only
person who rather differed from this opinion. He
had been secretly told that there were persons in
Syracuse who were friendly to the Athenians; and
though he did not very much depend upon them,
yet this knowledge made him more hopeful than
the other generals. Demosthenes then begged that
at least they might all remove to Catana, one of
the Sicilian cities in alliance with Athens, which
was much more healthy at that time than Syracuse;
but Nicias was so bent upon remaining where they
were, that every one at last gave way to him.

It was a most unfortunate resolution; and very
shortly afterwards Nicias himself saw what a mistake he had made. The Syracusans received fresh
succours from their allies, and from Peloponnesus,
and made ready to renew their attacks both by sea

and land. Then Nicias agreed that it would be well to retreat. With the utmost secrecy the Athenians carried on their preparations for departure. Every thing seemed to favour them, and the hour was fixed for the troops to embark. Just as it was near, an eclipse of the moon took place. The Athenians, knowing little or nothing of the cause of such an appearance, considered it an evil omen; and Nicias especially, always full of superstition, after consulting with the soothsayers who accompanied the army, expressed his fixed determination to remain where he then was till the next full moon.

That determination completed the ruin of the unhappy Athenians. The Syracusans found out that it was their intention to retreat, and resolved to force them to a battle before they went. A sea fight took place, in which, although the Syracusans were at last routed, the Athenians lost eighteen ships with their crews, together with their general Eurymedon; and being then perfectly in despair, they had but one hope left, which was to force their way through the enemy's fleet out of the harbour, and, if possible, sail to Catana. In case this scheme failed, they were to burn their ships, and make their way over land to some part of the island which was friendly to them. The object of the Athenian commanders on this occasion was to make the battle as much like a land fight as possible; for the ships were crowded into such a small space that there was no room, whilst they were in the harbour, to turn and manage them as they were accustomed to do in the open sea. Grappling-irons, or iron hands, were therefore contrived by which they might seize the enemy's ships, and keep them close till they were taken. These and many other precautions, required by the great danger they were in, were carefully attended to; and when the men were about to embark, Nicias called them together to address them for the last time, and rouse them to courage in the approaching conflict.

All the motives which could make them either hope or fear were earnestly put before them. He spoke to them of their country, and reminded them that they were now on the eve of a battle which would decide whether or not they should ever see it again. "Their past misfortunes," he said, "were no reasonable ground for despondency, and their forces were still sufficient to encourage reasonable hopes. It only remained for all on board to do their duty. They must conquer. If they did not, their enemies would follow them to Attica, and the commonwealth of Athens would sink under their power. It was an occasion, therefore, worthy of every effort of skill and valour. Not one fleet, and one army, but the whole power, and the last hopes, and the great name of Athens were at stake, and in their hands."

The Syracusans, on their part, were no less careful than the Athenians. They had discovered the use which was to be made of the iron hands, and formed a plan for avoiding the mischief by stretching a screen of hides over the sterns of their vessels, so that the grappling-irons might not be able to get hold of them. The commanders also addressed their men, and cheered them with the prospect of a complete victory, and the hope of revenging themselves for all they had suffered; and in this state of excited, eager feeling on both sides, the battle began.

Demosthenes took the command of the Athenian fleet, and Nicias remained on shore with a body of troops to guard the camp, in case of the battle being lost. But he could not station himself at his post without once more summoning round him the cap-

tains of the vessels, addressing each by his name, and
exhorting them to courage yet more earnestly, as
he spoke to them of their wives and children, their
hearths and altars, all that they held dear and sacred,
which was now either to be lost or saved.

The Athenians began the battle by a violent
attack on the bar, at the entrance of the harbour,
the great obstacle to their escape, which was guarded
by some of the Syracusan ships. Their efforts were
so great that they overpowered their enemies, and
nearly succeeded in breaking the fastenings of the
bar. But they were interrupted by the sudden approach of the whole Syracusan fleet, and the battle
then raged on all sides.

The difficulty of moving in the narrow space
within the harbour, — the mingling of friends and
foes, — the din of sounds, which drowned the voices
of the commanders, — caused a scene of disorder beyond all that can be imagined. The Athenians, both
men and officers, fought desperately, each one as if
the event of the battle depended solely on his own
exertions; and all urging one another to force the
outlet by which they were to find a passage to their
homes. The general tumult was increased by the
voices of those who stood upon the shore and
watched the battle. As their friends or their foes
appeared victorious, the air rang with shouts of joy
or cries of terror. But at last all doubts were ended.
The Athenians were seen pursued by their enemies,
and making their way to the shore; and one fearful
wail of agony from their comrades on land, told
that all was lost.

That was the last battle between the Athenians
and the Syracusans. The Syracusans sailed back to
the city, and raised a trophy of triumph; and the
Athenians, forgetting even to send a herald to
recover the dead bodies of their countrymen, in

order that they might be buried,—a duty which was quite sacred in the eyes of the Greeks,—turned all their thoughts to an immediate retreat by land. They did not however set out at once, for the Syracusans sent false messages to them, bidding them beware of marching at night; and so induced them to delay, in order that they might themselves go before them and block up the passes.

It was not till the third day after the battle that the retreat of the Athenians began; and very sad it must have been. To look upon the bodies of their friends which it then struck them as impiety to leave unburied, was a heavy trial; but there was another yet greater,—the parting from the sick and the wounded. There were few, indeed, who could restrain their tears, as they heard these unhappy men entreating to be taken, and saw them drag themselves feebly along after the army, and then drop down from fatigue with cries of bitter grief. Many probably recalled, with mournful thoughts, the triumphant pride with which they had set forth from Athens,—the glittering arms, the wondering crowds, the solemn prayer, and the glad song of triumph, now exchanged for shame, and suffering, and fear.

Nicias, though almost overcome by pain of body and anguish of mind, did his very utmost to cheer his troops. He walked along the lines, speaking loudly that all might hear him, and exhorting them not to give way to despondency. "He, himself, was not," he said, "conscious of any offence against the gods, or against his fellow-creatures, yet he was suffering equally with themselves. But he confidently expected deliverance, for he had not deserved punishment; and, in like manner, they might hope that the misfortunes they had already endured had been sufficient to satisfy the envy and to move the pity of the gods, and that their affairs would soon take a favourable turn. Let them once reach the part of the island which was peopled by their friends, and they would be safe, and might look forward to a return to their homes, and a joyful meeting with their families."

This speech no doubt was an encouragement to the Athenians, though it would have been very little comfort to Christians to hear their misfortunes spoken of as caused by the envy of the gods. Nothing indeed sounds more dreary and hopeless to us than the consolations with which the heathens of old endeavoured to support themselves under calamity. They had great notions of the power of their deities, but of the Love of the One True God they had never heard.

The army was now formed into a hollow square, with the baggage and the persons belonging to the camp, who were not soldiers, in the middle. They were only able to march five miles the first day, being stopped by parties of Syracusans who followed them. The next day they only went half the distance, as they waited in a little plain to collect provisions and lay in a supply of water. So they advanced with great difficulty,—Gylippus and the Syracusans blocking up their way, and preventing them from procuring sufficient food.

The Athenian generals soon saw that their only hope of safety was to march by night; and they lighted fires in the camp to deceive the enemy, and then again set forward. But in this night march Nicias and Demosthenes were unfortunately separated; and whilst Nicias led on his troops in good order, Demosthenes followed with his, less regularly, at a distance behind. The Syracusans pursued, and the next morning came up with Demosthenes before noon. The Athenians were surrounded, and driven into an olive ground, enclosed by a wall, with a road running along the high ground above it, from which they could easily be attacked. Here, finding the strength of his soldiers utterly exhausted, Demosthenes humbled himself to submit. Six thousand men laid down their arms on the express condition that they were to be saved from any violent death, whether by bloodshed, chains, or hunger.

Nicias was overtaken the next day, and told that Demosthenes had surrendered. He refused at first to believe the fact; but, when he found that it was actually true, he endeavoured to make terms with the Syracusans, and sent a message to them to propose that Athens should pay all the expenses of the war, if they might be allowed to retreat. The Syracusans refused the offer, and still followed. The Athenians moved on till the next morning, when, reaching the banks of a little stream, they rushed forward to quench the raging thirst from which they were suffering. In their eagerness they fell one upon another, and numbers were trampled under foot and suffocated. The Syracusans threw themselves upon them; but they still struggled, not to escape from death, but to snatch from each other a draught of the tainted water. Then, at last, Nicias surrendered, making no terms with Gylippus, except that the slaughter of his unfortunate men should be stopped.

Neither Nicias nor Demosthenes made any agreement as to their own fate. Gylippus would willingly have carried them back with him to Sparta as proofs of his victory, but he could not follow his own wishes. The Syracusans urged that they should be condemned to death, and the sentence was passed and executed. The fate of Nicias is one of the saddest to be met with in the history of Greece, or perhaps of any other country. He had talent, prudence, wealth, honour, and amiability; and it seems that he ought to have been of the utmost service to his country. But his timidity and superstition interfered with these advantages, and in the end brought ruin upon himself and upon his native land. The miseries endured by the prisoners were, however, enough to make us pity them even more than Nicias and Demosthenes.

A considerable number contrived to escape, but those who were kept were placed in a dreadful prison, which was, in fact, a quarry hollowed in the side of the hill Epipolæ. It was a hundred feet in depth, and the rock was so steep that there was not the slightest possibility of escape. Here they were exposed to the scorching rays of the sun by day, and the chilly, damp air by night. So little food was given them that they could scarcely be kept alive, and the thirst they suffered was more terrible than can be described. The greater number were after some weeks sold as slaves. Some, it is said, gained their freedom, or induced their enemies to show them favour, by repeating the verses of the poet Euripides, which so charmed the Sicilians that, for the sake of the poet, they were willing to be kind to his unhappy fellow countrymen.

CHAP. XXVI.

THE RETURN OF ALCIBIADES.

B.C. 407.

Whilst all these terrible events were happening in Sicily, the Athenians were managing their affairs at home without any suspicion of the greatness of the misfortune which had befallen them. One morning, however, a stranger landed in Piræus, and going to a barber's shop to be shaved, began to talk about the Sicilian expedition, and mentioned the loss of the Athenians as if it were a fact which every one must know. The barber hastened directly to the archons, who brought him before an Assembly of the people to tell what he knew; but, as he could give no account of the person that had brought the information, he was considered as a false witness, and it is said that he was put to the torture as a punishment. The sad news was confirmed soon afterwards by other persons who had escaped from Sicily; yet it was long before the Athenians could really be brought to believe it. When, however, they were at last convinced of the fact, their regret for the past was only overpowered by their fears for the future. The victorious Spartans might, they knew, soon be expected to appear before the port of Piræus, whilst their armies and those of their allies were at the same time carrying on the war in Greece. The Athenians had no money, no ships, no soldiers,—one might have supposed that their spirits must have sunk completely. But they did not. The people seemed to have gained wisdom by their misfortunes. Without delay they chose certain persons of sense and discretion to advise what was to be done; and then every man set to work to provide against the dangers which threatened them, by building new ships, saving as much money as possible, and taking other measures for safety.

The Spartans, being a slow-moving, cautious people, did not follow up their success as quickly as the Athenians probably would have done under the same circumstances. Yet they had everything in their favour. Even in Attica itself they had obtained a fixed settlement; for they possessed a fortress, called Decelea, so near to Athens that they could almost see from it the great public processions of the Athenians on their festival days; and from this fortress they could sally forth and annoy their enemies at any moment. What was still more important, they were every day gaining over to their cause the small states and islands which had formerly been subject to Athens; and they had entered into a treaty with two great Persian satraps, or governors, who were wishing to weaken the power of Athens. Alcibiades was the chief adviser of the Spartans at this time; and when the Athenians, having somewhat recovered their strength, began to revenge themselves upon their subjects and allies for having deserted them, he was a distinguished person in the numerous battles and sieges which took place. Alcibiades was not, however, liked by the Spartans. Agis, one of the kings, was his personal enemy, and the people suspected him of treachery. This suspicion was not quite unfounded. Alcibiades had but one wish in going over to the Spartans, — that of humbling his own countrymen till they should be sorry for their conduct, and recall him. He did not, therefore, wish to see the Spartans too powerful; and when he found it probable that they might be so, he secretly gave counsel to the Persian governors not to help them too much; saying "that it would be much more advantageous for Persia to let Sparta and Athens quarrel with and so weaken each other." Having gained influence by this advice, he next sent secret envoys to Athens, who informed the people how intimate he was with the Persian governor, and suggested to them that if they would recall him, and make such changes in the government as he might propose, he would persuade the powerful Persian nobles to take part with Athens rather than with Sparta. In this way Alcibiades worked for his own selfish purposes, and was treacherous to every one whenever it suited him.

The Athenians were at first very unwilling to consent to the proposals of Alcibiades; but Pisander, one of the envoys, persuaded them that the prosperity of the state entirely depended upon the support of the Persian king, and that no one would be able to obtain this support for them as well as Alcibiades; and at last they consented that Pisander should enter into a treaty with Alcibiades, and find out through him what the king of Persia would require if they were to enter into an alliance with that country. This treaty came to nothing, for the claims of the Persians were much greater than the Athenians would agree to; and it seemed as if an obstacle was now placed in the way of the return of Alcibiades to Athens. But the question as to the change of government was not in consequence set at rest, for Alcibiades was not the only Athenian who desired to see an alteration made in it. There were always some who wished for what is called an oligarchy—that is, the government of a few persons of rank and influence—instead of a democracy, or the government of the people: and now, although Alcibiades was absent, these persons joined together, and by working secretly to bring over others to their notions, at length succeeded in their object; and Four Hundred new rulers were appointed, who were to rule with absolute power. It was endeavoured also to make the same changes in the government of the island of Samos, where the Athenian fleet was then stationed, and which was subject to Athens; but in that island, and amongst the soldiers and seamen, there were more persons in favour of the old form of government than the new.

The disturbances caused by these two parties were very great, yet they proved extremely useful to Alcibiades. Whether the government of Athens was an oligarchy or a democracy was of much less consequence to him than his own return; and, therefore, when the inhabitants of Samos, who favoured the old government, sent to him to beg that he would come to them and give them his advice and assistance, he immediately went. There was a great public meeting held at Samos to receive him; and, as usual, he made a boastful, untrue speech, declaring that he had great influence with Tissaphernes, the chief Persian satrap in Asia Minor, and that Tissaphernes had told him that if he could only rely on the Athenians, they should not want pay for their seamen,—no, not if he should be forced to turn the furniture of his palace into money for them,—and that he would bring his fleet to help them instead of the Spartans. All this was to be done, however, only if Alcibiades was recalled.

The real truth was, that Tissaphernes was wavering between Sparta and Athens,—doing, in fact, what Alcibiades himself had recommended,—sometimes appearing to favour one, and sometimes the other. But the people of Samos believed all that they were told, and, having made Alcibiades their general, sent him to make a treaty with Tissaphernes.

In the meantime the new rulers at Athens made themselves very much disliked by their severity, and people began to suspect them of holding communications with the Spartans. The feeling excited against them increased every day, and there seemed a prospect of a civil war, when a new alarm was caused at Athens by the news that the Spartans had gained a victory by sea off the island of Euboea, which was subject to Athens, and that the people of Eubœa had revolted. The consternation of the people at this intelligence was beyond description. With two parties hating each other at home, and an enemy gaining such triumphs over them abroad, the state seemed on the brink of ruin. Something, they saw, must instantly be done to restore peace amongst themselves; and they immediately agreed to do away with their four hundred rulers, and to make the government more like what it was before,—though not so much of a democracy as it had been. The laws and regulations were not all settled then; the principal alteration was the removal of the four hundred persons who were so much disliked. A decree was, however, passed, most important to Alcibiades,—that all exiles should be recalled; and ambassadors were sent to the army at Samos, to tell the changes which had taken place, and to beg that the war with Sparta, might be carried on vigorously.

Alcibiades was now openly acknowledged as an Athenian general, but it was not till three years afterwards, B. C. 407, that he returned to Athens. During that time he served his country greatly, by defeating the Peloponnesians many times, both by sea and land. On one occasion he was so entirely victorious that one of the Spartan officers gave the following short account of the sad situation of himself and his men: "Our good luck is gone; Mindarus, the general, is dead, the men are starving, and we know not what to do." This may well be called a Laconic epistle. The Lacedæmonians, or people of Laconia, were celebrated for their short way of expressing themselves, and our word laconic, or short, is derived from them.

In one point, however, Alcibiades failed. He was not able to bring over the Persians to the Athenian cause. Though he offered presents to the

Persian satrap, whom he called his friend, and tried to make the Spartans suspicious of him, and by that means to cause a quarrel, yet he never succeeded in really destroying the alliance between Persia and Sparta. Still, he was entirely restored to the favour of his countrymen, and when, after all his victories, he returned to Athens, it was as a conqueror, and not as an exile. As he sailed into the port of Piræus, with the ships he had taken, laden with prisoners and stored with treasures, the crowds which flocked to the shore to receive him were almost as many as those which had assembled to witness his departure for Sicily. Every eye was turned upon him, and the greater number of those present were willing to forget his faults, and to consider him merely as an injured person, who had been punished from the malice of his enemies. They followed him with shouts of joy, showering garlands of flowers upon his head, as he proceeded from Piræus to the city, there to present himself before the public Assembly; and a speech which he then made, asserting his innocence, and bewailing his misfortunes, touched every heart. Not one of his enemies dared to raise a voice against him; the priests were ordered to recant their curses; his property was restored; a golden crown was decreed to him; the records of the accusations against him were thrown into the sea, and he was appointed commander-in-chief of all the armies of the state, both by sea and land.

Alcibiades was now in the position which he had so long and earnestly desired; and his first act was a wise one, for it was an endeavour to show his respect for religion. In former days there had been, at stated periods a solemn procession from Athens to Eleusis, where the sacred rites were performed, which Alcibiades was said to have profaned. Since the Spartans had obtained possession of the fortress of Decelea, this procession had been given up, from the fear of surprise and interruption from the enemy. Alcibiades now undertook to restore the procession, and to perform all the ancient ceremonies; and, having taken every precaution against danger, he with a body of soldiers, escorted the priests and their attendants to Eleusis, and thus enabled them to return to all their ancient customs. The Spartan commander at Decelea was either not strong enough to interrupt them, or probably he felt it would be irreligious to do so; and Alcibiades, having done what was so well pleasing to his fellow citizens, rose even higher in their favour than before.

CHAP. XXVII.

THE BATTLE OF ARGINUSÆ, AND THE UNJUST SENTENCE AGAINST THE ATHENIAN GENERALS.

B.C. 406.

WHEN the Spartans found that Alcibiades was restored to his country, they felt that it would be necessary to take some vigorous measures for carrying on the war; and especially to fix upon a general who might be fitted to oppose him. The person they appointed was Lysander, a man not very unlike Alcibiades, for he was clever and agreeable in manner, but wanting in real truth and honesty of purpose. There was another cause also which made the Spartans particularly anxious to have a clever commander just at this time. The Persian king, Darius, had sent one of his younger sons, named Cyrus, to help the Lacedæmonians in the war, and to govern all the country on the sea coast of Asia Minor. But the Spartans were rather afraid that Tissaphernes, the satrap who had once been the friend of Alcibiades, would try to injure their cause with the young prince, for he was never heartily an ally of the Spartans, although he had not actually broken off the alliance with them. It was necessary therefore, that the Spartans should have some clever person to keep up the friendship of Cyrus, and there was no one more likely to do this than Lysander. He was accordingly sent to the coast of Asia Minor, with the Spartan fleet, and from thence he proceeded to Sardis, where Cyrus was. The young prince received him most graciously, promising, according to the eastern mode of speaking, that sooner than he would allow the Spartans to want money, he would melt down the precious metals which ornamented his throne. Lysander was encouraged by this to beg that some additional pay might be given to the men who served in the war, as he thought that the crews of the Athenian vessels would be induced to desert to them, if they had hope of higher pay, Cyrus replied " that he was bound by the king's orders, and that it was settled by treaty how much money should be given to the Lacedæmonians to assist them in keeping up their fleet, so that it was not in his power to grant Lysander's request." Lysander, of course, could say no more at that moment. But there was a great entertainment given by Cyrus the same day to the Spartan ambassadors, and before the banquet was finished, Cyrus, who was much pleased with Lysander, gave the cup, out of which he had been drinking, into his hands, according to the Greek custom of showing hospitality and kindness, and begged Lysander to tell him what he could do to oblige him. Lysander seized the opportunity to repeat his request, and this time it was granted. The seamen received additional pay, and money was given by Cyrus besides, which was of the greatest service to the Spartans.

Alcibiades on his part took care to increase the Athenian fleet, and to keep a watch upon his enemies; but now, when he had obtained the great object of his wishes, success seemed to forsake him. The Athenians were defeated in several engagements, and the people, who were always changeable, laid the blame on Alcibiades. It was said that he gave up the guidance of the war to persons who were not able to manage it, and that he himself only thought of pleasure and self indulgence; and these charges were probably not altogether false, for he was always bent upon gratifying himself, as well as serving his country. He was removed from his command, and instead of returning to Athens sailed away to the Chersonesus, where he had built himself a stronghold to which he might retire in case of necessity, for no doubt he was long before aware that his favour with the Athenians was not likely to last.

Conon was the name of the general who succeeded Alcibiades, and nine colleagues were joined with him, who became celebrated on acccount of a most severe and unjust sentence, which was passed upon several of them in the following year. But before we speak of this, we must go back to Lysander, who still remained with the Spartan fleet off the coast of Asia Minor. Being a very selfish and ambitious man, he cared little for his country's glory, except so far as it might increase his own; and just then his thoughts were less turned to the carrying on of the war than to the formation of a league with some of the principal men in the Greek cities in Asia, by which they might assist each other in destroying Athens, and then gain absolute power for themselves. He was full of these schemes when the time for which he held his command came to an end, and another commander, Callicratidas, was sent to take his place. Callicratidas was as unlike Lysander as possible. He was brave, honourable, and unselfish, earnestly desirous of his country's good, and hating every thing like deceit. Lysander disliked him extremely, and did all he could to tease and dishearten him. He sent back to Cyrus the money which the Persian prince had granted him, and so left Callicratidas without any, and he also instructed his allies to withold their help from the new general. Callicratidas suffered a great deal of inconvenience in consequence of Lysander's selfishness, and was obliged to make a journey to Sardis, to see Cyrus, and ask for the money he wanted. Cyrus kept him there some days without giving him an audience. Whenever he called at the palace he was told to wait till the next day, and when he came again he was put off till the day after. One day when he went there, a banquet was going on, and he was informed that Cyrus was drinking. "I will wait till he has finished his draught," said Callicratidas: but although he did wait, he was not treated any better; and at last, quite worn out, he went away bewailing the wretched condition of the Greeks, who were obliged to humble themselves to the barbarians, for the sake of money; and declaring, that if ever he returned home safely, he would exert all his power to make peace with Athens.

If Callicratidas had lived, the fate of both Athens and Sparta might have been very different from what it was. But he was killed the same year in which he undertook his command in a great sea fight near the Arginusæ, three small islands off the coast of Æolis, in Asia Minor.

It is said that a soothsayer warned him before the battle that an evil omen had been observed, and that he would probably be slain. But Callicratidas would not be alarmed, and replied that "Sparta would suffer no hurt from his death, but that he should be dishonoured by flight."

The battle of Arginusæ was the greatest that had, up to that time, been fought between the fleets of Athens and Sparta. The Athenians were completely victorious, but they lost a great number of their men, and it was this loss that occasioned the harsh sentence, which has before been mentioned, to be passed upon the generals. The Athenians were indeed delighted at the victory, and rewarded the slaves who had served in the battle most generously; but they said that many lives might have been saved if the generals had shown proper attention to a number of poor men who were left clinging to the Athenian vessels which were disabled in the conflict; and they complained bitterly of the dead having been left unburied. The fact was that after the battle the generals, thinking it right to pursue their enemies, sailed away from the Arginusæ, leaving special directions with some of the inferior officers, to go to the wrecks and take care of the poor men. A storm came on, which prevented the officers from obeying the orders, and in consequence the unfortunate men perished, and the dead were left unburied. Theramenes, one of the officers who had been told to attend to these duties, was the foremost in accusing the generals of having neglected them. Upon being brought to trial, the generals stated the facts just as they had occurred, and pleaded that if any person were to blame, it must be the officers and not the generals;

though they did not themselves see that there had been a fault in either, since they all would have done their duty if the storm had not prevented them. Several witnesses were called who proved that this statement was true, and the people seemed inclined to favour the generals; but unfortunately, the trial was not concluded on that day, because it was growing dark, and there was not light enough to see how many persons held up their hands for the generals, and how many against them. Some days passed before there was another Assembly of the people, and in that time Theramenes and the other enemies of the generals worked in every way possible to excite a feeling against them. When the Assembly met again, all those who had lost friends in the battle came forward to make an appeal against the generals. One man declared that he had been preserved by clinging to a meal tub, and that his comrades, whom he saw sinking near him, entreated him, if he lived, to tell the Athenians that their generals had left the brave defenders of their country to perish. This caused a loud outcry, and the clamour of the people was so great that they would not listen to any thing said in defence of the unfortunate commanders. The magistrates gave way, all except one, the upright, fearless philosopher, Socrates, who protested that the way in which the trial was carried on was illegal, and refused to join in it. But his one voice was of no avail against the shouts of the multitude. Eight of the generals who commanded in the battle were condemned to death, and six, who were present, were immediately executed.

CHAP. XXVIII.

THE BATTLE OF ÆGOS POTAMI.

B.C. 405.

This great national sin was followed by the ruin of Athens. The people, indeed, repented of their cruel haste, and when they found, as they soon did, that the accusations brought against the generals were false, they passed decrees against those who had urged their trial. But they could not restore the lives so unjustly taken, and neither did they succeed in punishing the false accusers, who all at that time escaped. Theramenes especially remained a favourite with the people, though we shall find that the vengeance of Heaven did overtake him in the end.

For some time after the battle of Arginusæ the Athenian fleet was left without a rival. Early, however, in the summer of the next year Lysander was again appointed to command the Spartans. He did not take the title of admiral, as it was against the Spartan laws that the same person should hold that office twice; but by his influence with Cyrus he obtained sufficient assistance to enable him to carry on the war with as much energy as ever. The battle which at last ended the long Peloponnesian war, is called the battle of Ægos Potami. It was fought near Sestos, in Asia Minor; but it can scarcely be called a regular engagement, and it would probably never have taken place if the Athenians had not been strangely negligent. Their fleet and that of the Spartans had both been sailing along the coast and chasing each other; and the Athenians having landed at Ægos Potami, which was merely an open beach, proceeded at their leisure to Sestos to buy provisions. The Spartans watched them, but did not attempt to disturb them, and the Athenians, growing more careless, landed in the same manner another day, and wandered farther up the country. The fortified dwelling of Alcibiades was near this part of the coast, and from his tower he could see all that went on. Observing the false security of the Athenians, he came down to the sea coast to give them warning, and advised them to remove their camp to Sestos, which was friendly to them. The Athenian commanders, however, would not listen to him, but bade him remember that they were the generals, and not he. So Alcibiades went back to his tower, and the Athenians continued to wander about the country at their will. On the fifth day, Lysander gave orders that the vessels which had been sent every day to watch the movements of the Athenians should, as soon as they saw them wandering over the country, return to the middle of the channel and hoist a shield. This was a signal for the whole Spartan fleet. They collected for battle and attacked the Athenian fleet. Conon alone, of six generals who were in command, saw the danger in time and escaped. The crews of the other vessels were too far off to be brought back, and the ships, being nearly empty, were easily taken. A body of Spartan troops also landed and pursued the Athenians who had gone on shore in every direction; and the greater part were taken prisoners. As many as 3,000 were put to death in revenge for cruelties which had before been shown to the Spartans.

Conon, as he sailed away, carried away with him, in token of his zeal for his country's cause, the large sails of the enemy's fleet, which he found on a headland near. He then took refuge at Cyprus, whilst one vessel alone proceeded to Athens to bear the sad tidings of the country's ruin.

The ill-omened ship reached Piræus at night, but the fatal news spread rapidly; and the streets of the city and the port were soon filled with anxious groups, whilst the air resounded with wailing and lamentations. None, it is said, went to rest on that night; and much cause indeed there was to mourn. The fleet on which all their hopes had been placed, was destroyed, and they had no means of restoring it. Resistance was no longer in their power. They had but to prepare for the arrival of Lysander, and the horrors of a long siege.

Lysander appeared, and Athens was blockaded both by sea and land. Offers of peace were made, but they were rejected; for one of the points on which Lysander mostly insisted was, that the Long Walls, built by Themistocles, between Athens and Piræus, should be pulled down. The Long Walls were considered the great defence of the city; they had been erected when Athens was in the height of her triumph after the Persian war, and the Athenians could not consent to such a sacrifice. The siege continued, and famine began to be felt. Again the Athenians endeavoured to make terms, but they could obtain none better. The Long Walls, and the fortifications of Piræus, were to be destroyed; the ships, all but twelve, were to be given up; and Athens was to follow whithersoever Sparta might lead. These were the demands of the haughty conquerors,—and to these at length the Athenians submitted; and Lysander sailed triumphantly into the port of Piræus. Joyful music sounded, and foreigners, crowned with chaplets and dressed as for a festival, looked on gladly whilst the Long Walls and the strong fortifications of Athens were levelled with the ground. "That day," they said, "was the beginning of Grecian liberty." But if the power of foreseeing future events had been granted them, they would have known that the work of destruction over which they rejoiced, was but the first of those scenes of ruin and misery which marked the downfall not of Athens only, but of all the states of Greece.

CHAP. XXIX.

THE GOVERNMENT OF THE THIRTY TYRANTS.

B.C. 404.

WHEN the walls of Athens were pulled down, Lysander proposed his plan for the government of the people he had conquered. Thirty persons were appointed as chief rulers, who were to govern according to the laws which the Spartans should think fit to ordain. Theramenes, the accuser of the generals, was one of the thirty. He had gained the favour of Lysander before Athens was taken, and now he was looked upon entirely as a friend of the Spartans. He did not, however, long remain so. Though he was a weak, bad man, yet he was not as cruel as many of the other rulers, the Tyrants, as they were soon called; and the measures which they proposed soon shocked and disgusted him. Lysander himself sailed away to Samos as soon as the government was settled, in order to force the inhabitants to submit to the Spartans; and his colleagues carried out their plans without scruple in his absence.

They wished the Athenians to forget their ancient freedom and greatness, and, therefore, they removed what was called the "Bema," or standing place, from which the speakers used to address the people, from its place looking towards Salamis and the sea, to a situation where nothing of the kind could be seen. But they could not succeed in blotting out from the memories of those whom they oppressed the glorious days when they were conquerors of the Persian armies, and honoured both at home and abroad, and if anything else had been necessary to make the Athenians long for freedom, it would have been the conduct of the Thirty Tyrants. Yet the new rulers only began their severe measures by degrees. They accused many persons of crimes, and caused them to be condemned and executed; but these were generally low and bad people, whom every one was glad to see punished. After a time, however, they caused men to be arrested merely because they had been heard to express a liking for the old government, and these likewise were tried and condemned; no one daring to defend them, as all the offices of importance were in the hands of the tyrants. Lysander, when he returned to Athens, upheld these cruel proceedings. The best and wisest men in Athens were singled out for destruction, and their fellow countrymen were compelled to assist the tyrants against them. Socrates, however, refused. On one occasion, being ordered to go to Salamis to arrest an innocent man, instead of obeying the commands of the tyrants, he returned to his home, and left it to others to execute the order.

A pupil of Socrates, Critias, who had once been taught by him, but would not listen to his advice, was one of the worst of the tyrants, and it was with him that Theramenes first quarrelled. The dispute was caused by the following circumstance. As there was very little money left in Athens, the tyrants despoiled the temples of their riches; and when this did not satisfy them, it was proposed that each of them should fix upon one wealthy foreigner living in Athens, and after putting him to death, should take possession of his property. Theramenes was invited to join in the guilty scheme, but he refused. Though he had done many very wrong things in his lifetime, he could not consent to such horrible wickedness as this, and the consequence was that his colleagues determined to rid themselves of him.

Every precaution was taken to prevent his escaping them. On a fixed day the council chamber was surrounded by a band of daring young men, armed with daggers; and Critias then came forward, and accused Theramenes of being a traitor to his country, and an enemy to the government. Theramenes defended himself upon the whole satisfactorily, but Critias was determined upon his death, and succeeded in obtaining a sentence of condemnation against him. The ministers of justice were summoned, and, without allowing any delay, Theramenes was compelled to drink the poison prepared for him. We may pity him as he suffered at last in a good cause, but it is impossible to forget that he was only undergoing the same punishment which he had himself inflicted upon others.

Soon after the death of Theramenes, the thirty tyrants were freed from another of their enemies, Alcibiades, who did not return to Athens after its fall, as many other exiles did. The tyrants were suspicious of him, and sentenced him to banishment. Not thinking himself safe in Europe, Alcibiades crossed over to Asia, and took refuge with one of the great Persian satraps. Some time afterwards, a house in which he was sleeping was set on fire in the night, and when he rushed out he found himself surrounded by a body of armed men, who immediately murdered him. Some say this was done by the order of the Persian governor; others, that a few persons whom he had offended took this means of revenging themselves. He left a son of the same name, but very inferior to himself in talent.

The cruelty of the tyrants increased when those whom they feared were dead; but they were not long allowed to follow their wicked designs. Amongst the persons whom the tyrants had banished was one named Thrasybulus, a noble, honourable man, who had distinguished himself very much in the Peloponnesian war. He was at Thebes when the cruelty of the tyrants drove hundreds of the Athenian citizens into exile, and hearing so much of the wretchedness of his country, he resolved to undertake its deliverance. His friends at Thebes supplied him with arms and money, and about seventy of the exiles joined him. With this small body Thrasybulus crossed the frontier, and seized a fortress built on a hill that projected from the side of Mount Parnes, and which was not more than twelve or thirteen miles from Athens.

The tyrants were not much alarmed, for it seemed as if they must be able at once to crush such a feeble enemy. But the task was not by any means as easy as they had expected. Their first attack upon the fortress was repulsed, and then a heavy fall of snow came, which obliged them to go back to Attica. After this Thrasybulus was joined by a much larger number of exiles, and was able to sally forth boldly against his enemies, and at last a regular battle took place in Piræus, in which Critias was killed. Thrasybulus and his soldiers showed much mercy to those who fought against them, and would take nothing from the slain except the arms which they needed themselves. When the dead bodies on both sides were given back, a friend of the exiles, who was possessed of a surprisingly powerful voice, took the opportunity to proclaim silence, and to entreat the Athenians no longer to serve the tyrants who oppressed them, but to join the cause of Thrasybulus. The address touched the hearts of all, and the commander of the troops, perceiving the effect it was likely to have, refused to allow his men to listen to it longer, and led them back to the city.

The tyrants were now so frightened that they left Athens and retired to Eleusis, and ten new rulers were appointed in their places. But this change did not help Thrasybulus and the exiles. The new governors were not more favourable to them than the tyrants had been, and messengers were dispatched to Sparta, both from Eleusis and Athens, begging that aid might be sent against Thrasybulus. Lysander was then at Sparta, and his wish was that the tyrants should be supported. But he was looked upon with great jealousy by his fellow countrymen, and although they allowed him to raise troops which were to serve against the exiles, they, at the same time, took care that the enterprise should not succeed. Pausanias, one of the Spartan kings, accompanied Lysander to Attica with a large force, apparently intending to besiege Piræus, which was in the possession of Thrasybulus, but at the same time he contrived to let the exiles know his friendly feelings for them; and he secretly found means to encourage those persons in the city who wished for peace, to hold a meeting and send him an address begging for it.

When the address was brought to Pausanias, a kinsman of Nicias appeared in the Spartan camp bringing with him some little children, descendants of Nicias, whose parents had been murdered by the tyrants. One he placed on the king's knee, and and the others by his side, and then he begged for protection against the cruel men who had deprived the poor children of their natural guardians. This entreaty was more powerful than any set speech, Pausanias, with the consent of the whole army, except Lysander and his friends, granted the exiles a truce for the time, and ambassadors were sent to Sparta who settled the terms of a regular peace, which restored the Athenians to freedom, and enabled them to settle their government as they thought best.

A general reconciliation was published at the time of the peace, from which none were excluded except the tyrants and a few other persons who had enjoyed power in the state, and used it to a bad purpose. Even they were to be allowed to live peaceably at Eleusis. When these arrangements were made, Pausanias sent away his forces, and the exiles triumphantly entered the city, and offered thanks and sacrifices to Athene, their protecting goddess; and once more the Athenians began to look upon themselves, if not as a free and powerful people, such as they once were, yet at least as safe from cruel oppression. The tyrants, indeed, did not at once submit to be thus deprived of their power, and tried many times to recover it; but their efforts were of no use, and we are told that they were all in the end put to death.

CHAP. XXX.

THE DEATH OF SOCRATES.

B.C. 399.

AFTER having experienced so much suffering under the thirty tyrants, the Athenians were naturally very anxious to return to their old form of government, and one of the first decrees passed by the people in their public Assembly declared, that from henceforth the country should be ruled according to the ancient institutions. But although they improved their laws, and restored their old customs, they could not bring back their former prosperity. They had no money, no colonies nor allies; and the Spartans were watching them with a great deal of jealousy, lest they should find means to regain the power they had lost. The character of the people, too, had, in many ways, altered for the worse. They were more bent upon serving their own interests at the sacrifice of the general good; men who had influence were often known to receive bribes to induce them to decide against what was right; and there was a great deal of injustice shown to rich persons, in accusing them of crimes and then seizing their estates for the public treasury. The habits of the citizens, also, were often very luxurious in public, and very wicked in private life. But the Athenians were not all corrupted; some saw these evils and mourned over them, and did their best to remedy them; and amongst these was Aristophanes, a writer of comedies. His plays were full of wit, and amused the people extremely, yet they had a really serious meaning, and were intended to show the folly and sinfulness of many of the Athenian customs. Socrates also laboured as much as possible to give his countrymen higher notions of their duties, and of religion. And yet, strange to say, Aristophanes and Socrates were not friends, and Aristophanes even wrote a play, called " The Clouds," in which he brought in Socrates and all his oddities, and turned them into ridicule.

The reason of this seems to have been that Aristophanes did not understand the ideas which Socrates had about religion, and fancied that he was one of a very bad class of men called Sophists, who have before been mentioned. The Sophists were clever in argument, but had little reverence for religion, and instead of keeping up clear distinctions between right and wrong, they used to pride themselves upon being able to argue ingeniously in favour of whatever they wished. Our word sophistical, which means making an action appear right when in truth it is wrong, is derived from the way in which the Sophists argued.

Now Socrates was not at all a Sophist, but it was true that he had notions of religion different from those of his fellow countrymen. He did not profess to give up the worship of the gods of the Athenians, or refuse to join in their common religious ceremonies, for it had never been revealed to him that they were wrong; but he had a great idea of the existence of one Supreme God, the Maker and Governor of the world; and when he spoke of his belief in " One God," it seemed like a new religion to those who worshipped many gods. In this way Socrates was at last looked upon as a corrupter of the religious principles of his countrymen.

For many years there had been complaints made of him; but it was not till the year B.C. 399, two years, that is, after the expulsion of the thirty tyrants, that any regular accusation was brought forward. Then a charge was made by some persons who were very desirous of keeping up the ancient religion, in these words: "Socrates is guilty of not believing in the gods which the state believes in, and of introducing other new divinities: he is moreover guilty of corrupting the young." The punishment proposed for these crimes was death.

From the first Socrates appears to have been certain that the charge would be believed, and that he should be condemned. He defended himself, indeed, but he made no appeals for mercy, such as were common in those days; but rather demanded reward and honour. The public feeling was strongly against him. He was known to have been the teacher of Alcibiades and Critias, who had brought great evils on their country; and no one remembered that both these men had turned away from him, offended, because he reproved their vices. The people had such a clear remembrance of the miseries endured under the thirty tyrants, that any person at all connected with them, as Socrates was with Critias, was looked upon with dread and dislike.

Sentence of death was passed; and he was condemned to drink the juice of hemlock, a strong poison. Socrates heard the decree unmoved; and when one of his friends broke out into lamentations that he should die innocent, he merely replied with a smile, "Would you have me die guilty? My enemies may kill me, but they cannot hurt me." The execution of the sentence was, however, delayed for a little time, in consequence of a yearly religious custom of sending offerings to the temple of Apollo, at Delos. From the moment that the vessel, which carried these offerings, departed, until its return, no criminal was allowed to be executed. The punishment of Socrates was, therefore, put off for thirty days, and during this time many of his friends entreated him to make his escape, which he might have done without difficulty. But Socrates was then seventy years old, and he could not bear to save a life which he knew could not be long, by breaking the laws that he had hitherto so carefully upheld. The hours of his imprisonment were cheered by the society of his friends; and when at length it was announced to him that the vessel from Delos was returned, he continued as calm and cheerful as before, and passed the day in conversing upon the most solemn subjects, chiefly relating to the life after death, in which he firmly believed.

As the hour for drinking the hemlock—which was at sunset—drew near, Crito, one of his great friends, asked if he had anything to arrange respecting his burial: "That which you please," replied Socrates, "if you can lay hold of me, and I escape not from your hands;" and looking at his friends with a smile, he added, "Crito always imagines that I am what he is going to see dead in a little while. He confounds me with my body, and therefore asks me how I would be interred."

The cup of poison was brought to him. He took it without the least change of countenance, spent a few minutes in silent prayer, and drank off the contents. His friends burst into tears, but Socrates gently reproved them, reminding them that it was a duty to die peaceably and with thankfulness to the gods. After walking up and down the room for some time the poison began to take effect, and he stretched himself upon his bed and covered his face. But as he found his last moments drawing near, he uncovered it again, and addressing Crito, reminded him of an offering due to Æsculapius, the god of medicine: "Discharge that now for me," he said, "and forget it not." These were his last words, and strange though they may seem to us, yet they were a proof of the sincerity with which Socrates desired to fulfil every possible religious duty, whatever reason he might have had in his own mind to doubt whether it was absolutely necessary.

The Athenians, as usual, repented their sentence when it was too late. The accusers of Socrates were punished; one being condemned to death, and the others banished; and a statue of brass, the work of Lysippus, a celebrated statuary, was placed in one of the most public parts of the city. The general respect, indeed, at length rose to such a height, that a chapel was dedicated to him, and he was worshipped as a demi-god.

CHAP. XXXI.

THE RETREAT OF THE TEN THOUSAND GREEKS.

B.C. 401.

WE must now return to some events which took place a year before the death of Socrates, when a body of Greeks were engaged in an expedition in Persia. The facts do not belong to the history of any particular state, but have become celebrated from the hardships which the Greeks endured, the fortitude which they showed, and the great skill of Xenophon, the general who led them back to Europe.

The expedition was undertaken in the service of Cyrus, commonly called Cyrus the Younger, who rebelled against his brother, Artaxerxes, king of Persia. Artaxerxes was the rightful heir, but

Cyrus, was the favourite of his mother, Parysatis, and she it was who encouraged him in his rebellion. We have seen before that Cyrus had been connected with the affairs of Greece, especially with those of the Spartans, of whose bravery and talents he had in consequence formed a high opinion. When he began to plan his rebellion, his thoughts naturally turned to the Greeks; for he felt that with their help he might succeed in dethroning his brother, but without it he could scarcely hope to do so. Cyrus was at that time living amongst the Greeks in Asia Minor, as he was governor of some of the provinces there. His winning manners, his hospitality, and his courage and energy, won the affections of many, and especially gained the goodwill of Clearchus, a Spartan, who, for several offences, had been obliged to leave his country. Lysander also was friendly to the Persian prince, and no doubt used all his influence in his favour; for, in the end, the Spartan government was persuaded to send ships and men, to join the forces which Cyrus was collecting from amongst the Greeks in Asia.

Still Cyrus did not venture to declare his real purpose. It was supposed by all, except his particular friends, that he was preparing to subdue one of the rebellious provinces in Asia Minor; and even when the troops were assembled, and had set out on their march from Sardis, where Cyrus held his court, by far the greater number were ignorant what they were about to do. As they proceeded on their journey, however, they began to suspect the truth, for it was very evident that Cyrus had no intention of subduing any revolted province. The Greeks refused to follow him further. "It was not," they said, "for the purpose of fighting against the king that they had entered his service;"

and the soldiers under Clearchus, especially, became so angry that they threatened to stone him.

Clearchus soothed them by declaring that he did not wish to do any thing against their inclinations; and as it was still not positively known that Cyrus was in rebellion against his brother the troops moved on again.

Artaxerxes was well aware of the plans of Cyrus. He had collected large forces, and was quite prepared to oppose him; and after Cyrus and the Greeks had undergone great hardships in a long and weary march, the two armies met at a village called Cunaxa, about sixty or seventy miles from Babylon.

The Greeks by this time had no doubt of the object for which they were to fight, but Cyrus had gained them over by many flattering words, and the offer of high rewards. The soldiers were promised a crown of gold in addition to the more solid recompenses they might expect; and the generals and officers were exhorted to show themselves worthy of the high esteem which Cyrus felt for them, and which rendered them, he said, of more account in his eyes than a whole host of barbarians. The only caution he gave them was not to be startled by the clamour of the enemy, for this was all they would find formidable in the onset. "Indeed," he added, "he was almost ashamed to think, how contemptible the Asiatics would appear to them in every thing but the sound of their voices."

Some persons seemed to doubt, before the armies met, whether Artaxerxes would risk a battle, and Clearchus asked Cyrus what he thought upon the subject. Cyrus himself was quite certain. "If Artaxerxes," he said, "is the son of Darius and Parysatis, and my brother, I certainly shall not become master of all he possesses without a struggle." Yet in spite of this expectation Cyrus was at last taken by surprise, for on reaching Cunaxa, near which the army was to halt and rest, a Persian officer, high in his favour, rode up to the camp at full speed, his horse covered with foam, calling out to all he met, that the king's army was approaching in order of battle. The tidings were heard with great consternation, for it was feared that Artaxerxes would attack them before they could recover from the disorder of the march. Cyrus alighted instantly from his chariot, and put on his armour; and springing upon his horse, gave orders for the army to form in the line of battle. He himself was placed in the centre with a guard of six hundred horsemen, and distinguished from them only by wearing the tiara instead of a helmet.

It was towards the middle of the afternoon, that a cloud of dust gave notice that the army of Artaxerxes was actually drawing near. Then, a dark mass was seen moving steadily forwards, brightened at times by the sparkling light which flashed from the armour and the weapons of the soldiers. Contrary to the expectation of Cyrus, the army of Artaxerxes advanced in perfect silence, whilst the Greeks raised the Pæan or battle song, and joined in shouts, which, with the clashing of their spears against their shields, startled both the horses and the drivers of the enemy's chariots. When the battle began, Cyrus kept his attention fixed upon Artaxerxes. His own guards were dispersed in the confusion of the battle, and he found himself left with a few officers near the spot where his brother was stationed. The moment that Cyrus perceived the king, he spurred his horse forward, exclaiming, "I see the man." The two brothers met. Artaxerxes was wounded and thrown from his horse, but his attendants raised him from the ground, and reseated him. Nearly at the same

Y

moment a javelin was cast, either by Artaxerxes or one of his attendants, which wounded Cyrus, and he fell; and in a few minutes he was overpowered and slain.

The whole account of the battle strikes us as unnatural and shocking. Artaxerxes, was always anxious for the honour, as he called it, of having killed his brother; and when the head and right hand of Cyrus were, according to the Persian custom, cut off and brought to him, it is said, that he seized the head by the hair and held it up as a proof of his victory.

The history of this war is given by Xenophon, a Greek historian, who, as we shall presently see, was a very important person concerned in it. He speaks highly of the good qualities of Cyrus, and says that he commanded the love and respect of his followers; but it is impossible for us to forget that he was a rebellious subject, and an unnatural brother, and sacrificed the highest duties to his ambition.

The situation of the Greeks after the battle of Cunaxa was very perplexing. They were in the midst of an enemy's country, with nothing to be gained by going forward, and very little hope of safety if they went back. Their first idea was to supply the place of Cyrus by offering to place Ariæus, one of his great friends and companions, on the Persian throne; but this offer Ariæus refused. Artaxerxes sent envoys to them to propose that they should lay down their arms and submit; adding that "if they did so, they might afterwards be employed in his service." But the Greeks would not agree to this proposal. "If they were to be the king's friends," they said, "they should be more serviceable to him with their arms than without them; and if they were his enemies they would need them to defend themselves."

Retreat seemed the only course possible, and retreat was determined upon. Clearchus took the command. They were then two thousand miles from the sea coast, by the road along which they had come; and that by which they were to return would be much longer, as they were obliged to go out of their way to avoid the enemy.

It was a most discouraging undertaking, but after the first setting out it seemed more hopeful than could have been expected; for the king, seeing they were not to be daunted by any dangers, sent messengers after them to propose a truce for a little while; and even consented to give them guides, who would conduct them to places where they might obtain provisions.

Tissaphernes, also, the great Persian satrap, came to them, with some other persons of distinction, and professing great friendship for them, obtained permission from Artaxerxes for their safe return to their own country, on condition of their doing no mischief in the king's territories, and paying for every thing they took.

All this appeared very satisfactory, but the Greeks could not help having a suspicion that these fair offers were not thoroughly sincere.

Tissaphernes was to escort them on their way with a body of his own men, and Ariæus, the Persian, also travelled with them. Ariæus had received offers of pardon from Artaxerxes for the offence of which he had been guilty in assisting Cyrus; and now that he felt safe, he did not show the Greeks the same kindness which he had done before.

As they all journeyed on, several circumstances occurred to make the Greeks more and more suspicious of the Persians, and Clearchus at length thought it advisable to speak openly to Tissaphernes, and tell him what they feared. Tissaphernes was not angry. He only begged Clearchus to reflect on the absurdity of such suspicions. "Supposing," he said, "that it was the king's wish to destroy them, there were means enough to do so without having recourse to treachery, which would be impious in the sight of the gods, and infamous in the eyes of men. But they need really be under no uneasiness, for, owing to the influence of Tissaphernes himself, they might be quite sure now that they were safe."

Clearchus was convinced. He was even anxious that the persons who had raised the suspicions should be discovered and punished, and it was agreed that Clearchus should bring his principal officers before Tissaphernes the next day; and that both should then point out the persons whom they knew to have said things to excite the distrust of the army. The officers who were proved to be guilty, were to be punished as traitors.

After this arrangement Tissaphernes detained Clearchus to sup with him, loaded him with kindness, and sent him to the camp the next morning perfectly satisfied.

The soldiers, however, were not equally pleased when they heard what had passed. Even amongst the common men there were some who saw the danger that might befall them if they placed their chief officers in the power of Tissaphernes. But Clearchus was not to be persuaded. He had selfish reasons for persisting in his intentions. He suspected one of his officers to be his enemy, and he hoped that by taking him before Tissaphernes, he might be convicted as a traitor. Four of the generals, and twenty of the inferior officers, consented to accompany Clearchus, the rest refused. When they came to the head quarters of Tissaphernes, the generals and Clearchus were admitted within, the inferior officers remained without, and with them a body of Greek soldiers who had followed from curiosity. They had not been there long before a signal was given, the generals were arrested, and the unfortunate officers and men who had accompanied them were massacred; whilst a troop of Persian horsemen galloped over the plain, around the Persian camp, and cut down every Greek who fell in their way.

The news of this treachery quickly reached the Greek camp. In the utmost consternation the soldiers seized their arms, expecting that the enemy would soon turn upon them. But this was not the case. The generals were kept prisoners, and were all sent to Artaxerxes, and afterwards killed; but the soldiers were only required to lay down their arms. This however they would not do. Notwithstanding the extreme danger they were in, at a distance of hundreds of miles from their country, without provisions or guides, without even a single horseman to assist them in fighting their way, they were still bent upon a retreat. Yet the hearts of all were very heavy: few could sleep that night, and few even found energy sufficient to taste food, or even to light a fire; but throwing themselves on the ground, wherever they might chance to be, they spent the long hours of darkness in mournful thoughts of their homes, their parents, and children, and friends, whom in all human probability they would never see again.

Ten thousand Greeks were left in this state of extreme peril, but help was found for them at the last minute. Xenophon, an Athenian, and a pupil of Socrates, who had accompanied the army merely for his own pleasure, was spending that night, like his companions, lost in gloomy thoughts, when he fell asleep for a short time, and awoke after a vivid dream, which gave another turn to his ideas.

"Why," he said to himself, "should I be lying here, while the night is wearing away, and the enemy may be expected to fall upon us at daybreak. No one is making any preparation for resistance, and if I wait for a more experienced general to step forward, the time for action will have passed away." As these considerations pressed upon his mind, he rose, and calling together a few officers, urged them at once to make provision for defence, and to appoint leaders to fill the places of those they had lost; by which means, he said, they would do much towards keeping up the spirits of their men. The proposal was received with great satisfaction, and the remainder of the Greek officers being called together, they appointed five new generals, Xenophon being one, and then proceeded to consider what was next to be done.

Xenophon was still their adviser. He was a man of astonishing eloquence, as well as talent and courage, and when he addressed the assembly, all were inclined to listen and obey. The danger they were in was plain to all, but Xenophon was full of hope and confidence, and inspired those who heard him with something of his own spirit. He insisted much upon the necessity of order and obedience, saying that the enemy had doubtless wished to introduce disorder into the camp, by depriving them of their generals; but he trusted the Persians would find that in the room of one Clearchus, there were now ten thousand men always on the watch to repress any breach of discipline. Besides this advice, he also suggested that they should burn their waggons, their tents, and all the baggage which was not absolutely necessary, as such things would delay their march, and encumber them if they were called upon to fight.

The soldiers left the assembly to follow the advice of Xenophon. Every thing that could possibly be spared was set on fire, and soon after the ten thousand Greeks proceeded on their retreat.

The courage, patience, firmness, and mildness of Xenophon, are plainly discovered from the account which he himself afterwards wrote of the celebrated retreat. The troops marched forward through the enemy's country, followed by Tissaphernes, and often attacked by the natives of the places through which they passed; and when, after immense difficulty, they reached Armenia, where Tissaphernes ceased to pursue them, they suffered as much from the intense coldness of the weather, as they had done before from the forces of their enemies. The snow lay six feet deep on their road, and many died from the effects of the piercing air, and the sharpness of the keen north wind. On they went, keeping to the north of Armenia, and forcing their way through savage tribes, sword in hand, till at length they arrived at a lofty ridge of mountains, known by the name of the Sacred Mountain. The foremost ranks had reached the summit, when Xenophon, who was behind, perceived them suddenly stop. His first idea was that they had come in sight of an enemy, and he rode forward to learn the cause of the delay. Loud shouts struck his ear, mingled with the joyful exclamation of "the sea! the sea!"

The waters of the Euxine lay beneath them. They were in the neighbourhood of Greek cities, and their dangers were nearly over. Both men and officers embraced each other with tears of joy, and joined in rearing a pile of stones on the top of the mountain, on which they placed the weapons of their prisoners, and other offerings, as a tribute of gratitude to the gods, and in remembrance of their deliverance.

Out of the 10,000 Greeks who began the retreat

together, about 8,600 survived its perils. These had been friends in distress, but when the common danger was over they began to quarrel, and Xenophon had great difficulty in keeping them together as long as it was necessary. They dispersed by degrees, and some of them entered the service of a prince of Thrace. Xenophon himself, instead of being received with honour by his fellow-citizens at Athens, was sent into banishment, probably because the Athenians were angry with him for having taken a share in the expedition of Cyrus, and perhaps, also, because they were jealous of the interest which he shewed in the affairs of Sparta. The Spartans gave him a grant of land, and a home in a pleasant valley, not far from the plain of Olympia; and here he afterwards built a small temple; after the model of the great temple of Diana, at Ephesus; and placed in it an image, of cypress wood, of the same form as the great golden image which is mentioned in the Acts of the Apostles. A grove of fruit trees surrounded the temple; and woods abounding with game, and fields, through which flowed a little stream of water, were spread around it. In this peaceful abode Xenophon lived for many years, dividing his time between his books and his friends, and the amusement of hunting; and setting an example, which we might do well to follow, in making religion—such as he understood it to be—his principal care. There are different stories told of the end of his life, but there is great reason to believe that in his old age he was restored to his native city.

CHAP. XXXII.

THE PEACE OF ANTALCIDAS.

B.C. 387.

WHILST the 10,000 Greeks were thus making their way with difficulty to their own country, Tissaphernes was rewarded for his services, and was made governor of the provinces which had before been subject to Cyrus. As a part of this government he claimed dominion over several of the Greek cities in Asia, but instead of submitting to him, they declared they would be independent, and sought for help from the Spartans. This brought on a war between Sparta and Persia, which was carried on chiefly in Asia Minor. Agesilaus, one of the Spartan kings, had the chief command a great part of the time, but Lysander accompanied him as one of his advisers. Lysander and Agesilaus did not long continue friends. Lysander, having had, in former times, a great influence over the Greek cities in Asia, was received on his arrival with much homage, and Agesilaus became jealous of him, and showed his ill-feeling by refusing to grant any petitions which were made to him through Lysander. Lysander reproached him with this unkindness, and begged to be sent away to some other place, where he might not be exposed to such humiliation; and to this the Spartan king agreed. Lysander was sent to the Hellespont, and Agesilaus carried on the war without him.

It was his object, so he said, to make the Greek cities independent of Persia, but he also seems to have had an intention of attacking the whole power of the Persian empire; and he so far succeeded as

to gain a great victory near Sardis, which made
him feel that if the Spartan government would only
give him full assistance, he might even become the
conqueror of Persia. This victory gained by the
Spartans caused the ruin of Tissaphernes. He had
always been hated by Parysatis, the mother of
Artaxerxes and Cyrus, for having taken part against
Cyrus, her favourite son; and now she persuaded
the king that Tissaphernes was a traitor, and deserved to die. Certainly Tissaphernes was of a
treacherous disposition, for he was continually de-
ceiving all persons he was connected with; pretending to befriend them, when in reality he thought
of nothing but his own interests. He had not,
however, been faithless on this occasion; yet the
weak Persian monarch yielded to his cruel mother's
arguments, and Tissaphernes was killed.

The Persian governors of provinces were so
powerful that they were almost kings; and the governor who succeeded Tissaphernes wished to make
peace with Agesilaus, as if he was quite independent
of his master, the king of Persia. But peace was
not what Agesilaus desired; and the Persian satrap,
finding himself in great difficulty, and wishing,
above all things, to divert the attention of the
Spartans from his own province, sent messengers
secretly to Greece to stir up the different states,
and persuade some, and bribe others, to undertake
a war against Sparta at home.

It was not a difficult task, for the Spartans were
at this time by no means liked in Greece. They
had accused the Athenians of being harsh and
tyrannical in their time of power, but they do not
seem to have been at all better themselves. They
had quarrelled with the people of Elis, and made
that state subject to them, although it had always
before been peculiarly safe and guarded, because

of the temple at Olympia, which belonged to it. The Eleans, therefore, had no love for the Spartans; Argos was always an enemy; Corinth, Arcadia, and Achaia, had many complaints to make; and Athens, of course, was quite ready to put herself at the head of the confederacy, and endeavour to humble the pride of her ancient rival.

The Spartans had not one sincere friend abroad, neither were they safe in their own dominions. There was a strong feeling of hatred amongst the lower orders against the higher classes, and a short time before a terrible conspiracy had been discovered, the first we hear of in Sparta, by which it was intended to murder the king, who was then in the city, the senators, the ephors, and, in fact, all those who really had a title to the name of Spartan. For we must remember that although all the inhabitants of Laconia, both those in the city, and those in the country, were often spoken of as Spartans, yet, strictly speaking, only the citizens had a claim to be so called, or were allowed to have any real authority in the state, since they were the descendants of that race of Dorians who, in former years, had invaded and conquered Laconia. The conspirators were discovered, and the leaders were seized, tortured, and put to death. But though the evil was, in this way, stopped for the time, yet the very fact of there being such a plot showed how much the government and the chief persons in the state were out of favour with the people.

The war which the Persian governor tried to excite broke out at last, in consequence of some quarrels amongst the smaller states, but it spread quickly. Lysander took the command of the Spartan armies, but in one of the early battles he was slain, and then the Spartans, being greatly in want of a skilful general, sent to recal Agesilaus from Asia.

This was a terrible blow to the ambitious plans which Agesilaus was so bent upon carrying out. All that he had done hitherto had answered his wishes. He was gaining friends amongst the Persians, and had really a fair prospect of attaining his object of conquering the empire; but the command of the ephors could not be disobeyed, and without any delay he prepared to go back to Sparta, leaving about 4000 men to guard the Greek cities, and promising to return as soon as possible.

The Spartans, in the meantime, had been very active, and before Agesilaus reached Greece a battle had been fought near Corinth, in which they were so victorious that it seemed as if the dread of their name alone was enough to overpower all resistance. Agesilaus, also, as he advanced through Thrace and Macedonia, overcame the barbarous tribes who opposed him, and appeared to carry victory with him. But just as he arrived at the borders of Bœotia he received intelligence of an event which not only caused him great personal sorrow, but was also a terrible public calamity. This event was the destruction of the Spartan fleet, and the death of its admiral, who was his brother-in-law. At any time this loss would have been felt very deeply, but Agesilaus knew that he had, in a great measure, to blame himself for it. Whilst he was in Asia he had taken great pains to collect the fleet, and so far had acted wisely and rightly; but afterwards it became his duty to appoint an admiral, and instead of choosing the person whom he knew to be most fitted for that office, he appointed Pisander, because he was his wife's brother, and he was fond of him.

Now the consequences of this fault were to be felt

not by himself alone, but by hundreds of others.
Pisander had very little experience, whilst the
Persians had the advantage of a most admirable
commander, — no less a person than Conon, the
Athenian, who had escaped to Cyprus after the
battle of Ægospotami, in which the Athenian fleet
was destroyed, and had since entered the service
of the king of Persia, hoping by his help to free
Athens from the power of Sparta.

When Conon and Pisander met in battle, which
they did off the coast of Syria, after Agesilaus left
Asia, Pisander was unable to contend with the skilful Athenian. Some of his allies took to flight,
others were driven on shore. Pisander remained
to the last on board his ship, and died like a Spartan, sword in hand; but personal courage could not
restore what Sparta had lost by the battle, and the
news of the misfortune must have been a sad blow
to the hopes of the country.

The Spartans continued the war by land with
considerable success for several years, chiefly in the
neighbourhood of Corinth, but they never recovered
their losses by sea. Conon, whose great wish was
to restore the greatness of his own state, persuaded
the Persians that if the Long Walls of Athens, which
had been destroyed by Lysander, could be rebuilt,
it would do more to humble the Spartans than any
victory. Having obtained sufficient money from
them for his purpose, he sailed to Athens, and the
walls were rebuilt; even the crews of the ships
which he took with him assisting in the work. The
Spartans now looked upon Conon as their great
enemy, and longed to rid themselves of him, and
before long their wish was attained. The Persians
began to think of making peace, and terms were
proposed which Conon did not approve. He said
so openly, and this was considered to be speaking

z

against the king. He was seized and put in prison, and though he afterwards escaped, yet he took no part again in the war, and died in Cyprus. The Athenians showed their gratitude to him for his services by erecting a brazen statue to his memory. The peace which Conon so much disliked was at length concluded in the year B.C. 387. It is generally called the peace of Antalcidas, because Antalcidas, a clever Spartan, was the person who principally arranged it.

All parties were tired of the war, and all had reasons for wishing it to be at an end, since they began to see that no advantage could be gained from it.

But the peace which was made was certainly not what might have been expected. The war had been begun for the purpose, it was said, of making the Greek cities in Asia Minor independent of the Persian king; but when a meeting of deputies from Greece was held, to hear what the king of Persia was willing to agree to, the following decree was read to them:

"King Artaxerxes thinks it right that the Greek cities in Asia, and the islands of Clazomenæ and Cyprus, should belong to himself; but that all the other Greek cities, both small and great, should be left independent, with the exception of Lemnos, Imbrus, and Scyrus; and that these should, as of old, belong to the Athenians. If any state refuse to accept this peace, I will make war against it."

Thus the king of Persia spoke proudly, as if he was the person to decide upon the affairs of Greece; and the Greek cities in Asia Minor were left just as much subject to him as they were when the war began.

CHAP. XXXIII.

THE BATTLE OF LEUCTRA.

B.C. 371.

THE Lacedæmonians, considering their state as the most important in Grece, took upon themselves to see that every one else complied with the terms of the peace of Antalcidas; and, as usual, they behaved selfishly and haughtily. The city of Mantinea, in Arcadia, had not been friendly to them in the late war; and now, though peace was established, the Spartans revenged themselves by ordering that the walls of the city should be thrown down. The Mantineans resisted, and the Spartans sent an army against them. The city was taken by means of an embankment, which stopped the course of a small stream, and turned the water against the brick walls so as to make them crack and totter. The Mantineans propped up the walls, but nothing that they could do could save them, and at last they were obliged to yield; the city was destroyed, and the inhabitants dispersed amongst four different villages.

In this way the Spartans showed that they were determined to be supreme in Greece. Whenever disputes arose, they were sure to interfere, in order to gain power; whatever they might order they expected to be instantly obeyed; and the only good thing we hear of them is, that they permitted the Platæans to return to their land and rebuild their city.

They were now at the greatest height of their greatness, but their downfall was near at hand. Like the Athenians they had used power tyranni-

cally, and the punishment of their great fault was
soon to fall upon them.

An act of injustice was the first cause of their
misfortunes. For five years they had been carrying on a war with Olynthus, a Greek city in Macedonia. It was not begun on their own account, but
in order to assist some of the enemies of the Olynthians, who had applied to them for help. It
happened, during this war, that a Spartan army, on
its way to Olynthus, was passing near the city of
Thebes, which was then disturbed by the quarrels
of two parties of citizens. The leader of one of
these parties, thinking that the Spartans would be
likely to favour him, held a communication with
the general of the army, and offered to betray
Thebes into his hands. Of course this was not
done with the idea that the Spartans were always
to remain the masters of Thebes, but only that they
were to assist the leader who professed to be their
friend. The Spartans, however, having once gained
an entrance into Thebes, resolved to keep it; and,
in spite of the injustice of the action, they took the
citadel for their own, and made themselves governors
of the place.

There were at that time in Thebes, two persons
of great talent, high birth, and noble principles,
who were also distinguished for their affection for
each other. Pelopidas was a rich man, fond of
action, and desirous of glory. Epaminondas was
very poor, of a quiet, thoughtful disposition, yet
always willing to exert himself when his duty required it. They had long been attached to each
other, and had served together in war, and lived in
great intimacy amidst all the anxieties of those
troubled times; yet Epaminondas would never consent to accept money from his friend, and Pelopidas,
instead of being angry with him, only tried to imi-

into his habits, and practice the same temperance and self-denial. The affection of Epaminondas for Pelopidas was especially shown at the siege of Mantinea, when the Thebans assisted the Spartans. Pelopidas was wounded, and fell, and Epaminondas believed him to be dead. But he would not even then forsake him; and throwing himself upon the body of Pelopidas, he continued to shield it until he was nearly overpowered, and would probably have been killed, but for the happy arrival of some Spartans, who saved them both.

When the Spartans, as we mentioned before, seized the citadel of Thebes, Pelopidas fled with several other persons to Athens. Epaminondas remained at Thebes, hoping that he might be the means of preventing violence. He kept up a constant correspondence, however, with his friends at Athens, who were full of impatience to revenge themselves upon the Spartans. The accounts which they received of the cruelty and wickedness of the Spartan leaders at Thebes, increased this feeling every day; and a plan was formed by Pelopidas and some of his friends, to rescue their native city. But Epaminondas, though he wished for the success of the project, would not take part in it, fearing that it would only be executed by means of a tumult, in which, probably, innocent persons would be killed. Pelopidas did not feel the same scruples, and all the necessary arrangements being made for obtaining help from Athens, if necessary, he and a small number of chosen companions disguised themselves as hunters, and set out for Thebes. One of his friends in the city, who had been prepared beforehand for their arrival, offered them his house for a hiding place; and another invited two of the Spartan leaders to a banquet. When the evening came, some of the companions of Pelopidas issued forth from their place of concealment, and were admitted, by the help of their friends, to the banqueting room, when they immediately rushed upon the two Spartans and killed them. Pelopidas with two companions went, in the meantime, to the house of another Spartan leader, and having gained admittance, though with some difficulty, killed him; and then proceeded to punish a fourth in the same terrible manner. After this they set a number of their friends at liberty, who had been put in prison by the Spartans, and went through the streets proclaiming the downfall of the tyrants, and inviting all true Thebans to join them.

The citizens remained quiet during the night, not understanding all that was going on, but when the morning came, and they all met together, their joy was unbounded. The exiles were received with shouts of triumph, and Pelopidas and two of his friends were chosen to be chief rulers with the title of Bœotarchs, — an ancient name for the governors of the different cities in Bœotia. Some Athenian troops now marched to Thebes to assist the inhabitants, and the Spartans were obliged to give up the citadel; and, as a matter of course, war was declared against Thebes by the Spartan government. Agesilaus was offered the command of the army, but he declined, saying, that he was too old: though the truth probably was, that he did not like to have any thing to do with a war which had been caused by such wrong conduct. He was afterwards, however, induced to alter his determination.

The Athenians seemed at first disinclined to assist the Thebans. The favour they had already shown them was only granted by two of their generals, who did not ask the consent of the people, and who were afterwards severely punished for what they had done. Probably, the Athenians did not want to bring upon themselves the anger of the Spartans; but though they kept aloof for a little while, they were at last induced to declare themselves in favour of Thebes, by a false alarm which the Thebans themselves caused, and which made them think that the Spartans were going to attack them. If this had been true, of course they could not have done better than join with Thebes. When once they had determined upon war, the Athenians carried it on for some time vigorously. Alliances were concluded with a number of important islands and seaport cities, and Athens again began to be looked upon as the head of the Grecian states. Yet the inferior states were still considered independent, for none of them would have been willing to own themselves subjects of Athens, knowing how hardly they had been treated by her in former days. Neither were the Thebans at all backward in their efforts against Sparta. Pelopidas was an excellent commander, and with his help, and that of Epaminondas, a well trained army was raised, amongst which were a body of young men distinguished above all others, called the "Sacred Band." There were three hundred of them, all friends, and remarkable for bravery, and love of their native land. The Sacred Band were the chief support of the Thebans in this long war, and succeeded in rendering the name of their country glorious throughout Greece.

The Theban war lasted sixteen years, and though it began merely with an attempt of the Thebans to set themselves free from the power of the Spartans, yet, before it was ended, the power of Thebes was so increased, that it was considered able to rival both Athens and Sparta. This was entirely owing to Epaminondas and Pelopidas. The Athenians assisted them at times, but when they felt that it was necessary for their own interest to have peace, they entered into treaty with the Spartans, and left the Thebans to themselves. The Athenians had not, indeed, much reason to be satisfied with the conduct of the Thebans, who attacked the allies of Athens without scruple, whenever they had any cause of complaint against them. Plataea was treated with especial harshness, for the inhabitants, not wishing to become subject to Thebes, put themselves under the protection of Athens, and were in consequence compelled by the Thebans to quit their city, the walls of which were once more levelled with the ground. This certainly does not appear like the conduct of friends and allies, interested in the same cause; and the fact appears to be that the Thebans were becoming ambitious, and the Athenians jealous and envious, so that it was impossible for them long to remain united.

One of the most celebrated battles of the Thebans was fought at a time when the other states of Greece had made peace with each other, and the Thebans were left to carry on the war with Sparta by themselves. They also might have had peace if they would have agreed to allow the principal towns in Bœotia to be free and independent; but like Athens and Sparta they desired to be chief over all others. It may be said that they had some right on their side, for they had long been considered supreme in Bœotia.

The battle before mentioned was fought between the Thebans and Spartans at Leuctra, in Bœotia, in the year B.C. 371. It was one of the most remarkable of the many battles in Greece. The Thebans were completely victorious, though the Spartans were superior to them in number. Their success was chiefly owing to the skilfulness of Epaminondas, who was one of their commanders, and the courage of Pelopidas and the Sacred Band. For a long time it was doubtful which side would be the conqueror; but after a great struggle Epaminondas cheered his men by exclaiming "Only one step forward," and led them on to victory. The Spartan general was killed, together with between one and two thousand soldiers, many of whom were amongst the chief persons in the state, being Spartan citizens and not merely Lacedæmonians.

The Spartan soldiers could scarcely be brought to own that they were defeated, and wished to prevent their enemies from raising a trophy of victory; but their commander saw that it would be unwise to attempt any thing of the kind; and, according to the Greek custom of acknowledging that a battle was lost, sent a message to Epaminondas begging that they might be allowed to bury their slain. Epaminondas gave the permission, but insisted that the allies of Sparta should carry off their dead first. He did this to prevent the Spartans from concealing the greatness of their loss; for when the allies came to bury their dead, it was seen how large a number of those who were killed were Spartans.

CHAP. XXXIV.

THE BATTLE OF MANTINEA.

B.C. 362.

The messenger who carried to Sparta the account of the battle of Leuctra, found the people engaged in celebrating one of their great festivals. They were assembled in the theatre, and a performance was going on. The ephors neither allowed the entertainment to be stopped, nor in any way cut short the amusements of the day. When the names of the slain were given to their friends, the women were commanded to refrain from the public wailings and lamentations, which were usually considered the proper mode of expressing grief; and the only persons who showed any open signs of sorrow before the strangers assembled at the festival, were the relations of the survivors. Those whose friends had fallen looked cheerful and hopeful. But in spite of all this assumed spirit, the loss of the battle of Leuctra was felt to be a great public misfortune. The power of Sparta over the other states of Peloponnesus was now gone, for so great a defeat had shown every one that Spartans were not invincible; and the natural consequence was, that those who had hitherto submitted to her humbly, began to think of making themselves independent.

The Arcadians were the first to exert themselves. Up to this time Arcadia had been divided into different districts, or cantons, something like the cantons of Switzerland. Now, it was proposed to unite these cantons together, as one great state, and build a capital city, to be called Megalopolis, or the great city; which was to be peopled by inhabitants from the other Arcadian towns; and in which the great council of the nation, consisting of ten thousand persons, was to be held.

Epaminondas and the Thebans entered warmly into this scheme, for it seemed very desirable to have a state in Peloponnesus sufficiently powerful to resist the ambition of Sparta. The Spartans, indeed, had great cause for alarm. Enemies were springing up all around them. The Arcadians assisted the inhabitants of Mantinea to rebuild and return to their city, and the Spartans could not prevent it; and when war was declared by them against Mantinea, a whole army of Thebans, with numerous allies, marched into Peloponnesus, under pretence of protecting Mantinea, and invaded Laconia.

The great object, however, of Epaminondas in this expedition was to restore the Messenians, who had so often and so long been crushed by the Spartans, that they had almost ceased to be a distinct people. They were scattered over various parts of Greece, but Epaminondas now invited them to return, and proposed that Ithome, their ancient fortress, should be rebuilt, and that Messenia should again become an independent state.

The surprise and consternation of the Spartans when the army of Epaminondas entered Laconia and encamped quite near to Sparta, was beyond every thing great. They saw the dwellings, in the neighbourhood of the city, which were chiefly villas, belonging to rich persons, plundered and destroyed; and they could watch their enemies, as they moved along the banks of the river Eurotas, which flowed close to Sparta. It was the first time for several hundred years — indeed ever since the conquest of Peloponnesus by the Dorians — that the fires of an enemy's camp had ever been seen from Sparta; and the inhabitants had been taught to believe that their land could never be invaded, nor their city taken.

The Thebans remained for some days near Sparta, hoping to induce the Spartans to engage in a regular battle; but this they were not willing to do, and Epaminondas then thought it would be wiser to move further away from the capital. For some weeks he and his army ravaged Peloponnesus, and during that time Epaminondas, with great solemnity, laid the foundation-stone of the city of Messene, on the spot where the ancient Ithome had stood. Portions of the buildings which were then begun remain to this day, and all who see them speak

with surprise and admiration of their size and
strength, and the solid manner in which the stones
are put together.

The restoration of the Messenians to their country, and the building of Messene, were considered
very great works, and many of the Greeks believed
that Aristomenes, the ancient Messenian hero, had
foretold them before his death.

The Spartans, in their distress at the presence of
an invading army, sent to Athens to beg for assistance; but although aid was granted them it did not
arrive in time to be of much service. Epaminondas
had no intention of remaining long in Peloponnesus,
and having fulfilled the purpose for which he came,
he led his troops back to their own land, and neither
the Spartans nor the Athenians were able to stop
him. His reward on his return was very different
from that which might have been expected. Some
base-minded people were envious of his successes, and
brought a charge against him, and against Pelopidas
also, of having kept their command as Beotarchs,
three months beyond the year, which was the fixed
time for that office. Both were acquitted, for no
one could honestly say that they had done any
harm. Epaminondas was indifferent in the matter,
and declared himself willing to die, if the names of
Leuctra, Sparta, and Messene, and the deeds by
which he was connected with them, might be inscribed upon his tomb. Pelopidas was more indignant, and exerted himself afterwards to have
his accusers punished.

Three times after this first enterprise the Thebans, under Epaminondas, invaded Peloponnesus,
but all things did not continue as favourable to
their cause as they were at first. The Athenians
openly assisted the Spartans; the Arcadians wished
to be first themselves, and so were not anxious to

increase the power of Thebes; and the attention of Epaminondas was distracted by a new enemy who had sprung up in Thessaly.

Thessaly, like Greece, was originally divided into a number of different states and cities, which were really independent of each other, though they professed sometimes to be united. About this time, however, these states had become subject to one family, the members of which succeeded each other in the government, as if they were kings, or rather tyrants, for they were ambitious and cruel. The last of this family was such a monster of wickedness, that the people of Thessaly would no longer submit to him. They rebelled, and called in the aid of the king of Macedonia, who helped them for a short time, but was then obliged to return to his own country, which was in a very disturbed state, from the many rivals contending for his throne.

The Thessalians next applied to the Thebans for assistance, and obtained it, for Pelopidas was sent with an army into Thessaly. There was no battle fought, for the tyrant was awed by Pelopidas, and consented to every thing which was required. Pelopidas was then summoned to Macedonia, to settle the disputes there, and after having successfully arranged all these important matters, he went back to Greece.

But he was not long to remain quiet. The tyrant of Thessaly became as cruel as ever, after he was left to himself; and when Pelopidas returned again to Thessaly, hoping once more to restore peace and happiness to the country, the tyrant threw him, and a friend who accompanied him, into prison.

It was then that Epaminondas was obliged to leave the affairs of Peloponnesus, and undertake an expedition into Thessaly to release his friend. This was more difficult than might at first have been imagined,—for the tyrant was very powerful in his own country,—and was moreover assisted by the Athenians,—and Thessaly was invaded twice before the prisoners were set free.

Greece at this time appears to have been entirely distracted by the selfishness of the different states. There seems to have been no idea of any common interest; and those who, in former days, would have been most indignant at the thought of allowing any foreign power to interfere with them, now apparently looked upon such help as a matter of course.

Both the Thebans and the Spartans sent ambassadors to Persia to solicit the king's support; and Pelopidas himself, after his release from prison, was not ashamed to be one of the envoys.

The Persian king was inclined to favour the Thebans, for they had been friendly to Persia for many years. He settled with Pelopidas the terms of peace which ought to be proposed to the other states; but no one would agree to them, and the war went on.

The Arcadians now thought themselves strong enough to be independent of Thebes, and continued their contests with Sparta without help. But one great battle, in which they were defeated, quite crushed them, and destroyed all their prospect of being a great and independent state. This battle was called the Tearless Battle, because not a single Lacedæmonian is said to have been killed in it.

All this time Epaminondas had been steadily working for one great object,—that of making Thebes supreme over the other states of Greece; but this object was discovered, and disliked by all persons who wished for the prosperity of Peloponnesus. They saw that Epaminondas desired to make them weak, in order that his own state might be strong; and many, who before dreaded the power of Sparta, now were inclined to join with her.

The power of Thebes had risen rapidly, and it was destined rapidly to decay. The fourth invasion of Peloponnesus which Epaminondas undertook, put an end to all his plans of greatness. He had attacked his enemies several times without gaining any decided advantage, and the period for which he was given the command of the army was nearly over. He could not bear to return home without having obtained a victory, and when he met his enemy's forces near Mantinea, he resolved to risk a general battle. His men heard the determination with the greatest delight. They burnished their arms, and adorned themselves as if preparing for a festival, and went forward eagerly to meet their foes. The battle was fought about harvest time, on the 8th of July, B.C. 362. The Spartans, who were assisted also by the Athenians, were not aware of the intentions of the Thebans, and the furious attack routed them; but in the very moment of victory Epaminondas received a mortal wound. He was borne from the field, and carried to a rising ground from which he could overlook the scene of battle. Life was fast fleeting, but his eye still lighted up with enthusiasm, as he watched the movements of his troops. The shaft of the spear which had struck him remained in the wound, and the agony it caused was terrible; when it should be drawn out, death, he was told, would instantly follow. The anguish was endured till the friends who stood around him assured him that the triumph of Thebes was complete. "Then all is well," he exclaimed, and calmly drawing forth the weapon from his side, he almost immediately expired.

The character of Epaminondas is one of the best which we meet with in history. The struggles that he made for his country were begun to rescue her from the tyranny of a foreign state; and if, afterwards, he appears to have been too ambitious to extend her power, we must remember that all around him were striving for the same object for themselves; and that whenever he was able to rule others, he did it gently and moderately. Heathen nations and heathen men cannot be judged by the same rules as Christian states and people. Glory was the object they were taught to desire, and no one had ever ventured to suggest that the love of glory might be a sin.

Pelopidas died about two years before his friend. After his return from Persia he was again obliged to go to Thessaly, to defend the people against their tyrant, and he was then killed in battle. Like Epaminondas, his last contest was a victory, and the tyrant of Thessaly was afterwards compelled to submit entirely to the Thebans.

The Thessalians, in gratitude for the services he had rendered them, begged permission from the Thebans to bury him in Thessalian ground.

Agesilaus, king of Sparta, who had been the chief opponent of Epaminondas in the Theban war, died in the same year. He was eighty years old when he undertook an expedition to support some rebels, who had raised an insurrection in Egypt against the power of the king of Persia; and it was as he was returning home that he died in Africa. His constitution must have been naturally very strong, for he was capable of bearing immense fatigue; and his habits of life were so simple that he never could have injured it by self-indulgence. He was a very honourable, generous, amiable person; and one of the strongest features in his character was his great affection for his children. A friend one day found him riding with them upon a hobby-horse, and expressed his surprise that he should amuse himself in such a way. But Agesilaus only replied: "Do not speak upon that subject until you are a father yourself."

CHAP. XXXV.

COMMENCEMENT OF THE SACRED WAR.

B.C. 357.

It has been said that "the virtues of the Athenians perished when Epaminondas died," and the saying is in a great measure true, not only of Athens, but of all Greece. Peace was restored, the Thebans being no longer able to keep up the war; but when there ceased to be any call for great exertion, the Greeks, and especially the Athenians, sank into a state of indolence and luxury. At home the Athenians occupied themselves in attending law courts, and frequenting theatres; and when troops were wanted in time of war, instead of fighting themselves, they hired soldiers whom they could not afford to pay, and who did not in the least care whom they fought for, as long as they received their money.

A country in this state was, as it were, ready to be conquered by any one; and though the actual downfall of Greece did not take place immediately, yet the circumstances which led to it, may be clearly perceived after the battle of Mantinea, and the death of Epaminondas. At that time the Greeks were celebrated as the most civilised and refined people of Europe; and all who wished to be considered superior in mind, and acquirements, tried to imitate them.

Macedonia, a large country to the north of Thessaly, was then governed by a king named Philip, — a brother of that same monarch who assisted the Thessalians, before Pelopidas and the Thebans were called in to help them. There were great disputes in Macedonia when Philip was a boy, and Philip himself was sent away from his country, and brought up at Thebes; — it is said under the care of Epaminondas. This naturally led him to admire and like the manners, and talents, and refinements of the Greeks; and when, after some years, he was restored to his country, and became king, his most earnest wish was to civilise Macedonia, and make it one of the Grecian States; and then to extend its power over all the rest. Philip was just the person likely to carry out these purposes. He was very quick in understanding what was going on around him, very eloquent, and particularly clever in bringing other persons round to his opinions. Besides which he was in appearance handsome and dignified, his manners were agreeable, and he was strong enough to bear almost any fatigue.

When Philip first began to govern Macedon, he was not strictly speaking the king, for there was a little infant, his nephew, who was the rightful heir, and Philip professed to act only as the child's guardian. But the kingdom was then in a very dangerous condition; war was springing up all round, and there were many claimants for the throne; and in this perilous state, the Macedonians were not unwilling to set aside the little prince, and give the whole power of the government into the hands of a powerful monarch. So Philip, when he was about four and twenty years of age, became really king of Macedon without trouble; and his nephew was brought up at his court, and when he grew up married one of Philip's daughters.

The Athenians had been induced to assist one of Philip's rivals, but Philip did not wish in consequence to engage in a war with Athens, for this would have been difficult and troublesome. When some Athenian troops were taken prisoners by him in one of his battles, he treated them with the greatest kindness, made them presents, and set them at liberty; and when they returned home, he dispatched envoys with them, to say how little he wished to be the enemy of the Athenians, and to beg for their friendship. The Athenians were much flattered by the embassy, and readily agreed to become the friends of the Macedonian king. But they must soon have had cause to suspect Philip's sincerity. There was a town in Macedonia called Amphipolis, which had been colonised by the Athenians. It was a very important place, and one which they particularly desired to keep possession of; but the people had made themselves independent. Philip had a quarrel with Amphipolis, and besieged it; and when the Athenians were a little alarmed at this, he secretly assured them that he did not intend to keep it when it was taken, but would give it back to them. Amphipolis was taken, but Philip thought no more of his promise, and not only kept the city he had offered to restore, but turned his arms against Pydna, another Athenian city, and took that also. Happily for Philip the Athenians were at this time so much engaged that they were not able to revenge themselves for this conduct. Just when Philip was besieging Amphipolis, they were obliged to send troops to the island of Euboea, to assist in quelling some disturbances there, and soon afterwards a war, called the Social War, broke out, which lasted for three years, and fully required all their efforts.

The cause of this war was the dissatisfaction felt by some of the allies of Athens, on the sea coast of Asia Minor, and in the islands near. Athens was still superior at sea, and professed to protect these cities and states: but there was a great deal of oppression and injustice in the way in which they were treated, and in consequence some of the most powerful declared that they would guard themselves, and refused to pay the money which Athens required from the cities which she professed to take care of.

A war of course followed, for the Athenians would never submit to give up what they considered their right. But it was a very unfortunate one. They lost their best generals, and spent large sums of money, and in the end they were obliged to make peace, and allow their revolted allies to be independent.

That same year another war began, known by the name of the Sacred War, in which not only Athens, but nearly all the states of Greece took part.

The Sacred War continued for ten years, and was carried on with the greatest eagerness and bitterness. It began with a quarrel between Thebes and Phocis, who had long been secret enemies though they professed openly to be friends. The Thebans accused the Phocians of irreligion and irreverence, because they had ploughed up some land which was held sacred; and though they did not come forward themselves, they induced the Thessalians to bring the charge before the Amphyctionic council, or council of deputies from the different states, which met every year to settle religious disputes, and to make regulations for the public worship of the temple at Delphi.

The Phocians were condemned to pay a heavy fine, and, if they refused, their lands were to be seized. The Spartans also were threatened with the same punishment, for having neglected to pay a fine which had been imposed by the council, when the citadel of Thebes — the Cadmea, as it was called — was unjustly kept by them.

Neither the Spartans nor the Phocians took any notice of this sentence, and the council of the Amphictyons then summoned all the states of Greece to join in putting it into execution. The Athenians however refused. They sided with Sparta, and the Phocians, of course, were joined with them.

In the old times the Phocians had been considered the guardians of the city and the treasures at Delphi; and now, knowing that whoever had possession of the sacred city would be the most likely to be victorious in the war, they formed a plan for seizing it, together with the treasures of the temple. The enterprise succeeded, and this was the first step in the war; which, as far as the Spartans were concerned, was carried on chiefly in Peloponnesus. The Phocians were the most victorious at first in the Sacred War, for they had a great deal of money from the temple treasures, and could afford to hire troops to help them. They had also a skilful general, named Philomelus; but in the third year of the war Philomelus died, and not long afterwards a new enemy appeared against them, no less a person than Philip, king of Macedon. Philip had all this time been extending his power in Thessaly, till he had nearly conquered it, and now he found occasion to mix himself up with the Sacred War, under pretence of assisting some people in Thessaly who were enemies of the Phocians.

The interference of Philip was the most important circumstance of the Sacred War. The quarrels of the different states were of no consequence in comparison. He was considered the friend and ally of all who were opposed to Sparta, Athens, and Phocis; and when a powerful king becomes the ally of weak states, it is not at all difficult for him to make himself their master.

CHAP. XXXVI.

THE BATTLE OF CHÆRONEA.

B.C. 338.

The Athenians seem to have taken but little part in the Sacred War, till Philip of Macedon interfered. Then they were rather alarmed, and began to suspect what his real designs were; especially when they found that he was still trying to make himself master of several towns on the coasts of Macedonia and Thrace, which had been colonised from Athens, or were subject to her. Demosthenes, the orator, was the person who first made them perceive their danger. Demosthenes was the son of an Athenian merchant. In his childhood he was weak and sickly, and unable to join in the sports of his companions; and this probably may have induced him to give up more time to study, since he must have known that it would be impossible for him to distinguish himself as a soldier, and he had not money

enough to enable him to be luxurious. To be
eloquent was what he most desired, for by that
means he knew that he should gain great influence
over his fellow countrymen. But he had few natural gifts to make him hopeful of success. His
voice was not strong; he pronounced his words in
a way that made them difficult to be understood;
his sentences were confused and unpleasing; and
his manners awkward. At the end of his first
speech in public the people were full of laughter
and murmurs; and yet even then there were some
who discovered his great talents, and were friendly
enough to encourage him. One old man in particular, it is said, who remembered, when a boy, to
have heard Pericles speak, assured Demosthenes
that he reminded him of that great orator.

But without good instruction and great perse-
verance, Demosthenes, though he was extremely
clever, would have failed to obtain his wish. Happily for him he had both these advantages. A celebrated player in Athens undertook to correct his
faults, and Demosthenes listened to him humbly,
and set himself to work diligently. For a season he
withdrew from the society of his friends, and practised the most difficult and irksome methods to improve his pronunciation, and make himself graceful;
and when he again appeared in public he was pronounced an unrivalled orator. As a proof of his
great industry, we are told that he copied out the
history of Thucydides eight times, in order to improve himself by the beautiful style in which it was
written.

It was this clever unwearied orator who now
made it his great object to stir up the Athenians to
resist the power of Philip of Macedon. The speeches
which he made upon the subject were called Philip-
pics. They were full of energy and wisdom, and if

the Athenians had possessed the spirit of their ancestors, they would doubtless have been incited to resist Philip, as they had formerly resisted Darius and Xerxes. Philip indeed was powerful, but as Demosthenes reminded them, "there was no divinity about his greatness, to exempt it from the common vicissitudes of human affairs. Their tardiness and negligence had made Philip powerful, and as long as they continued passive, he would continue to encroach. It was, therefore, of the utmost importance that the citizens should not shrink, as they had been used to do, from military duty, but begin again, in part at least, to fight their own battles;— for the troops which they hired would plunder their allies, instead of seeking the enemy; and if their pay was not regularly furnished, would leave them, to engage in a more profitable service."

Demosthenes, besides this advice, gave a plan for carrying on the war, and stated how many ships should be prepared, and what number of soldiers collected. But it is not known what effect exactly his instructions had upon the Athenians. They do not appear to have had any strong warlike spirit remaining; and, indeed, some of the best men amongst them despaired of rousing the people to energy, and thought it would be wiser to make the best terms they could with Philip, and keep him as their friend, even if he were to be their master. Phocion, an orator almost as celebrated as Demosthenes, was one of the persons who took this view of public affairs. He was an upright, and benevolent, but stern-mannered man, who despised luxury, and hated flattery : yet even he could see no hope of successfully resisting the growing power of Philip of Macedon.

Demosthenes, it is said, quite trembled for the effect of his own speeches, whenever Phocion rose to address the people after him, and used to whisper to his friends: "Here comes the hatchet to my speech."

The Sacred War continued till the year B. C. 346. No one obtained any advantage from it, except Philip, who went on steadily gaining more and more influence in Greece,—assisting one state against another, and so making himself lord of both; whilst at the same time he contrived to deceive every one. The Athenians did at last rouse themselves in consequence of the speeches of Demosthenes, and called upon all the states of Greece to assist in opposing Philip, but no one would move; Philip had bribed them to be still, and even the Athenians were soothed for a time by the professions of friendly feeling which were made to them. It was Philip who was allowed to settle the terms of peace, when the Greeks grew tired of the Sacred War, and wished it to be brought to a close. The Phocians were as willing as the other states to allow of his interference, for he had promised to exert himself on their behalf with the council of the Amphictyons; but they found themselves grievously disappointed. Philip did nothing for them, and the council insisted upon a most cruel sentence against Phocis, which was carried into execution by Theban and Macedonian troops. Twenty-two towns were utterly destroyed; ten thousand captive Phocians were carried away to distant colonies; and the poor people who remained were obliged to cultivate the desolate country, in order to raise a large sum of money, which was to be paid to the temple at Delphi.

The Phocians were also declared to be no longer members of the Amphictyonic league, and Philip of Macedon stepped into their place, and had two votes. He also claimed to be the guardian of the city and temple at Delphi, and was made president of the Pythian games, instead of the Corinthians, who had assisted the Phocians, and so were thought unworthy of the honour.

But Philip was not to be permitted thus to rule Greece, without one effort being made against him. Now that he was a member of the Amphictyonic league, the council of the Amphictyons looked to him for support; and a few years after the end of the Sacred War, he was appointed by them to be the commander-in-chief of their forces, and to put in execution a decree which they had passed against the inhabitants of a small state, accused of an act of profanation.

Philip readily consented, for in fact he had been secretly working to bring about this quarrel, hoping to gain some advantage from it. But not contented with merely upholding the decree of the Amphictyons, he raised a much larger army than was necessary, and took possession of some towns over which he had no right. This act excited general indignation. Athenians, Thebans, Corinthians, with many of the smaller states, joined in one body against him;—others, who were favourable to Philip, refused to aid him, that they might not be called upon to fight against their own countrymen; but Sparta and several of the Peloponnesian states took no part in the quarrel. A battle was fought in the plain of Chæronea, in Bœotia, in the year B. C. 338, but it was fatal to the freedom of Greece. The Athenians had been long unaccustomed to war, and had no generals of any distinction; whilst the Macedonians were skilled in battle, and encouraged by the command of their king, and the presence of his son, the young prince Alexander.

The Thebans, it is said, kept their ground the longest. The Sacred Band fought to the last, and were cut off to a man. Demosthenes was amongst those who were engaged in the battle, and has been called a coward because he left the field; but he fled only when others did, and when all hope of victory was over.

The battle of Chæronea made Philip of Macedon the lord of Greece, for all now dreaded to oppose him. Yet he used his power gently. He even refused to listen to those advisers who would have persuaded him to treat Athens severely, saying:— "that they would have him destroy the theatre of his glory." All he required was, that the island of Samos should be given up to him, and that deputies should be sent the next year to a general meeting of the Greeks at Corinth. The government of Athens, he said, should remain as it had been before. Thebes was treated more hardly, and the states of Peloponnesus were obliged to submit to his arrangement of all their affairs, — not even Sparta daring to resist, though she professed to be free.

In the spring of the next year the deputies of all the Greek states, except Sparta, met on the Isthmus of Corinth, at Philip's command. There the king announced to them the great object of his ambition, which he declared to be the conquest of Persia. They were to assist in it, and he was to be their general, with unlimited power. Such a proposal was in fact a command. But another year passed before the plan was ready to be put in execution; and before that year was over, Philip's schemes of earthly glory were in one moment ended for ever.

He was celebrating a festival, — the marriage of his favourite daughter with the king of Epirus. The city of Ægea, the ancient capital of Macedonia, was crowded with strangers; — not only guests of the king, but envoys from the leading states of Greece, bearing presents of crowns of gold for the mighty monarch. The marriage was celebrated, and a banquet followed. Philip desired a player who was present to recite some piece of poetry, suited to the approaching expedition against the Persians. The man obeyed, and sang of power, luxury, pride, and wealth, but he spoke also of that death which "approaching unseen by hidden paths cuts off in an instant man's brightest hopes." On the morrow an entertainment was to take place in the theatre; spectators assembled at an early hour, and the building was crowded. A solemn procession advanced, bearing twelve images of the gods, with another representing the king, who himself followed, dressed in white robes, and a festal chaplet on his head.

The shouts of the multitude hailed his approach. At that moment a young man stepped forth from the crowd, drew a sword from beneath his garments, plunged it into the king's side,—and Philip of Macedon fell dead.

CHAP. XXXVII.

THE INVASION OF PERSIA BY ALEXANDER THE GREAT.

B.C. 334.

The news of Philip's death reached Athens when Demosthenes was mourning for the loss of an only daughter, who had died about seven days before. But all private sorrow gave way to the delight which the great orator felt at the thought that Greece was now freed from her dangerous master. Although the customs of his country required that he should still perform funeral rites for his child, he no sooner learnt that Philip was dead, than he dressed himself in white, placed a wreath on his head, and with a joyful countenance performed a solemn sacrifice at one of the public altars. The people shared his joy, — but they had little real cause to congratulate themselves; Philip indeed was dead; but the son who succeeded him inherited his ambition and his talents, and was destined to be the lord not of Greece only, but of the greater part of the known world.

From his childhood the young prince, Alexander, had shown the spirit of one born to rule. When he was quite a boy, a splendid horse, called Bucephalus, was sent from Thessaly to his father Philip, which proved so unmanageable that Philip proposed to return it. Alexander, hearing this, asked permission to try his skill in taming the animal. He went up to it, soothed it with his voice, stroked it gently, and turned it from the sun, so that it might not see its own shadow, which had frightened it, and then, springing upon its back, and giving it the rein, galloped away, and returned safely. When he brought back the horse, perfectly tamed, it is said that Philip shed tears of joy, and, embracing Alexander, exclaimed, "My son, seek a kingdom more worthy of thee, for Macedon is below thy merit." Yet Alexander and his father were not friends in after years. Philip, who was married several times, treated his wife, the mother of Alexander, with disrespect; and she, being a woman of a fierce temper, encouraged her son almost to rebel against his father. Alexander always suspected that Philip wished to prevent him from succeeding to the throne, but there does not seem to have been any real cause for such an idea; — and certainly Philip did not at all neglect his son, but gave him an education fit for a prince who was to rule over a powerful kingdom.

Aristotle, the philosopher, was his tutor. He was

a native of Stagira, a town in Macedonia, — and as
celebrated for his wisdom as Alexander afterwards
was for his conquests. Whilst Philip of Macedon was
brought up at Thebes, Aristotle was living at Athens.
There had been some connection between them before, for the father of Aristotle was physician to
Philip's father; but it was in Greece that they
formed the friendship which lasted even when
Philip became king. It seems that Philip fixed upon
Aristotle to be the tutor of his son, as soon as
the young prince was born; for we are told that in
the letter in which he informed Aristotle of the
birth of his child, he added, "that he thanked the
gods less for the son they had given him, than that
he had been born when he might have Aristotle for
his teacher." Alexander had the greatest possible
reverence for his tutor, and used to say of him "that
he loved him no less than his father; for to the one
he owed life, to the other the art of living." In his
outward appearance Aristotle would not have excited much admiration, for he was short and slight;
he had small eyes, and rather a sarcastic expression of countenance, and lisped when he spoke.
Much of his wisdom was derived from Socrates.
He was not taught by that great man himself, but
he was a pupil of Plato, a philosopher who was one
of the chief friends that Socrates had; and who
taught publicly in Athens after Socrates was dead.
Aristotle and Plato had different opinions upon
many very important subjects, but they both believed in the existence of one Great God, the Lord
of all in Heaven and earth. Aristotle knew a great
deal about natural history and medicine, and the
wonderful things which are seen in nature. His
History of Animals is one of his most excellent
works. Plato thought and taught more of the
things which concern the human mind. Aristotle

returned to Athens after he had instructed Alexander, and used to deliver lectures whilst walking up and down the shady walks which surrounded the Lyceum. His scholars were, from this circumstance, called Peripatetics, which meant persons who walked about. Plato travelled a good deal, and when he was at Athens gave lectures in a place called the Academy, which was something like the Lyceum.

When Philip of Macedon died, Alexander was only twenty years of age, but even then he was more fit to be a king than many sovereigns who have reigned for years. He was noble, generous, brave, energetic, and affectionate; and, though glory and conquest were his great object, we must not so much blame him for his ambition, as make allowance for his education. His father Philip had striven for years to increase his dominions, and the persons who surrounded Alexander from infancy had encouraged his natural love of warlike fame. Even Aristotle does not seem to have checked him, though he must soon have perceived the object which his pupil had most at heart. When ambassadors from Persia came to Macedonia whilst Philip was living, Alexander asked no questions concerning the splendour of the Persian court, the beauty of the hanging gardens, the luxuries and enjoyments of the great monarch: he inquired only what was the state of his army, the condition of the country, what the distances were from one place to another, and whether the roads were good; and the ambassadors returned home, more alarmed at the open ambition of Alexander, than the cunning wisdom of his father.

And now that Philip was dead, no obstacle remained to prevent Alexander from indulging his desire of glory. He was at once acknowledged king of Macedon; and although Demosthenes

endeavoured to stir up the Greeks to a last effort
for freedom, they remembered too well their defeat
at Chæronea, to be easily roused to rebellion
against a prince so powerful. They did, after a
time, plan a revolt, but Alexander no sooner heard
of it than he marched into Greece himself, and so
awed the different states by his presence, that, instead of opposing him, they only thought how best
to appease his anger. In this way every thing
seemed to yield to him; and when a meeting of
deputies from the Grecian states, like that which
Philip had before assembled, was held at Corinth,
he was declared commander-in-chief of the Grecian
forces, by the consent of every state except Sparta.

It was in vain to think of resistance whilst
Alexander lived, but soon after the meeting at
Corinth, whilst the king was absent upon an expedition against the countries to the north and west of
Macedonia, a report was spread that he was dead.
The Thebans and Athenians instantly determined
to set themselves free from the power of Macedon.
War was declared against that country, but in an
incredibly short space of time Alexander, whom all
supposed to be dead, appeared with his army before
the gates of Thebes. The city was taken by storm,
the walls were razed to the ground, the inhabitants
were sold for slaves, and only the temples, and one
house, that of Pindar, the Theban poet, were spared.
This destruction was in a great measure caused
by some Greek allies of Alexander, who were ancient enemies of Thebes, and persuaded the Macedonian king to treat the inhabitants thus harshly.
But it was a terrible warning to the rest of Greece,
and the Athenians, when they heard of it, lost no
time in sending ambassadors to beg for mercy.
Alexander treated them kindly: he had no wish
to make enemies who might rise up against him

whilst he was in Asia; for it was that country which was still the object of his ambition. The great project of the invasion of Persia was constantly in his mind, as it had been in that of his father, and at last the time arrived when he might undertake it.

In the spring of the year B.C. 334, he crossed the Hellespont, and landed in Asia with an army of about 30,000 foot soldiers and 5000 horsemen, and with only a small sum of money; — his treasures having been divided amongst his friends before he set out. They were but slight preparations, compared with those which Xerxes had made for the conquest of Greece; but Alexander had a confident spirit, and when he was asked what, amongst all his treasures, he had kept for himself, his answer was "hope."

In the whole of Alexander's army there were only about 7000 Greeks, so that the account of his conquests can scarcely be considered as belonging to the history of Greece; but it may be as well shortly to describe them, as they are so universally celebrated.

CHAP. XXXVIII.

THE BATTLE OF ISSUS.

B.C. 333.

PERSIA was governed by a king named Darius Codomanus, who was a member of the royal family, though not the son of the last king, and had been raised to the throne by the influence of one of the great Persian officers. Darius Codomanus was a man of considerable talent, and much beloved; but though the kings of Persia possessed an immense empire, the different provinces were nearly independent of their sovereign, and would seldom unite together for any one purpose; so that in fact Darius had less real power than many princes whose dominions have been less extensive.

He was, however, able to raise great armies, and when the news of the approach of the Macedonians reached him, he sent a large force, under an experienced officer, to oppose Alexander; and prepared himself to follow. But Alexander's success began at the very opening of his expedition, for the Greek cities on the coast of Asia Minor were all favourable to him, and he had but to march from one to the other and receive their submission. The first battle with the Persians was fought on the banks of the Granicus, a little river of Mysia, which flowed into the Propontis, or Sea of Marmora. Alexander was completely victorious, and before the Persian army could recover from their defeat their general was seized with a fatal disease and died, and no one was left able at that moment to take his place. The Macedonian king passed on through Asia Minor, overcoming every difficulty, and at length reached Gordium, the ancient capital of Phrygia. In this city an incident took place which gave rise to a proverb in common use in these days. In very early times, when there were great disturbances in Phrygia, an oracle had informed the people who were holding a public assembly, that a waggon would bring them a king, who should at the same time put an end to all their troubles. Directly afterwards Midas, the son of Gordius, a poor peasant, appeared, coming in his waggon to the assembly, with his father and mother. All present instantly acknowledged him as their king, and Gordius, being very grateful, dedicated the waggon as a thank-offering to the god Zeus.

The pole of this waggon was fastened to the yoke by a knot of bark, and there was a prophecy, generally believed amongst the people, that whoever should untie the knot would be the lord of Asia. When Alexander came to Gordium, he took care to prove that the prophecy related to himself, for he drew his sword and cut the knot in two. And from this circumstance has arisen the saying of "cutting the Gordian knot" when a person finds himself in a difficulty, and gets out of it not by patience, but by some hasty action. But Darius was not willing that Alexander should make himself lord of Asia without a further struggle. At Babylon, half a million of men were collected, under the command of the king of Persia himself; and as Alexander advanced into the country, the two armies met at the pass of Issus, leading from Cilicia into Syria. It was a most fatal battle for the Persians. Their army was routed; Darius fled, and his mother, his wife, and his children were taken prisoners. The conduct of Alexander on this occasion does him more honour than all his victories. When he heard the princesses lamenting in their tent over Darius, whom they supposed to be dead, he immediately sent one of his great officers to tell them that the Persian monarch had fled away in safety; and to assure them that he desired to treat them with the honours due to their high station, and had no wish to deprive them of any of the ornaments which they valued.

After the battle of Issus Alexander proceeded onwards to Damascus, which was betrayed to him by the Persian governor. There he found a treasure which had been left by Darius, consisting of money, splendid dresses belonging to the king and his nobles, and other valuables, sufficient to load seven thousand beasts of burden. There were also in Damascus a number of Persian ladies of high rank, with their children and servants; and several hundred persons of the lower classes, — cooks, confectioners, perfumers, chaplet weavers, music girls, and others, who were appointed to wait upon Darius, and provide him with the luxuries he had been accustomed to enjoy; all these now belonged to Alexander.

The unfortunate Darius, alarmed at such rapid success, began to think of peace. Messengers were sent to remonstrate with Alexander upon his invasion of Persia, and to inform him that it was the wish of Darius to become his friend and ally; and humbly to entreat that the mother, the wife, and the children of the Persian king, might be restored to him.

The answer of Alexander was full of the pride of a conqueror. "Darius," he said, "might, himself, have come to him as to the lord of Asia. He would promise him safety, and he might then ask with confidence for his mother, wife, children, and whatever else he could desire. In future Darius must address him as the king of Asia, in the style not of an equal, but of a subject; or he must expect to be treated as an enemy. If, however, the question of sovereignty were disputed, they may try the event of another contest. Darius might rest assured that Alexander would seek him wherever he might be found."

This reply, of course, caused the continuance of the war. Darius began to collect another army, and Alexander proceeded to Tyre which he besieged for seven months. This city, famous for its riches, and the trade which its inhabitants carried on with distant countries, stood on an island about half a mile from the main land. It was considered almost impossible to take it, but Alexander commanded a mole, or causeway, to be raised across the strait so that his troops might approach the walls; and when that was destroyed by the Tyrians, who set fire to some wooden towers which were built upon it, he gave orders for another to be begun; and at length, with the help of ships, brought from Sidon, the city was surrounded, the walls were broken down, and Tyre, which is described in the Bible as "full of wisdom, and perfect in beauty," was cast to the ground.*

There were two cities called Tyre; and the destruction of both was foretold, long before it took place, by the prophet Ezekiel. The ancient city stood on the main-land, and was destroyed by Nebuchadnezzar king of Babylon; and it was from these ruins that Alexander took the materials which he used to form a causeway when he besieged Tyre on the island. This circumstance is particularly foretold by the prophet when he says of the first Tyre, "They shall lay thy stones, and thy timber, and thy dust in the midst of the water." "I will also scrape her dust from her." "Though thou shalt be sought for, yet shalt thou never be found again." (Ezekiel, xxvi. 4. 12. 21.)

Darius now again sent ambassadors to Alexander. They offered the Macedonian monarch an enormous sum of money, the provinces to the west of the river Euphrates, and the daughter of Darius to be his wife. Alexander informed his council of these proposals. Parmenio, his most trusted general, declared that if he were Alexander he should accept them. "So should I," replied the king, "were I Parmenio." His love of conquest was in no way satisfied by the successes he had obtained, and his reply to Darius was proud as it had been before. "The gold and the land which were offered him

---

* Ezekiel, xxviii. 12—17.

were," he said, "already his own; nor would he accept a part of his treasures, or his empire, instead of the whole. If he chose to marry the princess, he did not need her father's consent. If Darius desired to receive his favour, he must come in person as a suppliant."

Darius gave up all hope of peace, and Alexander proceeded on his victorious course. From Tyre he proceeded to Gaza, and from thence marched northward to Jerusalem. Palestine was at that time subject to Persia; and the high priest of the Jews, who was also their governor, had refused to assist Alexander with troops and provisions, when he was besieging Tyre. Alexander was determined to revenge himself for this refusal; but as he approached the city, we are told by the Jewish historian Josephus, that he was met by the greater number of the inhabitants, dressed in white festival robes; with the Priests, and Levites, and the High Priest at their head, in their sacred garments. As the procession advanced Alexander was struck with awe. The figure of the High Priest reminded him of one which he had before seen in a dream that he was little likely to forget, for in it he was promised success in his vast enterprise. Instead of receiving the High Priest as his enemy, the king went forward alone to meet him, and bent before him. He was convinced now that the God whom the Jews served was a God of Might; and, accompanying the High Priest to the temple, he sacrificed there according to the Jewish rites; and, after bestowing gifts upon the Priests, and granting privileges to the nation, he left Jerusalem and proceeded on his way to Egypt. That country at once submitted to him, for the people hated the Persians, and longed to throw off their yoke; and then it was that Alexander founded a city, to which he gave the name of Alexandria, desiring

that it should carry his remembrance to the most
distant ages.

Leaving Egypt he advanced further into Africa,
across pathless sands, and under a burning sky,
till, in the midst of the desert of Lybia, he reached a
green, pleasant, watered valley, where, enclosed by
woods, stood the temple of the Egyptian god Ammon.

The oracle of Ammon was greatly celebrated,
and Alexander desired to visit it, that he might
inquire whether his enterprises were likely to succeed, and if they were according to the will of the
god. We do not know the exact questions he
asked, nor the answers he received; but no doubt
the priests flattered him, and said what they
knew would please him; for Alexander, on leaving the temple, gave offerings for the service of the
god, and assured his followers that he was well
satisfied with all that he had heard

CHAP. XXXIX.

THE BATTLE OF ARBELA, OR GAUGAMELA.

B. C. 330.

HAVING now secured the countries subject to
Darius, Alexander's next wish was to return and
complete the conquest of Persia itself. He accordingly left Egypt, passed again through Palestine
and Phœnicia, and met Darius in Assyria near the
river Tigris. The battle which was there fought
is generally called the battle of Arbela, though in
fact it took place at a distance of fifty miles from
that place. The Persian king had by this time
collected a vast host, consisting not of luxurious
Persians, but of hardy mountaineers, from the

borders of the Caspian Sea, and the distant confines of India. Powerful bodies of horsemen, scythed chariots, and even elephants, were brought to oppose the great conqueror of Asia; but no preparation disturbed the security of Alexander. After surveying his enemy's forces, and making his own arrangements the evening before the battle, he slept as peacefully as if secure from every danger; and when Parmenio roused him in the morning, and expressed surprise that he should have rested as well at such a moment as if he had gained a victory, Alexander replied, "Is it not as good as a victory to have overtaken the enemy?"

The feelings of Darius were very different. Being afraid that Alexander would attack him during the night, he made his troops remain under arms in order of battle; and though he visited them by torch-light, and tried to cheer them, yet, when the morning came, he found them wearied and dispirited. Their sad anticipations were soon realised when the battle began. Though the Persians fought very bravely, the Macedonians were so much better trained, that it was impossible to withstand them. One body, called the Macedonian phalanx, it was almost impossible to overcome. It consisted of a large body of men, who stood one behind another with long spears. These spears reached so far before them, that the spear of a man who was the sixth from the front could still project beyond his comrade in the first line. Thus the front ranks were defended, on all sides, by those who were behind them; and when they all moved forward together, their power was too great for ordinary soldiers, however brave, to resist.

It was the phalanx which completely routed the Persians at the battle of Arbela. The shock of its attack spread fear and disorder amongst the enemy; and Darius, finding himself in danger, alighted from his chariot, and, mounting a fleet horse which was kept in readiness for him, fled from the field of battle. His family were still left in the power of Alexander; but the queen, who was the most beautiful woman in Asia, had died many months before. It is said that when Darius heard of the noble way in which she had been treated, and the splendid funeral which his enemy had ordered for her, he lifted up his hands to heaven, and prayed that, if his kingdom was to pass from himself, it might be transferred to Alexander. That prayer was now to be granted. Darius, indeed, was in safety, but his power was gone. From Arbela Alexander marched to Babylon, and for a short time his soldiers were permitted to rest, and enjoy all the splendour and luxury of that great city. From Babylon he proceeded to Susa, where still greater treasures were in store for him,—gold and silver to an immense amount uncoined, and dresses, so rich and valuable, that the wardrobe of one of the chief officers alone was deemed a present fit for Alexander's favourite Parmenio.

Soon after his arrival at Babylon, fresh troops arrived from Europe. With them came fifty noble Macedonian boys, who were to be the king's pages; besides a present, sent to Alexander from his sisters, of some articles of dress which they had made themselves,—a work which the Persian ladies would have thought it a disgrace to undertake.

Sisygambis, the mother of Darius, and her grandchildren, were left at Susa, in their own palace, whilst Alexander advanced further through the Persian dominions. The distant provinces had never been entirely subject to Darius, and they were now inclined to rebel against Alexander;

but the very sight of the Macedonian soldiers filled them with terror, and those who came out, prepared to resist, fled as Alexander drew near.

Persepolis was his next object, a place even richer than Babylon and Susa; for the treasures collected there by the Persian monarchs were seldom touched. A number of Greeks met him at this place, who had been transported thither from Asia Minor, and, as a punishment for some offence they had committed, had been barbarously mutilated. This sight naturally caused the anger of Alexander; but the revenge which he took was a disgrace to him. One evening, after drinking largely at a banquet till he lost his reason, he was persuaded by a wicked woman, named Thais, who was present, that it would be a glorious thing to show his indignation by setting fire to the royal palace. Alexander started up, half in jest and half in earnest, and seizing a torch, led the way to the palace, and threw the brand into the splendid building. The flames spread rapidly and widely; and Alexander, repenting of his mad act, gave orders that the fire should be stopped. But the mischief which his folly had caused could not be repaired. The palace was not, indeed, burnt to the ground, but its splendour was entirely destroyed.

Whilst Alexander was thus making his way through the country, Darius had fled to Ecbatana He seems to have had little thought of again raising an army, and probably intended to retrea' from the country entirely, and seek for refuge on the other side of the Oxus, a river which flowed between the provinces of Sogdiana and Bactria, to the north-east of Persia, and fell into the Caspian Sea.

But he was not destined to live in security. One of his own officers, named Bessus, became a traitor to him, seized him, chained him, and then took all authority upon himself.

Alexander heard what had been done, and set out in pursuit of the rebel. His approach caused the greatest consternation to Bessus and his followers. They determined to flee, and pressed Darius to mount a horse and accompany them.

The unfortunate king, however, trusted more to the mercy of Alexander than to that of his false subjects. He refused, and the conspirators then wounded him mortally, and left him in his chariot.

He died before Alexander saw him. The noble spirit of the Macedonian king was deeply touched with the misfortunes of his rival. He threw his own cloak over the dead body of Darius, and ordered that he should be buried in the sepulchre of his ancestors, with the magnificence suited to a monarch. He afterwards took charge of the education of his children, and married his daughter.

CHAP. XL.

ALEXANDER DEFEATS PORUS.

B. C. 325.

ALEXANDER was now, in the eyes of the Persians, their lawful monarch; or at least they were willing to acknowledge him as such; for it was seldom that the throne of Persia descended peaceably from the father to the son; and though the kings were generally members of one family, yet they often gained their power by bloodshed and rebellion.

But Alexander was not yet at liberty to rest, even if he had desired it, for Bessus, who had rebelled against Darius, was still in arms. Alexander pursued him through the countries bordering on the Caspian Sea, and at last took him prisoner; and, after making him stand with a clog round his neck in the road by which the army passed, he caused him to be scourged, and then placed him in the custody of some relations of Darius, by whose wish he was afterwards tortured and killed in the most cruel manner.

It was during this expedition that Alexander allowed himself to be led into an action which must always be a stain upon his name. Accusations of treason were brought against his faithful general, Parmenio. They were unproved, but Alexander gave way to suspicion, and most cruelly and unjustly caused Parmenio's son, whom he disliked, to be tortured, in order to obtain some evidence against Parmenio himself. The son was executed, and sentence of death was passed upon Parmenio, who was then absent. This sentence was carried out very treacherously. A letter was dispatched to him, forged in the name of the son who had just been killed; and, whilst he was reading it, the officers who brought it fell upon him and slew him, and then carried his head to the king. Several other persons were accused of being concerned in this conspiracy; it is supposed in consequence of the jealous spirit of Olympias, Alexander's mother, whom he had left behind him in Europe, and who, it is known, often tried to make him distrust his officers. Alexander was excessively fond of his mother, though he did not like her to be regent of Macedonia, fearing her proud hasty temper. As it was, she often interfered with the regent Antipater, and Antipater wrote complaints of her to Alexander; but the king's love for his mother was stronger than his anger at her behaviour, and he was once heard to say, that Antipater did not know how soon ten thousand letters were blotted out by a single tear of a mother. Alexander had now no more enemies to fear, but his desire for conquest was still unsatisfied. From the countries near the Caspian Sea, he marched with his army, through the midst of barbarous lands and warlike tribes, till he reached the northwest of India, known to us by the name of Affghanistan. Wherever he passed he was a conqueror. But although he could subdue others he could not always subdue himself; and about this time we are told of a most fatal burst of rage to which he gave way when intoxicated at a banquet. An officer, the brother of his nurse, who had been his playfellow in childhood, and had once preserved his life, offended him by some provoking language; and Alexander seized a spear, from a soldier who was standing by, and thrust it through the body of his former friend. He had no sooner committed the deed than his reason returned; he retired to his chamber, threw himself on his bed in an agony of grief, and for three days refused to eat, or listen to any comfort. Now, as before, when he set fire to the palace at Persepolis, repentance came too late; though he might have learnt, from all he suffered, the terrible consequences of the habit of excessive drinking, which it seems was common at that time, and which deprived those who indulged in it of all self-command.

The conquest of India, which was at this period undertaken, had long been a great object with Alexander. The country was little known; but it was believed to be of immense extent, and to abound in wonders and riches. At the battle of Arbela, the Greeks for the first time saw elephants, which had been brought from the banks of the Indus, and the sight of these enormous and powerful animals no doubt increased their desire to visit the land from whence they came.

The greatest resistance which the Macedonians experienced in India was from a king who had a number of these animals in his army. Alexander had advanced victoriously through Affghanistan, passing through a city built on the same spot as that which we call Cabul, — where, in the year 1842, the English were cruelly massacred by the Affghans; — and as he went on some of the natives opposed him, and others were willing to become his allies, and in either case he made himself their lord. But after crossing the Indus he was met by Porus, an Indian prince, who proudly defied his power, and collected an army to withstand him, in which there were between two and three hundred elephants. Porus trusted much to the fear which he thought the Macedonians would have of these animals; and for a time it seemed as if even the phalanx could not stand against them. At last, however, the poor animals, being wounded, became quite frantic, and turned in fury upon their Indian masters as well as upon the Macedonians. Many were killed, and the rest were quite exhausted; and the army of Porus, having lost the help upon which it chiefly depended, was completely routed. Porus, hopeless of escape, gave himself up to Alexander. When brought into the king's presence, and allowed to name the requests which he wished to have granted, his only reply was, "that he desired to be treated as a king." Alexander observed "that this was no more than a king must do for his own sake," and bade him make some request for himself. But Porus declined. "All that he wished," he said, "was included in this."

Alexander restored him his kingdom, and even

added to it large dominions. Probably, besides admiring the dignity of the Indian prince, he was anxious to make him his friend, so that he might not always have cause to fear rebellion in these distant provinces. The country which was thus placed under the government of Porus is that now called the Punjaub.

The notions of Alexander as to the geography of the countries he had been passing through were very strange. When he found crocodiles in the Indus, he fancied that this river was a branch of the Nile; and in a letter, which he wrote to his mother, he told her that he thought he had discovered the land which contained the springs of the Nile. But as he travelled on he must have begun to suspect his mistake. He was still ignorant of the vast extent of country which lay beyond the Indus, but reports were brought of a powerful monarch, who dwelt on the other side of the Ganges; and although Alexander himself was only the more anxious to proceed, his Macedonian soldiers were by this time weary of the hardships they had endured. When they reached the banks of the river Zaradrus, now called the Sutlej, a general murmur arose amongst them. They could see no end to these distant expeditions, and their thoughts turned with an intense longing to their homes. The officers felt with the men, and one of them undertook to represent to Alexander all they were suffering, and to entreat him to give up his design. A speech was accordingly made to the king, setting forth the wishes of his soldiers. Alexander listened to what was said, and then retired angrily to his tent; and the next day, assembling his army, informed them that he would not force any one to accompany him, but that he was quite sure there would be many willing to go of their own accord. The rest might return, and say they had left the king in the midst of his enemies.

Even this appeal to their feelings was of no effect: the soldiers were still bent upon a retreat. Alexander remained three days within his tent, not even allowing his chief officers to come near him, and still hoping that the disposition of his men would change. But at the end of that time he was forced to yield. As an excuse for thus giving up his own will he declared that omens had been observed, which showed that it would be unfortunate to cross the river Zaradrus, and that in consequence it was his intention to go back.

The intelligence was received with shouts of delight, and Alexander,—after ordering twelve great altars to be built on the banks of the Zaradrus, and dedicated to the gods whom he believed had led him thus far victorious,— prepared to return to Persia. The portion of India which was conquered by Alexander is particularly interesting to us now, because of the war which has in later years been carried on there between the English, and the Affghans, and Sikhs. The battle of Chillianwallah, fought in 1848, between Lord Gough and the Sikhs, took place nearly on the same spot as that between Alexander and Porus.

Though Alexander had consented to return to Persia, he had no idea of going back through the countries he had conquered. His wish was to follow the course of the Indus, an enormous river into which many other rivers fall. The waters of the Zaradrus, after joining another river, at last fall into the Indus; so also do those of the Hydaspes; and it was on the Hydaspes that the king and a portion of his army embarked, in a fleet which was probably collected from the natives. The remainder of the forces, with about 200 elephants, advanced along the eastern bank.

It must have been a strange and beautiful sight. The Indians stood on the bank in wonder, watching the mass of vessels as they glided away from their sight, and were lost amidst the distant woods; and the shouts of Alexander's rowers mingled with the strains of warlike music, with which the natives showed their delight at a spectacle so splendid.

But, though the retreat was thus easily and happily begun, there was much to be borne before the Macedonian army again found itself in civilised countries.

The river on which Alexander had embarked, as was before said, joins the Indus. The nations on the banks of the Indus were hostile to him, and it was necessary therefore to conquer them; and when, after subduing them, Alexander at length reached the sea, there was still a dreary tract of country to be crossed by himself, and those of his troops who were to return to Persia by land. A portion of the army were to go by sea; and this was really a voyage of discovery, for Alexander only guessed that there was an open sea between the Indus and the Persian Gulf; there were no ships passing backwards and forwards between India and Persia, as there are now. Of course it was necessary to build vessels fitted for such an undertaking, since the galleys, in which the army had rowed down the Indus, would not have been at all fitted for the dangers of the sea. This was a work of some months; but there was a city called Pattala, at the mouth of the Indus, of which Alexander took possession; and there he formed a harbour, and built his vessels. When all was ready, Nearchus, a great friend of the king, was made commander of the expedition.

Alexander did not, however, see his fleet sail.

The wind was not favourable, and they were obliged to delay; and as he did not think it desirable for the rest of the army to wait so long at Pattala, he began his march with them first. His plan was, to pass along the sea coast, and through the country then called Gedrosia, which lay to the east of the Persian Gulf. The difficulties of this march were terrible. The heat was so great that, to avoid it, the army generally moved at night; the sand which the men often walked upon, was in the daytime so burning that it blistered their feet; whilst at night it was driven by the wind into long ridges, and numbers of the animals died under the fatigue of wading through them. The carriages were broken up, because they could not be dragged along, and there were then no means of conveying the sick; and as their companions became at last careless of them, they were often left to perish in the sandy waste.

But the greatest distress of all was caused by the scarcity of water. Numbers of men and animals expired from thirst, and when the soldiers came in sight of water, several were known to drink till they died.

Alexander bore his full share of all these hardships. He walked on foot with his troops, and gave them an example of fortitude which they could not help admiring and trying to imitate. On one occasion, some soldiers who had been sent to search for water, discovered a little in the bed of a torrent, and brought it in a helmet to the king; Alexander was parched and faint with thirst, but he could not bring himself to indulge in a luxury which others were not to share; and whilst many were gazing upon him, — longing, doubtless, that they could be in his place, — he poured the delicious draught on the ground.

The perils of the sea voyage were not less than

those of the land journey. The troops of Nearchus having landed for a short time, met those of Alexander in the district of Caramania, or Kerman, which joined Gedrosia. They had only been separated a few months, but the forces of Nearchus were so altered in consequence of all they had suffered, that their countrymen did not know them again. The trials of all were then, however, nearly over. They parted, but it was with the hope of soon meeting again in safety. Nearchus pursued his voyage up the Persian Gulf, and Alexander proceeded to Susa, where many important affairs awaited him.

CHAP. XLI.

DEATH OF ALEXANDER THE GREAT AT BABYLON.

B.C. 323.

As was naturally to be expected, the governors who had ruled the empire during the absence of Alexander, had not all been faithful to him, or governed with wisdom and gentleness. When the king returned, numerous complaints reached him from all quarters, and it was evident that a great spirit of disloyalty prevailed both amongst the Persians and Macedonians. It must have been a most difficult task even for Alexander to please two distinct nations, of different habits and language, so suddenly mixed together; but as he had braved distant evils, so he was now ready to overcome those which were nearer.

It was necessary, if possible, to make the Persians and Macedonians one people; and with this object, Alexander encouraged his officers to take Persian ladies for their wives, and appointed a great festival on which all the marriages were to be celebrated publicly.

On this day he celebrated his own marriage with Statira, the daughter of Darius; and that of Hephæstion, his dearest friend, with Statira's sister. Another of his generals married a niece of Darius; and, in fact, more than a hundred Macedonians of rank were at this time united to the great Persian families. Not contented with this, Alexander also induced 10,000 private soldiers of his army to marry Asiatic women; giving their wives portions, and allowing their weddings to be celebrated at the same time, and in the same place as his own.

It must certainly have been the largest and grandest marriage party that ever was known. A gorgeous tent, supported by pillars sixty feet high, was erected on a plain near the city of Susa. It was hung with the richest silks, and sparkled with gold and silver. The 10,000 soldiers were entertained in an outer court. The marriages were celebrated according to the Persian usage, and afterwards, the king gave his hand to Statira; and saluted her as his wife, and the officers followed his example. This completed the ceremony. A magnificent banquet followed, and the festivities altogether lasted for five days. Statira was not the only wife of Alexander, for according to the Persian custom, he had several, who were, however, all considered inferior to her.

Notwithstanding these endeavours to preserve peace, Alexander could not succeed in satisfying his Macedonian officers. They were still full of jealousy, and caused him much vexation by their suspicion and discontent. But a private grief which befell him about this time, seems to have been more deeply felt by him than any public calamity. This was the loss of his friend Hephæstion, who died unexpectedly of a fever. Hephæstion does not appear to have been a great or a good man, but Alexander's fondness for him was excessive. When he died, the king was for a long time inconsolable, and seemed to find his only comfort in paying the most extravagant honours to his friend's memory. A general mourning was ordered to be observed throughout all Alexander's Asiatic dominions; and the same signs of lamentation were shown as were common upon the death of a Persian king. Amongst others, the horses and mules were shorn; and the walls of Ecbatana, the city in which Hephæstion died, were divested of their battlements.

The officers of the court, seeing the king so engrossed in grief, endeavoured, in many ways, to divert his mind. But although he roused himself sufficiently to make an expedition against some rebellious mountaineers, he was still often absorbed in gloomy thoughts. On his return from the mountains he went to Babylon, and there pleased himself by erecting a funeral pile for his friend, so splendid that none of the wonderful buildings of the East had ever surpassed it. It was a square tower, about 200 feet high, divided into thirty stories, and covered on the outside with groups of figures, larger than life, and other ornaments; all being made of gold, ivory, or similar valuable materials. On the top were a set of statues, so contrived that they sent forth strains of sad, soft music.

Alexander's energy seemed to return after this, and he occupied himself with plans for exploring the coast of Arabia, and the shores of the Caspian Sea. His dominions were now so great, and his power was so vast, that those who were accustomed to worship their great heroes did not hesitate to own him as a god. Envoys arrived from Greece to offer him golden crowns, and, salute him with the name of a deity. At that moment the Almighty Lord of All had decreed that Alexander's death should be close at hand.

Shortly after the arrival of the Grecian envoys, a grand banquet was given at Babylon to the Macedonian and Persian officers. Alexander, as was his custom, continued with them till a late hour, drinking. The following evening the same revels were continued at the house of one of his intimate friends; and at the close of this banquet, the symptoms of a fever, which had probably been upon him for several days, showed themselves so strongly that he did not return to his palace.

For several days he continued extremely ill, but did not think himself in danger. His thoughts were still bent upon the new expeditions he was planning, and orders concerning them were given to his generals, from day to day.

On the seventh day he felt himself dying. His generals were admitted to his chamber, and found him sensible, but speechless. His soldiers passed through the room, one by one, and he recognised and made signs to them, but could give them no parting words. All human aid was now of no avail. His empire was passing from him, and who was to inherit it?

This question none dared to ask;—but the last act of Alexander was to draw his ring from his finger and give it to Perdiccas, one of the most distinguished of his Macedonian generals.

With this faint intimation of his wishes, the great conqueror of the world expired.

Alexander the Great died in the year B.C. 323, at the age of 34. His empire was the largest ever possessed by one man, and he has continued to this day, perhaps, the most celebrated amongst earthly monarchs. Yet he was no sooner dead, than all his vast dominions seemed, as it were, to melt away. Though Perdiccas had received the ring, he was not allowed to hold the kingdom. The generals of Alexander contended for his throne, and divided his possessions. Every one forgot their monarch, and each thought only of himself; and the truest marks of affection for Alexander's memory were given by Sisygambis, the mother of his great enemy Darius. Upon being told that Alexander was dead, she seated herself on the ground, covered her face with a veil, refused to take food, and on the fifth day died.

Yet we must not think that because Alexander's empire was thus quickly broken up, therefore his conquests were of no importance. We cannot, indeed, consider it right that one man should invade the dominions of another, and rob him of his just inheritance; but however we may blame Alexander's ambition, we must confess that his power was of great use to the world. He spread the customs and tastes of the Greeks amongst the nations of the East; and in Alexandria, especially, all the treasures of Greek learning were in consequence collected and preserved, so that they have now come down to us. He also caused great activity in commerce, by forming harbours for vessels, and encouraging men to trade from one place to another. When he had conquered a country, it was his wish also to improve it; and, if he had never lived, the world would, probably, now be in a much less civilised state than it is. These are circumstances for which we ought to be very grateful; and persons who read history attentively will constantly find, as in this instance, that the faults of a monarch are ruled by the mercy of God, for the good not only of his own people, but of distant ages.

Amongst the anecdotes which have been related

of Alexander, there is one which can scarcely be omitted in any account of his life. It is connected with Diogenes, the Cynic philosopher. Diogenes was a native of Sinope, a town of Pontus, in Asia Minor; but a great part of his life was spent at Athens. He is said to have been a very extravagant, careless person when young; but he afterwards practised great self-denial, and used to live on the plainest food, and sleep in porticoes or in the streets; and at last, it is declared that he took up his residence in a large tub. His wish was, to make persons practise what they knew to be right, as well as talk about it; and, in spite of his strange habits, he was much respected. The name of Cynic was given him from his sharpness of manner when finding fault. As he was once sailing to the island of Ægina he was taken prisoner by some pirates, and by them sold as a slave to an inhabitant of Corinth. But he soon received his freedom, and continued to live in his master's house, taking care of his children. It was at Corinth that his interview with Alexander the Great, which has ever since been famous, is said to have taken place. The king began the conversation by saying, "I am Alexander the Great;" to which the philosopher replied, "And I am Diogenes the Cynic." Alexander then inquired whether he could benefit him in any way. "Yes," was the reply, "you can stand out of the sunshine." The king found that it was useless to offer any favour to a man who had so few wants; and, being full of admiration for him, is said to have exclaimed: "If I were not Alexander, I should wish to be Diogenes."

Diogenes was ninety years old when he died, at Corinth, B.C. 323.

CHAP. XLII.

ATHENS TAKEN BY ANTIPATER.

B.C. 322.

WE must now return to Greece, which, however, at this time scarcely merits the name of a separate and independent country. During the lifetime of Alexander, several attempts were made by the people to recover their freedom, but they were all unsuccessful. Antipater, the general who governed Macedonia, was always able to subdue them; and indeed Sparta and the Peloponnesian states were almost alone in their efforts, for the Athenians cared much more for their amusements than their liberty; and as long as they were allowed their games and festivals, were quite willing to remain quiet. Demosthenes still endeavoured, from time to time, to rouse their fears, and make them see the danger they were in, and he would even have desired that they should seek the favour of the king of Persia; but although his influence was very great, there were still other persons of importance in the state to oppose him. Phocion continued to take the Macedonian side in all public questions; and Æschines also, an orator, and a rival of Demosthenes, who had, years before, done every thing he could to gain the favour of Philip of Macedon, now thwarted Demosthenes on every opportunity, and at last caused a public enquiry to be made into his conduct.

Demosthenes had not much difficulty in defending himself, for his life had always been so pure, that every person who was not prejudiced must have been forced to own that he was innocent of any public offence.

Æschines lost his cause, and left Athens full of vexation, and went to live at Rhodes. It is said, that as he was about to embark, Demosthenes followed him with a purse of money, which he forced him to accept. Æschines was much touched by this kindness, and exclaimed: "How will it be possible for me not to regret a country, in which I leave an enemy more generous than I can hope to find friends in any other part of the world?"

A few years afterwards, Demosthenes was himself compelled to leave Athens. The circumstances which caused his misfortune were these:— Whilst Alexander was in Asia, one of his generals, who had behaved extremely ill, and was afraid of the king's displeasure, made his escape to Greece, bringing with him a large amount of treasures, with which he intended to bribe the Athenians to side with him against Alexander. At the time when this man arrived in Greece, the Greeks were in a state of extreme indignation against Alexander, who had sent an order to them to receive back all their exiles, whether they liked it or not. The way in which this order was given was sufficient in itself to rouse their anger; for Alexander was not acknowledged to be their king, and he had strictly promised not to interfere with their laws. A proclamation was published at the Olympic festival in the following style: "King Alexander to the exiles from the Greek cities. We were not the authors of your exile, but we will restore you to your homes,— all but those who are under a curse. And we have written to Antipater on the subject, that he may compel those cities which are unwilling, to receive you."

We can easily imagine how exceedingly angry the Greeks were when this proclamation was read. Several of the states began to talk of war, and when

Alexander's general, Harpalus, arrived at Athens, with his bribes, there were many persons willing to listen to him.

The greater number of the Athenians were, however, too much afraid of Antipater, the Macedonian governor, to take part with Harpalus. After a time an enquiry was made as to the persons who had received money from him, and amongst those who were accused was Demosthenes.

The accusation was not thoroughly proved, indeed there is every reason, from the character of Demosthenes, to believe that it was false. But he was condemned and sentenced to pay a fine; and as he could not do this, he would have been thrown into prison, if he had not fled from Athens, and sought for refuge at Trœzen, and in the island of Ægina. From these places he could still see Athens, and here he waited sadly, lingering day after day, on the coast or the cliffs, looking towards his beloved city, and longing for some change in public affairs which would enable him to return.

The death of Alexander must to him, especially, have appeared a happy event for Athens; and at the first, it certainly seemed as if the ancient spirit of the people was restored to them, and that they were about, with one consent, to rise up against the power of Macedon, and declare themselves free.

In an Assembly of the people, it was declared that Athens was ready to assert the liberty of Greece, and to deliver the cities which were held by Macedonian garrisons. All the citizens under forty years of age were called to arms, a large fleet was ordered to be made ready, and envoys were sent to the different states of Greece to announce that Athens was willing to take the front in the approaching war, and to risk everything for freedom.

Phocion however, looked on all this enthusiasm

with distrust. At first he would not believe that Alexander was really dead; and endeavoured to prevent the people from assembling immediately in council. He entreated them to have patience, to wait till they were quite certain the report was true. "If the king is dead to day," he said, " he will still be dead to-morrow, and the next day, so that we may deliberate at our leisure, and the more securely." And when at length they were assured of the fact, and the preparations for war had actually begun, Phocion still kept aloof and would express no pleasure or even hope of success, but only said, "that the preparations were well enough for a single course, but that he feared for the end of the race, seeing that the city had no more money, or ships, or men, to carry on the contest with if these should be lost."

The spirit of Demosthenes was as hopeful as that of Phocion was desponding. He was still an exile from Athens, but when he heard of the embassy which was sent to rouse the Peloponnesian states, all anger against his country vanished. Leaving his retreat, he joined the envoys as they went from city to city, and exerted his splendid talents in public speaking, to prevail on the different states to take up arms for the freedom of Greece.

The Athenians were full of gratitude for his services; and one of his kinsmen, seeing that the opinion of the public was in his favour, proposed that he should be recalled. The decree was passed, and a vessel was sent by public authority to bring him back. When he reached Piraeus a procession, headed by the chief persons in Athens, went to the port to receive him, and he was conducted to the city in triumph. It was a most joyful day for Demosthenes, and he delighted to compare his own return with that of Alcibiades. He had, himself, been restored to his former honours from a sense of gratitude; but Alcibiades was brought back from fear, because his countrymen knew he would be a powerful enemy if he was forced to remain an exile.

So far it seemed as if Demosthenes had judged rightly, and Phocion wrongly. Yet, in the end, events proved that the fears of Phocion were well founded.

Antipater was still governor in Macedonia, or rather we should call him regent, for he ruled in the name of two princes. One was a little infant, the son of Roxana, one of Alexander's wives, who was born after the king's death. The other was Aridæus Philip, a half brother of Alexander, who was made joint king with the infant prince. Aridæus was a very weak person, and no one would have thought much about him, if it had not been for his wife Eurydice, a clever, ambitious woman, who eagerly desired the power and grandeur of a throne.

But neither Aridæus nor the young prince Alexander had ever any actual authority in the empire. The great generals seized every thing, and carried on their wars just as they liked, without a thought for anything but their own interests.

When Antipater found that the Greeks were rising in rebellion, he collected an army and marched against them. Success was, for a time, entirely with the Greeks; but it did not remain with them. The power of Antipater could not be resisted by a people whose spirit was so much lessened; and, after a short struggle, the Athenians were compelled to entreat for peace, and to submit to whatever conditions Antipater thought fit to insist upon.

They had no personal danger to fear; but the commands of Antipater must have been very bitter to those who had once so gloried in their power and freedom. A Macedonian garrison was stationed in one of the ports of the city; a large number of persons, who had once been citizens, and allowed to take part in the government, and vote in the public assembly, were now declared unfit for this privilege, because of their poverty; and many of them left Athens in consequence, and went to live in a distant land; whilst some of the chief persons in the state were regularly banished.

Demosthenes knew well that he could not escape, when so much suffering was going on around him. Before the Macedonian garrison arrived, he retired from the city, and sought refuge, as before, at Ægina. From thence he proceeded to a small island, near Trœzen. Here one of Antipater's followers, named Archias, found him. Archias had once been a player, and was now one of an infamous set of men, who received the name of Exile Hunters, from the task which they undertook of finding out and slaying the exiles, who were the enemies of Antipater. Demosthenes knew that Archias was coming, and waited his arrival in a temple dedicated to the god Poseidon. Archias at first tried to deceive him; and spoke to him as a friend, and endeavoured to persuade him to leave his retreat; promising, at the same time, to intercede with Antipater for him. Demosthenes listened for a time, and then replied, "Archias, you never won me by your acting, nor will you now by your promises." The player found that his purpose was discovered, and threatened instead of promising. Demosthenes was still quite unmoved, and only begged to have time given him that he might write a letter to his friends. Taking up the reed with which he was accustomed to write, he put the end of it in his mouth and bit it. Then, bending his head, he covered his face with his robe. Archias imagined that he was delaying from fear, and began to reproach him with cowardice. But Demosthenes, when biting the reed, had at the same time taken poison, which was laid upon the point; and now, uncovering his face, and rising, he said, "I quit thy sanctuary, Poseidon, still breathing, though Antipater and the Macedonians have not spared even it from pollution." He moved towards the door with a slow and trembling step, and, before he reached the threshold, fell with a groan and expired.

Many years passed before the Athenians were allowed to show the respect which they felt for their celebrated fellow citizen; but at length a bronze statue was erected to his memory, bearing this inscription: "Had but the strength of thy arm, Demosthenes, equalled thy spirit, never would Greece have sunk under the foreigner's yoke."

CHAP. XLIII.

ATHENS SUBMITS TO CASSANDER.

B.C. 318.

THE history of Athens from this time, is but a succession of struggles against the power of the Macedonian rulers. At first, indeed, after the submission to Antipater, every thing went on very quietly. The few citizens who were allowed to remain, were entirely under the influence of Phocion; and his good sense and high principles served to keep them tranquil, although they never could endure the sight of the Macedonian soldiers who were stationed at the port of Munychia. Phocion, however, had great reason to lament the part he had taken in public matters. He had urged the people to submit to the power of Macedon; and the governors of Macedon caused the ruin both of his country and himself. After the death of Antipater there were great disturbances in Macedonia, between his son, Cassander, and Polysperchon, one of Alexander's generals, whom Antipater, on his death bed, had appointed to succeed him as regent of Macedonia. Polysperchon, wishing to gain the favour of the Greeks, set forth a proclamation declaring that Greece should be free. Cassander, on the contrary, desired to treat the country as his father had done, and sent one of his friends to command the garrison in the port of Munychia. The Athenians were naturally inclined to favour Polysperchon, but Phocion would not join with them. He made no efforts to dislodge the garrison, though Polysperchon had sent him orders to do so; and at length the people were so angry that they accused him, and several persons who had sided with him, of treason. They were tried by the Assembly of the people, and condemned to death.

The feeling against Phocion was so strong that many persons, before lifting up their hands to vote against him, crowned themselves, as they were accustomed to do when about to take part in any joyful solemnity.

The sentence was executed with unusual haste, for, although it was a holiday, the people would not allow any delay. They insulted Phocion grossly as he was carried back to prison; but he bore every thing with the greatest meekness, and seemed only to feel sorrow for those who were to suffer with him. As a proof how little ill will he felt, it is said that, when he was asked if he had any message for his son, he replied, "Only tell him not to bear any grudge against the Athenians." The poison which was prepared was brought, but it was not sufficient for all who were to drink of it; and when the jailor required to be paid for bringing more, Phocion requested one of his friends to comply with the demand, observing, that "Athens was a place where one could not even die for nothing." This was the only remark that showed the bitterness of heart which he must really have felt. He may have greatly erred in his counsels for the good of his country, but no one could doubt that he acted from the purest motives.

Phocion was called "The Incorruptible," because he was never known to accept a bribe. There was another person, equally noted for integrity, who lived about the same time, but whose name is not so generally known, because he did not take so great a part in foreign affairs. Lycurgus, the Athenian, was, indeed, in many respects superior to Phocion. He was of noble birth, and possessed an ample fortune, but he lived, like Socrates, in the most simple manner himself, and took great pains to correct the luxurious habits of the people. No one, except Pericles, ever did as much as Lycurgus to adorn Athens with public buildings, or gave up as much of his attention to the improvement of the taste and learning of his fellow citizens. But his chief talent lay in a careful management of the public money. He was placed at the head of the treasury, and allowed to keep the office for twelve years, though, generally speaking, no one was permitted to hold it more than four. Enormous sums of money passed through his hands, but he was never known to have a flaw in his accounts; and his truth and integrity were so great, that private persons used to give their property in charge to him; and his witness was considered the best aid that any one could have in a court of law.

A short time before his death, he is said to have caused himself to be carried into the council chamber, where he called upon all persons to come forward and declare the charges they might have against him in his public character. Only one man was found to accuse him, and every thing which he said was disproved.

The Athenians, fallen though they were in many respects, could yet venerate a character like that of Lycurgus. They bestowed crowns and distinctions upon him during his life; and after his death he was honoured with a public funeral, a statue was erected to his memory, and peculiar privileges were granted to his family.

The contest between Cassander and Polysperchon continued for a considerable time, but Cassander was in the end victorious, and not only made himself master of Macedonia, but also contrived to murder Olympias, the mother of Alexander the Great, together with Roxana and her young son Alexander; so that no one was left who had a right to dispute his power.

Olympias was one of the most haughty and ambitious women that ever lived, and had made great efforts to overthrow the power of Antipater and his family, in order to secure all authority for herself and her grandson. The majesty of her appearance was so great that when she came forward, dressed in her royal robes, to meet the soldiers whom Cassander had ordered to kill her, they drew back overpowered; and Cassander was obliged to procure other persons to execute his commands. She deserves, however, but little pity, for she was supposed to have been concerned in the murder of her husband, Philip of Macedon; and it is certain that she caused the death of her step-son Aridæus Philip, and his wife Eurydice, who, as it was said, occupied the throne after the death of Alexander the Great.

Roxana, also, who was killed by Cassander, had behaved in the most treacherous and cruel manner to Statira, sometimes called Barsine, the daughter of Darius, who, like herself, was one of Alexander's wives, and whom she exceedingly hated. She invited Statira and her sister to come to her at Babylon, and sent them a very friendly letter, to induce them to accept the proposal; but, when the two princesses arrived, she caused them to be assassinated, and secretly buried. Now, when Cassander was in power, the same fate came upon Roxana and her son. It is very remarkable that not only was Alexander's empire rapidly broken to pieces by the quarrels of his generals, but all the members of his family died a violent death. The blessing of Heaven certainly did not rest upon his ambition and his conquests.

Though Cassander was a very bad man, his victory was, in some respects, good for the Athenians. He allowed one of their own citizens, Demetrius, of Phaleron, to govern them, and, for a time, they were tranquil and happy. But they could not long escape disturbance when so many disputes were going on around them.

Demetrius of Phaleron was a gentle governor, but he became unpopular from his extravagance; and when he had governed Athens for about ten years, another Demetrius, named Poliorcetes, or "the conqueror of cities," appeared unexpectedly at Athens, and took all his power from him.

This Demetrius Poliorcetes was the son of Antigonus, one of Alexander's generals, who tried to make himself lord of Asia. Antigonus and Cassander were at this time at war, and, as was always the case, both parties were anxious to gain possession of Greece. Demetrius Poliorcetes told the Athenians that he was come to restore their freedom, and the people, in great delight, received him with honour, presented him and his father with a golden crown, and ordered statues to be erected to them. Demetrius was a most fascinating person, but, in many respects, too like Alcibiades. The Athenians were charmed with his handsome face and his winning manners, and flattered and humoured him in the most shameful manner, even allowing him to live in a part of the Parthenon, or temple of Athene.

The inhabitants of Peloponnesus also received him as their deliverer, and he was chosen to be head of the Greek Confederacy. This state of things, however, did not last very long. Demetrius left Greece and joined his father, and assisted him in his wars; and when he came back to Athens again, he found that the feeling of the people was quite changed. Alexander's generals, it seems, had now taken to themselves the title of king; and Antigonus not only called himself a king, but allowed his son to do the same. The people of Athens knowing this, sent word to Demetrius that they had passed a decree not to admit any kings into their city. Demetrius sailed away then, but two years afterwards he came back with a fleet, and an army, and besieged the city and took it. The people were ordered to assemble in the theatre, and when they were all collected, Demetrius came forward on the stage and made them a speech. Every one expected that it would be full of reproaches and anger; but Demetrius addressed them in the mildest manner, assured them that he quite forgave them, and,— what was equally important to them just then,—made them a present of corn; for, whilst he had been besieging the city, the inhabitants were nearly starved. He allowed them to keep their old customs; but he was considered their master, and left a governor behind him to retain them in subjection.

Demetrius after this conquered Macedonia and the rest of Greece, but he was dethroned by Pyrrhus, king of Epirus. He still, however, carried on a war in Asia, with a small body of troops, against another of Alexander's generals, who was then king of Syria: but he was taken prisoner, and kept in captivity for two years; and at last growing quite weary, he took no pleasure in anything but excessive eating and drinking, and died in consequence.

CHAP. XLIV.

AGIS IV. ENDEAVOURS TO REFORM SPARTA.

B.C. 244.

THERE is little more to be told of the condition of Greece under the rule of the Macedonian kings, except an attempt made by the Spartans to bring back something like the ancient customs and strict discipline which had, by degrees, fallen into disuse. This took place about the year B.C. 244, thirty-nine years after the death of Demetrius Poliorcetes. Sparta had, up to this time, kept very much aloof from the wars which were going on around. The people still called themselves free, and they enjoyed their ancient form of government; but they had no power to assist others, and were often exposed to danger from the conquerors of the other states of Greece. In the year above mentioned, Agis IV., a descendant of Agesilaus, was one of the kings of Sparta. He was not twenty years of age when he came to the throne, and had been brought up in great luxury. But the honours of his rank, and the amusements suitable to his age, did not satisfy him. He was always thinking of the time when the Spartans were a brave and hardy people, and longing for some great change which might enable him to bring back the simple habits they had lost. One of the Ephors was his friend, and entered into his plans; and by his help Agis was able to make some very useful laws, by which the poor were relieved from the debts that many of them owed, whilst the lands of Laconia were more equally divided. These reforms were very much disliked by several of the chief persons in Sparta, and especially by the king who reigned with Agis; and when Agis was absent from the city they roused the people against him. On his return he was seized and brought to trial before the Ephors. He was asked whether he repented of his conduct; but he replied, that however fatal the issue of his undertaking might be to himself, he could never regret it. The Ephors then condemned him to death. He was carried off calm and unmoved. An attendant bewailed his fate; but the king consoled him saying, "that he was still superior to his murderers." They strangled him in the chamber of execution, and then brought his grandmother and his mother, who had also been sentenced to death for supporting him, to look upon his dead body. His grandmother was first killed, and his mother, having laid the corpse by the side of Agis, and given him her last kiss, bent her own neck to the cord, saying: "May it but bring good to Sparta." Agiatis, the young wife of Agis, who was both rich and beautiful, was forced, after the loss of her husband, to marry the son of the other king, though his father had been the greatest enemy of Agis, and the cause of his death. This, strange to say, was the occasion of a further attempt being made to carry out the plans for the reformation of the country. The second husband of Agiatis was named Cleomenes. He was very young when his father forced him to marry, and he became extremely fond of his wife, and took great interest in hearing all she had to tell him about Agis. He saw how wrongly his father had behaved, and determined, as soon as possible, to follow out the intentions of Agis, and make another effort to reform the Spartan institutions.

Cleomenes came to the throne after his father's death, and had then a better prospect of being able to fulfil his purpose; but he was obliged to proceed very carefully. What he most desired was, to diminish the authority of the Ephors, which had become much greater than it was originally meant to be. In order to obtain this end he knew that a war would be very desirable; as it would give him the opportunity of gaining victories, and so increasing his own power, until at last he might oblige the people to agree to any alterations in the government which he might consider necessary.

The opportunity of a war soon came. There was at this time a union amongst the chief towns in Achaia, called the Achæan league. Its object was to maintain the freedom of Greece. This league was not thought of much importance until Aratus, a citizen of Sicyon, persuaded his countrymen to become members of it. Aratus was a brave, noble-minded, and clever man, and was made strategus, or general, of the joint army; and after he had thus set the example of joining the league,

Corinth and some of the other Peloponnesian states did the same. The Lacedæmonians, however, kept aloof from it, and were afraid of its becoming too powerful, and this feeling of jealousy was the cause of a war.

Unfortunately for Greece the different states were now never able to stand alone; and when Aratus found that Cleomenes was likely to gain the advantage in the war, he opened a communication with Antigonus Doson, then king of Macedonia, hoping for his support. He thought that Antigonus would assist him, and still allow Greece to be free; and he was afraid that if Cleomenes gained the victory he would put an end to the Achæan league, and that Sparta would become supreme and tyrannical over the other Peloponnesian states. But it was a great mistake, and it ended in destroying his own object. Cleomenes gained several victories at first, and was able in consequence to make the alterations he wished in the state; for as he had an army at his command, he was too powerful to be opposed. Several of the Ephors were killed, which seemed a cruel act, but it was one which Cleomenes considered necessary for the good of the country, as they had used their power wrongly. The debts of the poor were forgiven, and the lands were divided afresh. Cleomenes gave up his own property, and set an example,— as indeed he had always been in the habit of doing,— of simplicity and frugality in his mode of life. Several important changes were besides made in the government, which Cleomenes thought would bring it back to what it had been originally; but many persons have considered, that he really gave too much power to the kings, and that the form of government which he established was more like a tyranny, or the rule of an absolute monarch, than anything else.

But however this might be, it did not last very long. When Antigonus, king of Macedonia, supported Aratus and the Achæan league, both together were too strong for Cleomenes. Not that the Spartans were left without any help from the other states of Greece. There was a league called the Ætolian league,—a confederacy among the cities of Ætolia,—which had existed a long time, and the members of this league now sided with Cleomenes. The Ætolians were a rude, uncivilised people, and had as frequently taken part with the Macedonian kings as against them. Their league was not much liked, though it was powerful, and their support, though it served to delay the conquests of Antigonus, could not save Sparta from the fate which awaited it.

Antigonus invaded Peloponnesus, and carried on the war with much vigour for more than two years.

After a battle, fought at Sellasia, a town in Laconia, in which Antigonus was completely the conqueror, Cleomenes gave up all hope, and even entreated his countrymen not to think of irritating the king of Macedonia, by a resistance which they knew must be vain. For himself, though he dared not remain in Greece, yet he was still, he said, determined, whether in life or death, to devote himself to the service of Sparta. A vessel had been kept in readiness for him in case of need, and he embarked in it, and went to Egypt, where he was kindly received by the king, who allowed him a pension, and promised to aid him to recover his kingdom. Cleomenes thus remained in safety for some time; but the king who next succeeded to the throne of Egypt became jealous of him, and kept him a prisoner; and Cleomenes, despairing of obtaining his freedom or returning to his country, endeavoured to excite an insurrection against the king, and, failing in this, killed himself. Agiatis, the wife of Cleomenes, died some years before him, and it is said that he mourned for her more than for all his misfortunes.

Antigonus treated the Spartans mercifully, but he restored the government of the Ephors. The cities of the Achæan league, also, were obliged to admit a Macedonian garrison within their walls, and were not able from that time to undertake any enterprise, or even to make a decree, without the consent of the king of Macedon. The citadel of Corinth, the Acrocorinthus, as it was called, was also given into the hands of the Macedonians; indeed, it was one of the first things which Antigonus insisted upon before he would assist Aratus and the Achæan league.

CHAP. XLV.

THE DEATH OF PHILOPŒMEN.

B.C. 182.

THE history of Greece is now drawing rapidly to a close; yet there is one celebrated name still to be mentioned, as assisting in her feeble and expiring efforts for freedom. It is that of Philopœmen, sometimes called the last of the Greeks. Philopœmen was a native of Megalopolis. He lost his father when he was very young, and was then brought up by two clever and kind friends, fellow citizens, who early inspired him with a dislike to an absolute government, and a desire for liberty. The example of Epaminondas was that which he was most anxious to follow, for Epaminondas was the founder of Megalopolis, and his memory was cherished by every inhabitant of the city. From his childhood Philopœmen delighted in war, and his reading was chiefly upon this subject; one of his favourite books being the history of Alexander's campaigns. His thoughts, also, were constantly dwelling upon it; and even when walking along a road, he would amuse himself with thinking how he should manage if he found himself in the same place, at the head of an army.

When Philopœmen was grown up to manhood, the wars between Cleomenes and the Achæan league had begun; and when he was about thirty years old, Megalopolis, his native city, which had always sided with the league, was besieged by Cleomenes, taken, and destroyed. This act filled the mind of Philopœmen with the most intense desire for vengeance. He joined eagerly in the war, and distinguished himself greatly at the battle of Sellasia; for, after his horse had been killed under him, he continued to fight on foot, and refused to leave the battle field, even when both his thighs had been transfixed with a javelin.

After Cleomenes fled from Sparta, and when Antigonus was lord of Peloponnesus, Philopœmen left Greece, and went to Crete, to learn more of the art of war by practice, as there were many contests just then between the cities of that island.

The Achæan and Ætolian leagues still existed, though their chief power was gone. The Ætolians were continually giving offence by their rude, lawless habits; in fact, there was a constant warfare between the members of the two leagues for several years, and when Philopœmen came back to Greece, he was made general of the Achæan league. The Achæans were supported by the king of Macedon, Philip V., who had succeeded Antigonus. He was considered the head of the Grecian states, as the

kings of Macedon had been before him; and for
this reason it seemed natural to apply to him in
cases of dispute. But, as it had always happened,
the interference of a person, who was in part a
foreigner, brought great evils upon the country; and
now the Greeks were to suffer, not only from the
king of Macedon, but from the Romans, who were
bent upon conquering Macedon.

Aratus had died before Philopœmen was made
general of the league. He quarrelled with Philip V.,
who was an extremely wicked man, and Philip
caused him to be poisoned; and now Philopœmen
seemed to be the only person in Greece really able
to guide and advise the people. His first object
was to reform the habits of the Achæans, who depended almost entirely upon the Macedonians, and
had become extremely luxurious, spending large
sums in dress and beautiful furniture, and caring
so little for war that they grudged the money
which they were obliged to lay out in arms. Philopœmen's influence was so great, that in a very
short space of time — only a few months, indeed —
he contrived entirely to change their notions. He
made the young men feel how absurd their habits
of life were, and he inspired them with such a
longing for military glory, that they began to take
pride in every thing connected with war. The
rich sent their plate to be melted down, that they
might employ the silver in decorating their arms;
and it was considered ridiculous to be seen in a
handsome dress except on parade. What was of
much greater importance, the young men were really
taught to be soldiers, and obliged to live the life
and practise the duties of their profession. In this
way Philopœmen exerted himself so successfully,
that, in about eight months' time, he had an army
fit for service, and was able to gain a victory over

the Spartans, who belonged to the Ætolian league, without the aid of Macedonia.

The Peloponnesians now began to look upon Philopœmen as the defender of Grecian liberty. But it was too late for him, or indeed for any one, to bring back the days of glory and freedom which were gone. Philip of Macedon was at this time at open war with the Romans, and the Romans brought armies into Macedonia, and from thence into Greece. Nearly all the Grecians sided with the Romans, but this only served to engage them in war, not for themselves, but for a foreign power which did not in the least care for their good.

The Romans were then the most powerful people in the world. Philip withstood them for a long time, but they defeated him entirely at a battle in Thessaly, and from that time Macedonia was subject to them. This battle is called the battle of Cynoscephalæ, from a ridge of mountains called Cynoscephalæ, or Dog's Heads, near which it was fought. The Greeks thought that this event would be for their advantage. The Romans professed that they meant Greece to be independent; and Flaminius, one of the Roman generals, caused the freedom of the country to be solemnly proclaimed at the Isthmian games. The delight of the people on this occasion was so great, that they almost crushed Flaminius with the quantity of garlands and flowers which they showered upon him, and their shouts of joy so rent the air, that birds which were flying over the heads of the people are said to have fallen to the ground.

There was one circumstance, however, which soon taught the Greeks that this hope of freedom was vain. The Romans insisted upon keeping possession of three Greek cities: — Chalcis in Eubœa, Demetrias in Thessaly, and Corinth; — which one of the Macedonian kings had been accustomed to call the fetters of Greece, because whoever possessed them could keep the people in entire subjection. So it was now. The Roman power took the place of the Macedonian, and whatever Rome ordered, Greece was obliged to submit to.

The Ætolians tried once to throw off the yoke, and begged for the assistance of Antiochus, king of Syria; and Antiochus came over to Greece, and several of the other Grecian states supported him. But nothing could stand against the power of the Romans. Antiochus was defeated, the Ætolians were obliged to pay a large sum of money, and give up all power of their own, and the Ætolian league was destroyed.

Thus it happened at last with the Achæan league also. Its members were stronger and better guided than those of the Ætolian league, and therefore it lasted longer. But it met with the same fate in the end.

The great sources of evil were the disputes amongst the Greeks themselves. Sparta had been obliged to join the Achæan league, but it was unwillingly, and there was always a jealousy between her and the other states. This ill feeling at length brought on an open quarrel, and a war, in which Philopœmen, who was the head of the Achæan league, took entire possession of the city of Sparta, altered the government, and obliged the Spartans to do away with the laws and institutions of Lycurgus.

The Spartans appealed to the Romans, as in former times the Greek states had been accustomed to appeal to the kings of Macedon. The Romans would not interfere by force of arms, and acted so as to make each party believe that they were in some degree favoured.

The Spartans now were powerless; but the Messenians carried on a war instead, and Philopœmen commanded an army against them. He was by this time an old man, having reached the age of seventy, but his energy still remained the same. A fever attacked him, and left him extremely weak, yet he was resolved to head an engagement against the Messenians, and exerted himself even beyond his strength. His troops, however, were forced to retreat, and Philopœmen fell from his horse, and, being stunned, was taken prisoner.

His enemies, the Messenians, carried him in triumph to Messene, exhibited him in the theatre as a spectacle to the multitude, and then threw him into a dungeon, — a kind of pit which had only an opening at the top, and was secured by a heavy stone. The next day a secret council was held, and it was resolved to destroy him. The executioner was sent to him with a cup of poison. Philopœmen inquired after the fate of some troops which he had intended to join if he had been successful in the last unfortunate engagement, and, having learned that they were in safety, he calmly drank the cup of poison and expired.

Such was the end of the "last of the Greeks." His death was soon followed by what may be considered the death of his country.

CHAP. XLVI.

CORINTH DESTROYED, AND GREECE MADE A ROMAN PROVINCE.

B.C. 146.

THE Romans were now so powerful in Greece, that when Perseus, king of Macedon, who succeeded his father Philip, made immense efforts to carry on a war against Rome, no city or state in Greece, except the towns in Bœotia, dared to give him assistance. He was joined by the Syrians, the Bithynians, the Carthaginians, the kings of Illyricum and Thrace, and even by some of the barbarous tribes on the Danube, but the Greeks were afraid. They dared not rebel against their great lords. Perhaps it was well for them that they did not; for Perseus experienced the same fate as every other monarch who resisted Rome. He was defeated at the battle of Pydna, in Macedon, and his country ceased to be an independent kingdom, and became a Roman province.

The Greeks were allowed to call themselves independent for a few years longer. They had so little power, that the Romans did not trouble themselves about them, unless they seemed at any time inclined to disobey their orders; then they interfered at once, and often very cruelly. On one occasion, more than a thousand of the first men in Greece were sent to Italy, to be tried for some offence they were accused of; and, when they arrived, instead of being put upon their trial, they were distributed amongst different towns, and actually kept there for seventeen years, in spite of all the petitions that their friends made for them.

Even at last, when they were allowed to return, the Roman government gave the permission from a feeling of proud indifference, and not from any kindness or sympathy. Cato, the censor, was the person who urged the senators to allow the exiles to go back, and all he said was, "Have we nothing better to do than to be deliberating a whole day about a few old Greeks, whether they shall be put in the grave here or in their own country?" This is sufficient to show the contemptuous feeling which the proud Romans entertained towards the Greeks in their fallen state; and yet they were not too proud to learn from them, for the Romans had very little knowledge themselves of painting and sculpture, and arts which required taste and elegance; and were indebted to the Greeks for almost all they knew about them. The tutors and governors of the families of the wealthy Romans were generally chosen from amongst the Greeks, and at last the Romans became as civilised as their teachers; but they never, as a nation, had the same perception of what was beautiful and graceful.

This connection between the two nations took place, however, chiefly after Greece became a Roman province, in the year B.C. 146.

The Athenians were, in fact, the cause of the change in the government of the country. They had become so weak and so poor, that they actually oppressed and pillaged one of their own towns. The other states interfered, and a war was the consequence. But the Romans did not choose them to carry on contests between themselves, and sent word that they would settle their disputes for them. This made the Greeks very angry, and for the last time the members of the Achæan league declared war against Rome.

Of course the contest was quite hopeless. The

Romans sent an army into Peloponnesus, and the consul, Lucius Mummius, gained a victory, not far from Corinth, which put an end to the Achæan league for ever. Corinth was first plundered, and then, on a signal given by the blast of a trumpet, it was set on fire. The men were killed, and the women and children, and any slaves who could be found in it, were sold.

Corinth was the richest city in Greece, and full of most beautiful paintings and works of art. The Roman consul carried them away, but he did not in the least know how to value them. The men made dice boards of some of the finest paintings; and, though Mummius kept others to adorn his triumph at Rome, he agreed with the men who had the charge of them, that if any were injured they should be replaced by others of the same value. He thought, surely, that paintings could easily be replaced by any one.

All Greece, as far as Macedonia and Epirus, was now formed into a Roman province, and called Achaia, by which name it is frequently mentioned in the Acts of the Apostles. The name must have been derived from the Achæan league, which lasted as long as the country could in any way pretend to be independent.

The history of Greece from this time is entirely mixed up with that of Rome. When the Roman Empire was divided, the eastern division was called the Greek Empire ; but this was only for the sake of distinction. Greece itself was still only a province subject to the emperors. The Turks entirely conquered the Greek Empire, when Constantinople, the capital, was taken by them in the year A. D. 1453, and they then became the lords of Greece.

Their government was very cruel, and the two nations felt the utmost hatred for each other. The

Greeks often rebelled, and at length several of the principal European kingdoms, pitying their condition, and remembering their former glory, united together, and compelled the Turks to set them free.

Otho, a son of the king of Bavaria, was chosen for their monarch, and Greece was raised into a kingdom, A. D. 1828.

CHAP. XLVII.

It will perhaps help to fix the history of Greece in our minds, if we endeavour to learn something of the dwellings, the manners, and customs of the people. The descriptions will be taken, principally, from those which have been given by different writers at the time of the Peloponnesian war, and afterwards. There is little said about these things by persons who wrote in the more early days.

In a Greek family, the women lived in private apartments by themselves. A Greek house, therefore, was always divided into two distinct portions, one for the men, and the other for the women. The house sometimes, but not always, stood back from the street; and there was generally an altar to Apollo before it,—or perhaps a laurel tree, which was sacred to Apollo, — or a head of the god Hermes, to mark the religious feeling of the inhabitants. A few steps led up to the front door, which generally were marked with some inscription, for the sake of a good omen. The front of the house was not wide, as the rooms went far back instead of extending sideways. The house door opened into a narrow passage, on one side of which were the stables, and on the other the porter's lodge. From the passage the peristyle, or court, was entered. This court was open to the sky in the centre, and there were porticoes all round it, which were used for exercise, and sometimes for dining in, and generally there was an altar in it on which sacrifices were offered to the household gods.

Round the peristyle were the apartments for the men, such as large banqueting rooms, parlours, picture galleries, and libraries, sleeping rooms, and sometimes store rooms.

A door opened from this first peristyle into another, which was given up for the women of the family. It was like that of the men, except that the porticoes went round three sides only, and on the fourth there was a kind of recess, which formed a vestibule to the other apartments. The rooms on each side of the vestibule were sleeping rooms. That on the right hand side was the principal bedchamber of the house, and any valuable articles of ornament were usually kept in it. Beyond these rooms were large apartments for working in wool, which formed part of the occupation of the household. The eating room, and other apartments, were built round the peristyle. Usually there was an upper story to the house, occupied by the slaves; the roof of this sometimes projected over the lower story, and formed balconies or verandahs. The stairs which led to the upper story were sometimes on the outside of the house. The roofs were generally flat, and it was customary to walk about upon them.

In the interior of the house there were sometimes curtains instead of doors. The principal openings for light and air were in the roofs of the peristyle, but windows were not uncommon. There were fire places, but it is supposed that chimneys were unknown, and that the smoke escaped through an opening in the roof of the apartment. Little portable stoves also were often used.

The houses of the rich people, who lived in the country, were much more magnificent than those in the town. Generally speaking, the Greeks in their best days lived in small plain houses, and employed their money and their taste on the temples and public buildings. The floors of the houses were of stone, and the walls were white, till about the time of Alcibiades, who is the first person mentioned as having caused them to be painted. The practice was not uncommon in the time of Plato and Xenophon, and about that period also we hear of painted ceilings.

The Greeks usually partook of three meals, answering very much to our breakfast, luncheon, and dinner. The first commonly consisted of bread dipped in unmixed wine; the second, — taken, probably, about twelve o'clock, — was of a light kind, and varied according to the habits of different persons; the third and principal meal, was often not eaten before sunset. The ordinary dinner for the family was cooked by the mistress of the house, or by female slaves under her direction; but for special occasions the Greeks had hired cooks. The Sicilian cooks were especially famous.

When any person was invited to an entertainment, he was always expected to bathe shortly before. We are particularly told of Socrates, that when he was going out to dinner, he washed and put on his shoes. Generally speaking, he went about barefooted. As soon as the guests arrived, their shoes or sandals were taken off by the slaves, and their feet were washed; and after this they reclined on couches, and the slaves brought them water to wash their hands. The Athenian and Spartan men were accustomed to recline at their meals, but the women and children sat. Only two persons reclined on the same couch. The dinner usually consisted of two courses. In the first were fish, poultry, and meat; the second was more like our dessert. The most common food among the Greeks was a kind of frumenty or soft cake, which was prepared in various ways. Wheaten or barley bread was also usual. Pork was their favourite meat, and sausages were very common. They were also fond of fish, and ate vegetables, such as cabbages, lettuces, beans, with mallows, and lentils. They had no knives or forks, but helped themselves with their fingers, and then wiped them on a piece of bread. They had spoons for soup, but sometimes they used a hollow piece of bread instead. The company did not all eat at the same table, but separate small tables were placed before each couch.

When the first course was finished, water was brought for the guests to wash their hands; and crowns made of garlands of flowers, were given to them, besides perfumes of different kinds. No one drank any wine till after the first course, when some strong unmixed wine was brought, in a large goblet, and every one drank a little, and then poured out a small quantity, as a libation, or drink-offering, to the gods. A sacred hymn of praise was usually sung at the same time.

The great amusement of the entertainment began with the dessert. The Greeks drank wine and talked after dinner as gentlemen now do in England; but they also diverted themselves by games, such as casting dice, or throwing up buckle stones, or draughts. Very often, also, they asked each other riddles, and the persons who found them out were rewarded with a crown, or a garland, or a kiss; and if they failed were obliged to drink either a cup of strong unmixed wine, or wine mixed with salt water. Music was also common on these occasions, and persons were hired to dance for the pleasure of the company.

But the great enjoyment of the evening was the wine. Persons were often invited to wine parties, or symposia, as they were called, and not to dinner; and one of the company was commonly chosen to conduct the revels, and was called the symposiarch. He it was who ordered everything. The wine was always mixed with a great deal of water, and kept very cool; and honey and spices were sometimes put into it. The strange part of the arrangement was, that every one was obliged to drink exactly as much as the symposiarch ordered. These symposia often ended in a very disorderly manner, and for that reason they were forbidden at Sparta.

We can tell little concerning the gardens of the Greeks, but it seems that they did not know much about flowers. Violets and roses were chiefly cultivated at Athens, because they were used in making garlands. They certainly had not the same ideas of beauty in a garden that we have, for one of their writers speaks of the practice of setting off the loveliness of roses and violets, by planting them side by side with leeks and onions.

Many private persons in Athens had large collections of books, and sometimes the public were allowed the use of them. Aristotle is said to have taught one of the kings of Egypt how to arrange a library; and, after his time, the library at Alexandria in Egypt, became the most celebrated in the world.

The dress of the Greeks was very simple. Their principal garment was called a chiton; but the Spartan chiton and the Athenian were not alike. The Spartan chiton was made of woollen stuff, very short, and without sleeves, and it was fastened over both shoulders by clasps or buckles; the Athenian chiton was a long loose dress with wide sleeves, and usually made of linen. The dresses of both men and women were originally very much alike, for in early days it was the custom for all to wear the Spartan, or, as it was called, the Dorian chiton. But the Athenian women were obliged afterwards to give up this dress, because, on one occasion, they were so angry with a man who returned, the only one alive, from a warlike expedition, that they killed him with the buckles which they wore on their shoulders. Both kinds of chiton were fastened round the waist with a girdle.

Besides the chiton the Greeks generally wore an upper garment, or pallium, which is often spoken of as a blanket or shawl. The shape was square, and it was of different colours and patterns. It was usually made of wool, and was often fastened with a brooch over the right shoulder. Persons who could afford it, wore a thin pallium in summer, and a warmer one in winter. The splendour of a person's dress was usually seen in the pallium. The women's were in general of a finer material and of brighter colours than the men's; but the men did not disdain sometimes to show their fondness for finery by adopting the dress of the women. Alcibiades was distinguished by his purple blanket, which trailed upon the ground and formed a train. Females often employed themselves in ornamenting the pallium, and used gold thread when they wished to make it particularly splendid. When a person was very unhappy, or suffering from any great agitation of mind, he often covered his face with the pallium which he wore; and it was also used to protect the head in case of rain. That which seems most strange to us is, that the same blanket which was worn as a garment by day, often served to sleep in at night. Blankets, or pallia, were also spread on the ground, and used for carpets. This was quite an Eastern fashion, and we find it mentioned in the Gospels, when the people at Jerusalem spread their garments upon the ground, on the occasion of our Blessed Lord's entrance into the City.

The use of shoes was by no means universal amongst the lower orders, but those which were worn by the upper classes, were, probably, very like our own, only more various in colour. There seems to have been just as much fashion in those days as in the present time, for we read of Persian shoes, and shoes of Alcibiades, and Sicyonian shoes, all of which were worn by ladies. Laconian or Spartan shoes, as we might easily guess, were men's shoes.

Greek bedsteads must have resembled French bedsteads in some respects, but the beds themselves were stuffed with wool or dried weeds. The bedsteads were generally made of wood, and sometimes very expensively ornamented; indeed, in the later periods of Grecian history, we hear of bedsteads of solid ivory, with silver feet. In spite, however, of this magnificence, the Asiatics used to declare that the Greeks did not know how to make a comfortable bed.

The practice of bathing was as common amongst the Greeks as amongst the Romans; but they had no splendid public buildings for the purpose. Persons of rank and wealth had private baths in their own houses, and it was customary for them to use two in succession, first a cold bath and then a warm one.

The Athenians were far more luxurious in their mode of living than the Spartans. The habits of the two people, indeed, were as different as English habits are from French or Italian.

The Athenians lived very much in public. They met in public places, and wandered about in the public gardens, and cared but little for the pleasures of home; but the Spartans, though they dined together, because it was one of the rules given them by Lycurgus, kept to themselves at other times. The Athenians were much the more agreeable, but the Spartans seem generally to have been the more respected.

The writing of the Greeks must have been like that of most other nations, before paper was invented. Waxen tablets were in common use, which were written upon with an iron instrument very like a pencil in appearance.

Slavery was commonly allowed amongst the Greeks. Their slaves were generally prisoners taken in war, and belonging to foreign nations; for it was a practice to restore their own countrymen to freedom, on payment of a sum of money. The slaves were in general tolerably well treated, except at Sparta. They were frequently employed in public works, but there were so many at Athens, that the poorest citizen had a slave to manage his household. Nicias had a thousand slaves in the mines alone.

CHRONOLOGICAL TABLE

OF THE

CONTEMPORARY EVENTS OF GRECIAN AND JEWISH HISTORY.

B.C.	Greece.	B.C.	Israel and Judah.			B.C.
1200						
1100	The Siege of Troy	1184	The Birth of Samuel			1171
1000			Saul David Solomon			1095 1065 1015
			Rehoboam			975
			Separation of the Kingdoms of Israel and Judah.			
			Judah.	B.C	Israel. Jeroboam	B.C. 974
			Abijam Asa	957 955		
					Nadab Baasha Elah Zimri Omri Ahab	954 953 930 929 929 918
900			Jehosaphat	914		
					Ahaziah Jehoram or Joram	897 896
			Jehoram or Joram Ahaziah or Jehoahas Athaliah Jehoash or Joash	889 885 884 878	Jehu	884
					Jehoahas Jehoash or Joash	856 839
800	The Laws of Lycurgus	825	Amaziah Uzziah or Azariah	838 810	Jeroboam II.	825
					Zachariah Shallum Menahem Pekahiah Pekah	773 772 772 761 759
	The 1st Messenian War	743	Jotham Ahaz Hezekiah	758 742 727	Hoshea	730
700					The Kingdom of Israel overthrown by the Assyrians	721

CHRONOLOGICAL TABLE.

B.C.	Greece.	B.C.	Judah.	B.C.	Israel.
600	The 2nd Messenian War	685	Manasseh	698	
			Amon	643	
	Solon gives laws to Athens	638	Josiah	641	
			Jehoahaz	610	
			Jehoiakim	610	
			Jeholakin or Jeconiah	599	
			Zedekiah	599	
			Judah carried captive to Babylon	588	
	Pisistratus Tyrant of Athens	560			
			Cyrus proclaims liberty to the Jews	536	
			Foundation of the second Temple	534	
500	Hippias expelled from Athens	510	Temple finished	515	
	The Burning of Sardis	499			
	The Battle of Marathon	490			
	The Battles of Thermopylæ and Salamis	480			
	The Battle of Platæa	479			
	Themistocles banished	471			
	Cimon banished	461	Ezra sent to govern Judæa	457	
			Nehemiah sent	446	
	The Building of the Parthenon, the Propylæa, &c.	438			
	The Beginning of the Peloponnesian War	431			
	The Plague at Athens	430			
	The Siege of Platæa begun	429			
	Pylos taken and fortified	425			
	The Peace of Nicias	421			
	Commencement of the Sicilian War	415			
	The Return of Alcibiades	407			
	The Battle of Arginusæ, and the unjust sentence against the Athenian Generals	406			
	The Battle of Ægos Potamoi	405			
	The Government of the Thirty Tyrants	401			
400	The Retreat of the Ten Thousand Greeks	401			

B.C.	Greece.	B.C.	Judah.	B.C.	Israel.
400	The Death of Socrates	399			
	The Peace of Antalcidas	387			
	The Battle of Leuctra	371			
	The Battle of Mantinea	362			
	Commencement of the Sacred War	357			
	The Battle of Chæronea	338			
	Invasion of Persia by Alexander the Great	334			
	The Battle of Issus	333			
	The Battle of Arbela or Gaugamela	330			
	Alexander defeats Porus	325			
	Death of Alexander the Great	323			
	Athens taken by Antipater	322			
	Athens submits to Cassander	318			
300	Agis IV. endeavours to reform Sparta	244			
	Death of Philopœmen	182	Cruel treatment of the Jews by Antiochus Epiphanes	170	
			Restoration of the daily Sacrifice, and purification of the Temple by Judas Maccabæus	165	
	Corinth destroyed, and Greece made a Roman Province	146			

www.ingramcontent.com/pod-product-compliance
Lightning Source LLC
Chambersburg PA
CBHW030302240426
43673CB00040B/1029